Bill Blanchard

Dear Padre

Dear Padre

Questions Catholics Ask

A REDEMPTORIST PASTORAL PUBLICATION

Compiled and Edited by Rev. Thomas M. Santa, C.Ss.R.

Liguori
LIGUORI, MISSOURI

Imprimi Potest:
Richard Thibodeau, C.Ss.R.
Provincial, Denver Province
The Redemptorists

Published by Liguori Publications
Liguori, Missouri
www.liguori.org
www.catholicbooksonline.com

Imprimatur:
Most Reverend Joseph F. Naumann
Auxiliary Bishop/Vicar General, Archdiocese of St. Louis

Copyright 2003 by Liguori Publications

Library of Congress Catalog Card Number: 2003100483

ISBN 0-7648-0987-3

The editor and publisher gratefully acknowledge permission to reprint/ reproduce copyrighted works granted by the publishers/sources listed on pages 269–270.

Printed in the United States of America
07 06 05 04 03   5 4 3 2 1
First edition

T his book is dedicated to Janice N. Graves (1942–2002). A prayerful and faith-filled woman, she was a Christian who believed in Jesus with her entire heart and soul. Although she was not a Catholic, her tireless dedication to the Word of God helped millions of Catholics to enjoy and learn about their faith each Sunday as they read "Dear Padre."

CONTENTS

FOREWORD

In December of 1989, I was sitting behind my desk at Liguori Publications anxiously awaiting the start of my first workweek. The phone rang. The telephone operator informed me that a priest was on the line and wanted to speak to the person who was in charge of the "Dear Padre" column. That was now me! I heard the clink of the line and then a deep, concerned voice said: "Father, I need to speak to you about last Sunday's 'Dear Padre' column. Thus began my twelve-year career as "The Padre."

From 1989 to 2002, I organized and wrote the "Dear Padre" column, which appeared in parish Sunday bulletins throughout the English-speaking world. On Monday mornings, I would receive phone calls from various pastors, parish priests, and parish staff members offering me theological advice or insight about the "Dear Padre" question and answer that had appeared in their Sunday bulletin that week. Many times, they would disagree with my column and share with me their version of what I should have written. Throughout the week, I would receive dozens of letters from the Catholic faithful, usually with the "Dear Padre" column cut out and their comments written on the top, bottom, and along the sides. Sometimes the comments were critical, sometimes thankful or encouraging. But the comments were always interesting. The Catholic public was very much alive and interested in its faith.

The short line-up of Dear Padre writers dates back to the birth of the "Dear Padre" column in the late 1970s. During this period, Liguori Publications had noticed through phone calls and letters that people were asking very basic questions about their Catholic faith. These were Catholics who grew up in the experiential years of religious education in the middle to late sixties. They were now adults, settled in communities, with their children attending very structured religious education classes. These parents found themselves unable to answer many of the religious questions that their children brought home from those classes. The parents would call their parish priest, the director of religious education, or even a Catholic publishing house to find the answers that would deepen their own knowledge of their Catholic faith and give them reasonable responses for their children.

Liguori Publications responded to this new climate of questioning with a book entitled _The Handbook for Today's Catholic_ and with a weekly column that would appear in the parish Sunday bulletin. The column was entitled "Dear Padre." This column was modeled after the many popular question-and-answer columns, such as "Ann Landers," that appeared in the daily newspapers. The response to these two products was overwhelming. The "Dear Padre" column quickly became a hit, surpassing the one million mark in readers, and has remained popular for the past twenty-five years.

During the twelve years that I took on the persona of "The Padre," I have witnessed the Catholic population becoming more and more questioning about their faith. This new Catholic public has challenged Catholic publishing houses to create a variety of catechetical aids. This has also pushed the Church to publish the new _Catechism of the Catholic Church_, so that once again there is an accepted interpretation of Catholic practice and belief that is available to all.

Rev. Thomas Santa, who is the editor and compiler of this book, led Liguori Publications as president and publisher through the years surrounding the publishing of the _Catechism of the Catholic Church_. Father Tom knows well the climate of the discerning Catholic and presents this compilation of _Dear Padre: Questions Catholics Ask_ in hope of deepening your understanding of your Catholic faith.

I hope that you enjoy reading and reflecting on the questions and answers presented here as much as I enjoyed writing them. And if you disagree with the answer, as people often do, please give "The Padre" a call.

PAUL COURY C.Ss.R.
THE PADRE (1989–2002)

INTRODUCTION

For over twenty-five years, many Catholics have turned to the pages of their Sunday bulletin, not only to reference the particular activities of their parish community but also to discover a familiar and comforting friend. The "Dear Padre" column, where each week one of the priest columnists would address a particular question or concern and clearly present the Catholic teaching and/or perspective, became a valuable and necessary catechetical resource. For some Catholics, the column became their primary reference point for understanding the Catholic point of view, since they had no access to other Catholic resource material. For others, the column was a supplemental resource—a resource they found to be reassuring and easy to understand.

This book compiles the results of more than twenty-five years of the "Dear Padre" column. From the early years, when the reforms of the Second Vatican Council were being implemented, all the way through to the present day, the dialogue between the priest columnist and the person in the pew who asked the question that formed the subject matter of the column, "Dear Padre" has been a source of sure footing. I hope this collection might demonstrate that assertion.

As I reviewed each of the columns and chose the particular subject matter that is included in the pages that follow, certain themes and concerns emerged.

The pastoral response of the priest columnist seemed always to be reassuring and comforting. You have the sense, when you read the answers given to the questions, that the priest is first and foremost a pastor, intent on framing his answer to the question, not so much with a scholarly twist or emphasis, but more importantly, in language that is easy to understand and comprehend.

The questions that are asked seem to be the kind of questions that people in the pew would ask; for the most part, they do not seem to be "canned" or "planted" in order to make a point. The questions are the type of questions that readers of the column could easily imagine themselves asking or being concerned about.

Particular attention seems to have been focused on the kind of questions that would not necessarily come from one extreme or another, but more often than not from somewhere in the middle of the gathered parish community. I would imagine that this was probably a decision made early on in the development process of the column, to try and avoid the extremes or the hot issues of the day, and focus instead on those issues that the majority of the parish community would find helpful and useful in their daily living.

However, that being said, every once in a while, over the period of twenty-five years, there would be a series of articles based on questions that did not seem to emerge from the community, but probably from the pen of the editor. More often than not, these questions dealt with certain issues of social justice, a particular dogmatic point, or a major Church event, that the editors considered to be important and which would fall into the category, "This is the kind of question that should be asked, and we need to have an answer for it." I can easily understand the impulse and the need for this kind of response, but I also respect the restraint that was demonstrated, for this seems not to have been the driving force or energy behind the column. The editors remained remarkably focused on the pastoral needs and concerns of the people of God, as those needs were made known to them, and not the other way around. In a very real sense, I think this contributes to the fact that the column remains refreshing, and seems not to be forced.

In compiling and editing the questions and answers that make up this collection, I had to make certain judgments. For example, although there were many questions, especially in the early years of the column, about the Second Vatican Council, I determined that this was not an overriding concern for today's reader, and so I chose not to include most of these questions. I also determined not to include any topic that seemed to be more historical than contemporary in nature. For example, questions about the millennium celebrations and the Church Jubilee Year were uppermost on people's minds in 1999 and 2000, but they seem not especially appropriate or necessary for this kind of collection.

Perhaps the single judgment I made that might cause some questioning is the decision not to include either the name of the particular priest who wrote the "Dear Padre" column or the date of the publication of the column. I wrestled with this concern but then determined that this book, although it reflects the work of individual priests, is more of a collaborative effort, truly a *Redemptorist Pastoral Publication*. For this reason, I do not note the name of the priest at the end of each answer, but I include a list of contributing priests at the end of the book. I hope that this was the correct decision and is accepted in the spirit in which it was made.

For those familiar with the "Dear Padre" column, this collection will probably bring back some fond memories along with being a helpful reference. However, for readers who never experienced the parish bulletin series, this collection is nevertheless both helpful and useful. I have arranged the questions and answers thematically, and envision that readers can refer to a particular question or, if they prefer, refer to a particular theme of interest. In either case, it is my hope that the arrangement will be helpful, and will make a contribution to your sense of Catholic life and practice.

THOMAS M. SANTA, C.SS.R.
REDEMPTORIST RETREAT AND RENEWAL CENTER
PICTURE ROCKS, TUCSON, ARIZONA

1

Advent and Christmas

INTRODUCTION
The Meaning of Advent

Advent is a liturgical season and a time of waiting and expectation, approximately four weeks in length, in preparation for the solemnity of the Nativity of the Lord. In the Roman Catholic Tradition, the season of Advent begins on the Sunday closest to the feast of the Apostle Andrew (November 30), and is considered the beginning of the liturgical year. Because it is a movable season, dependent as it is on the feast of an apostle, the season of Advent may begin as early as November 27, providing for a period of twenty-eight days of preparation, or as late as December 3, providing for a period of twenty-one days.

Advent is closely related to Christmas and cannot be considered apart from the feast. For example, the season of Advent didn't even exist until the birthday of Jesus was universally celebrated throughout Christianity on December 25. What's more, the word *advent* itself comes from the ancient names associated with the solemnity. *Adventus* (Latin for "coming"), *Epiphania*, and *Natale* are all synonymous for the Incarnation and also for the feast that celebrates the historical fact that the Word of God became flesh (human). Understood in this sense, the season of Advent is much more than a preparation period for a historical event, but is rather best understood as a period in celebration and preparation for the coming of God as an event of salvation.

For most Catholics, Advent is considered a time of spiritual preparation for Christmas. The emphasis during Advent is captured in a phrase that at first glance might not seem to have anything to do with Advent: "Remember to keep Christ in Christmas." This is an obvious reference to the commercial aspect of the days preceding Christmas day, which are counted off as "so many shopping days till Christmas." Advent is often cast as the spiritual tonic for the secular emphasis of the season.

Because of the compressed time frame and the fact that Advent, at least in the United States, is the period of time between two official civil holidays (Thanksgiving Day and Christmas), a festive mood seems to be prevalent. Unfortunately, many people have lost the spirit of the season and are unaware of the primary intent of this period of waiting. Perhaps because of a common pastoral emphasis, many consider the Advent season to be simply a time appropriate for the celebration of the sacrament of reconciliation, and they have lost the ascetical significance of the season. Most parishes, recognizing this popular understanding, offer opportunities for the private and the communal celebration of the sacrament during this time. Almost every other spiritual practice seems difficult, although not at all impossible, to implement. Nonetheless, the season of Advent is rich in spiritual traditions and practices and can be an important opportunity for growth and development.

Why Advent?

Can you give me more information about the Advent season? Why do we have Advent?

A Christmas Observer

Dear Observer,

Advent as we know it today developed many centuries after Jesus' life on earth. Because of the number of persons being baptized in the early Church, a practice developed of having another time for baptism in addition to the Easter Vigil. Christmas was chosen as another baptismal season. Since Lent served as a time of preparation for the baptisms at the Easter Vigil, the month before Christmas was set aside as a time for that same kind of preparation. Thus, the weeks leading up to Christmas became a time of penance and preparation. This is the source of the penitential aspect of Advent.

Combined with this penitential practice, of course, was the preparation for Christmas. The Sunday and weekday Scriptures during Advent recall the centuries of longing for the coming of the Messiah, the conception of John the Baptist, and the family history of Mary and Joseph. Today, the writings of the prophet Isaiah are featured during Advent because they so eloquently speak of Israel's longing for salvation.

Among the special signs and symbols that the Church uses to recall and enter into these central parts of our Christian heritage are the Advent wreath, vespers, reconciliation services, the O Antiphons, Scripture readings, the Jesse tree, the Giving tree, the Christmas tree, the crèche, gift-giving, and, of course, Midnight Mass. Hopefully, these symbols of the season will remind you of your own birth in baptism and your own commitment to living a life filled with peace and love.

The Great Dogmas

A very intellectual friend of mine told me that she loves the great dogmas of this Advent season. I smiled and agreed with her, but I didn't have the faintest idea what she was talking about.

In the Dark

Dear In the Dark,

The word *dogma* refers to teachings of the Church that are defined by an ecumenical council, including the pope, or by the pope acting as head of the Church apart from a council. The magisterium, the teaching authority of the Church, tells us that these "must be believed" truths have been divinely revealed to us. During Advent, we celebrate two dogmas: the Immaculate Conception of Mary, which we celebrate on December 8, and the Incarnation, one aspect of which, the actual birth of Christ, we are preparing for during this Advent season.

Both of these dogmas speak to us of God's extraordinary and intimate connection with the human family. God gifted Mary in a special manner because of her future role in becoming the Mother of God. Mary, from the first instant of her conception, was free from the stain of original sin. Her closeness to Jesus was established from the earliest moments of her existence. That we celebrate this feast in Advent is fortunate, because it speaks to us of God coming to dwell with us ordinary people in an extraordinary way. Mary is one of us, raised to a special level, but still one with our concerns and struggles.

The dogma of the Incarnation is most simply defined by Saint John. "The Word became flesh and lived among us" (Jn 1:14). During the calendar year, we first encounter and celebrate the Incarnation on March 25, at the Annunciation of the Lord. Scripture and Tradition hold that when Mary accepted the will of God by answering "yes" to the angel's announcement that she would bear "the Son of the Most High," Jesus was conceived in her womb, and "the Word became flesh" (Lk 1:26–38). During the season of Advent, we eagerly anticipate the result of the Incarnation, the birth of Jesus.

Many times, dogmas can seem sterile and disconnected from our lives. The practices and customs of Advent put an everyday face on the book definitions and remind us that the God of love lives in our midst.

May our meditations, acts of love, and prayer during this Advent season lead us to experience the humble love and strength of Mary, so that the Word will come alive for each and every one of us.

The O Antiphons

What are the O Antiphons and what is their connection to Advent and Christmas? Our parish announced an Advent service centering on these O Antiphons.

Don't Know "O"

Dear Don't Know,

The word *antiphon* is a Greek word meaning "answering voice." The antiphon is a verse that is usually taken from Scripture and recited before or after a psalm or canticle. The antiphons are used commonly when the morning and evening Liturgy of the Hours is prayed. The O Antiphons are special. They are the distinguished titles applied to Christ. These titles are taken directly from the Old Testament prophetic and wisdom books. You are probably already familiar with these O Antiphons, even though you might not realize it. We sing each of the O Antiphons in the Advent song, "O Come, O Come, Emmanuel."

In the seven evenings before the vigil of Christmas, the Church sings these series of special O Antiphons at the *Magnificat* during Vespers, the evening prayer of the Church. It is hoped that these will provide a strong daily meditation for the days leading up to Christmas. May the Christ Child be born again within you this Christmas morn!

What Are the Jesse Tree and the Giving Tree?

I noticed in our Sunday bulletin that our parish is setting up a "Jesse" tree and a "Giving" tree for Advent. What are these trees?

Lost in the Forest!

Dear Lost,

Parishes and families use the Jesse tree and the Giving tree as two distinct ways to prepare for the coming of Jesus, the child-king. We use the Jesse tree to remember Jesus' own royal family tree. The gospels of Matthew and Luke contain lists of the ancestors of Jesus. Matthew traces Jesus' genealogy back to Abraham (1:1–17), and Luke's goes back to Adam (3:23–28). Almost every ancestor is mentioned, of course, because the purpose is to connect Jesus to Abraham and to Adam. Primarily, this history puts us in touch with the continuous longing of the "chosen people" for a Messiah. Over the days of Advent, the names of significant persons in the Israelites' history and quotations from the Hebrew Testament are hung on the branches of the Jesse tree as a preparation for Christmas. Usually, the Jesse tree is placed in a prominent position, in the church or the home, so all can see the history of Jesus unfolding as we get closer and closer to Christmas.

The Giving tree challenges each family or member of the parish to buy a gift for someone in need. The parish sets up a tree that is decorated with tags indicating gifts for those in need. Clothing sizes and children's ages are connected with the requests on the tree, so that the givers can easily get the needed items and take their gifts to the parish church by a designated date. The gifts are then distributed before Christmas. The Giving tree unites us to the great message Jesus continues to give us at Christmas: Whatever you do to the least of these, you do to me (see Mt 25:40).

The Christmas Tree

Is there any spiritual significance in the Christmas tree? It seems like a lot of work and energy for just a bunch of branches with lights.

Humbug

Dear Humbug,

Our present-day Christmas tree tradition has its roots in the medieval religious "Paradise" play, in which a fir tree decorated with apples was used to symbolize the tree of the knowledge of good and evil in the Garden of Eden. This tree is mentioned in Genesis 2:9. The play told the story of Creation, of the sin of Adam and Eve, and of their expulsion from Paradise. It usually ended with the consoling promise of the coming of the Savior and the story of Bethlehem. Obviously, this made the Paradise play a favorite pageant for Advent.

The pageant was usually performed outside, in front of the church. If the pageant was performed inside the church, lighted candles were placed around the tree, and the play was actually staged within that circle of light. After these plays were no longer performed in the churches, the Paradise tree found its way into the homes of the faithful, becoming a symbol of the coming of the Savior.

By the fifteenth century, the fir tree, decorated with apples, was a common tradition. Gradually, small white wafers, symbolizing the Eucharist, were added to the apples as decorations for the tree. The meaning was richly symbolic and deeply rooted in faith and Scripture: the tree that bore the apples symbolizing the sin of Adam and Eve also bore the saving fruit of the Eucharist. Later, the wafers were replaced by pieces of white pastry in the forms of stars, angels, hearts, flowers, and bells.

By the middle of the seventeenth century, candles, representing Christ as the "Light of the World," were placed on the tree. Maybe this year, as you decorate your Christmas tree, you can remind your family of Jesus who is the Light and who feeds us even today.

The Twelve Days of Christmas

Does the song "The Twelve Days of Christmas" have any deep spiritual significance? A friend of mine, who loves history, mentioned to me that this song is really about the Christian faith.

Snooping

Dear Snooping,

The song "The Twelve Days of Christmas" comes out of the English tradition of celebrating the twelve days between Christmas and the Epiphany. This song became popular among Roman Catholics in the days when it was a crime in England to have any Catholic teaching material or any literature that was connected to the papacy. This song, "The Twelve Days of Christmas," carried hidden Christian messages. The "true love" in the song refers to God's love for us. In the first verse, "the partridge in a pear tree," refers to God's only Son, Jesus (how the wounded Jesus protected and redeemed us, as a partridge protects her young). So, in the song, God gives God's only Son, Jesus, to us on Christmas day.

During this Advent and Christmas season, let this song, "The Twelve Days of Christmas," ring with new spiritual meaning in your heart and soul!

What Do We Really Know About the Three Kings?

What do we really know about the three kings? Were they kings or astrologers? The gospels say that they believed in stars and dreams. Does this square with our faith?

Don

Dear Don,

Your excellent question makes us realize how much mere human tradition has "embellished" some of the events described in Sacred Scripture. Historically, the name *Magi* (singular, *magus*) designates members of an ancient Near Eastern priestly caste. In Matthew 2:1–12, they are presented as wise men and astrologers of noble disposition.

The number three has long been associated with the Magi in the Gospel. However, the Gospel infancy narratives never mention their number (though they did offer *three* gifts—gold, frankincense, and myrrh—to the Infant Christ). Saint Matthew is also silent regarding their names. However, in the eighth century, Western traditions began to call them Gaspar, Melchior, and Balthasar. Other Christian traditions have given them different names.

Though their gifts to Jesus indicate that their origin was South Arabia, it is doubtful that they were representatives of particular nations or of the major racial families. At the very least, the Magi represent the Gentile peoples coming from afar to find the true God in Jesus Christ. This is in contrast with King Herod and Israel. Both neglected this manifestation of God's presence even though it was in their midst.

Over the centuries, the Church has discouraged dependence upon dream interpretation and astrology as being superstitious at best. However, the fact that the Magi interpreted the stars and dreams does not necessarily contradict our Christian beliefs. They were unbelievers and therefore, at least until they offered homage to the Son of God in infancy, were not subject to God's law.

In fact, the Scriptures seem to allow for the interpretations of dreams as a possible way for God to communicate with individuals. Some examples are the patriarch Joseph, who interpreted Pharaoh's dreams (Gen 37–41); the prophet Daniel, who aided King Nebuchadnezzar (Dan 2–4); and Matthew's Gospel, where God instructed Saint Joseph through dreams (Mt 2).

As astrologers, the Magi were practitioners of a false science that claims to interpret the positions of the planets and stars and their effect on an individual's life. Astrology permeated ancient cultures, so it is not strange that astrologers appear in the Bible.

The Church responded to astrology by "Christianizing" certain aspects of it. For example, the Church deliberately called Christ the "Sun of Justice," thus replacing the pagan god *Sol* with the one, true God. In the fourth century, the Church deliberately placed the celebration of Christ's nativity on December 25, the birthday of the sun. We emphasize Jesus as the "Light of the World" and celebrate his feast every week on "Sun-day."

With the invention of the telescope, astrology's hold on people was seriously weakened. Today, astrology survives only among the credulous, while the science of astronomy has taken over the more serious aspects of astrology. Though the Magi would feel out of place today, their impact as witnesses to the most "cosmic" event in the history of the universe has been undeniable.

The Visit of the Three Kings

What is the real meaning of the visit of the three kings to Jesus? And does their visit have any meaning for us today?

Jack

Dear Jack,

At the most fundamental level, the three kings represent all the nations of the earth. These nations come and share their treasures with Jesus. In this context, the mission of the three kings can be seen as a challenge to all nations to recognize Jesus and share the treasures they have.

We can link the story of the three kings with another story in Scripture, that of the multiplication of the loaves (see Mt 14:13–21). In this story, the disciples represent the three kings. The disciples ask Jesus: "How can we possibly provide food for all these people?" But Jesus insists: "You yourselves give them food to eat." So the disciples divide up the five loaves and two fish they have in their possession and everyone has enough to eat.

The message of the Gospel is that when we share with one another the things that we have, it turns out that we have enough for all. We can look at it from a broader viewpoint: when one nation shares with another, there is enough for all. We all work toward this sense of sharing from our own corner of the world by not accumulating what we don't need and by making a conscious effort to share with those who have less than we have. We can contribute on a broader level by raising our voices and being heard through our political choices and through our involvement in local, national, and international issues.

We are not perfect, but the Lord does not demand perfection. The Lord asks for progress and for an honest effort. May the Lord strengthen us to share more at home and internationally, so that all of us may royally sit together at the King's banquet.

The Shopping Mania

Once again I feel overwhelmed by the commercial hype of Christmas. I struggle to keep a Christ-centered Christmas amid the shopping and gift expectations. Any suggestions for keeping Christ in my Christmas?

Shopping and Dropping

Dear Shopping and Dropping,

Here are some suggestions that might help you find some peace and remain centered amidst the shopping mania. As you read this, take the time to write out other suggestions for yourself.

It is our Advent task to make Christ, Emmanuel, present in our lives. We do this by centering on the love and peace that is within us and offering that to others. By staying centered and at peace, we will find the Christ Child even in the midst of the mania!

- Take time to pray. The churches are decorated with Advent wreaths, Jesse trees, and banners that accent the sense of longing during this season. Why not make it a part of your schedule to stop in daily for some quiet time and prayer. Jesus told us: "I will do whatever you ask in my name" (Jn 14:13).

- Plan to spend less money. Instead of buying many gifts, buy a few gifts, ones that you really enjoy buying. Let your family know that you intend to spend less money and want to enjoy your purchasing experience. Have them help you select really good gifts that have deep meaning.

- Downsize. Instead of going to the huge malls, plan to spend time investigating the smaller stores with more handcrafted items. Go to the stores that have a more personal touch.

- Be inspiring. Give gifts that focus more on Christ and Christmas. They could be beautiful, inspirational gift books; a Christian music CD; or tickets to a Christmas play or concert.

- Start a tradition. Make it a point to find a new Christmas tradition from a different culture and adopt that tradition for this season.

- Support your community. Go to the school Christmas plays, the local Christmas concerts (usually each college in the area has one), a poetry reading, or small group ensembles playing Christmas music.

- Volunteer. Give someone else a gift of unexpected kindness, compassion, and unconditional love. Visit someone who is sick, help in a soup kitchen, buy and wrap presents that will be given to the poor.

2
Angels

INTRODUCTION
Angels: Messengers From God

From the Greek word for "messenger," angels are often spoken of in the Bible. There are many Old Testament references to them (Gen 32:1; Isa 6; Tob 5). Of special note is the Gospel assertion that angels are spiritual beings (Mt 22:30) who always enjoy the vision of God in heaven (Mt 18:10) and who will accompany Jesus at his Second Coming (Mt 16:27). In the course of the centuries, theologians have described angels as created spirits without bodies, endowed with intellect and free will, inferior to God but superior to human beings. The Catholic Church professes that angels exist, but does not define any details about them (CCC 328–336).

What Does the Church Teach About Angels?

What does the Church teach about angels? Are we supposed to believe in them? Do they even exist? What is their purpose?

Mary

Dear Mary,

Our usual understanding of an angel might be what we find on a Christmas tree or a card we send on Valentine's Day. It is a tall individual with flowing robes and elongated wings. Because this image is so foreign to our daily experience, there is a tendency to place angels in the same make-believe category as unicorns or elves. If this is the case, it is most unfortunate and deprives us of a very important facet of our faith.

The word *angel* comes from the Greek *angelos*, which is the translation of the Hebrew "*mal'ak*," meaning "messenger." The primary function of angels, then, is to be messengers from God.

The Church officially teaches that angels exist as creatures of God. This was defined by the Fourth Lateran Council in 1215 and the First Vatican Council in 1869.

Angels are spirits who are intelligent creatures. Like every part of creation, they are less than God. Because they have free wills they have the capacity to reject God. That is why we believe that it was those angels who rejected God who are called demons in collaboration with Satan (Eph 2:2).

Our understanding of angels is based primarily on Scripture. Angels are often referred to in the Hebrew Scriptures. Most often they are sent in human form by God to intervene in people's lives by conveying a message, offering help, or protecting a person from harm. One well-known example was the angel Raphael, who accompanied Tobias on his journey (Tob 5).

In the Christian Scriptures the most famous instance of an angel was Gabriel. It was this angel who announced to Mary that she would be the Mother of God (Lk 1:26). Other instances of angelic intervention include appearances to the shepherds at the birth of Jesus (Lk 2:9) and to the witnesses at the tomb of Jesus (Lk 24:4).

Over the years, angels have been seen as providing a variety of services. Angels primarily serve God but also are believed to be of service to people in the form of guardian angels. A guardian angel is said to protect every person in a very singular manner. In Matthew 18:10 we read, "Take care that you do not despise one of these little ones; for, I tell you, in heaven their angels continually see the face of my Father in heaven."

Throughout the ages, the angels have been grouped into various classes or hierarchical orders such as seraphim, cherubim, thrones, dominations, archangels, and so on. As already pointed out, some even have names, such as Raphael, Gabriel, and Michael (who is known as the militant angel and guardian of the faithful). This information may be of interest to "angel buffs," but it is not intrinsic to our faith.

Reflecting on angels can serve a very important function in today's highly materialistic world. We live at a time that demands proof, that will believe nothing unless it can be proven without a doubt. Angels remind us that there is more to creation than what our senses show us. What we see, feel, hear, and taste is limited. There is a whole other reality that we believe exists. Angels remind us of the beautiful truth that we have a God who takes a personal, loving, all-abiding interest in us.

An Angel's Power

Recently, there have been some movies showing the power of angels. What, from a Catholic perspective, are the spiritual powers of angels?

Wondering

Dear Wondering,

There seems to be a true fascination about angelic beings in our world. I wonder if it is as possible to be just as fascinated with God, who created these wonderful beings. Angels not only serve God, but they comfort us who, according to the psalmist, are created a little lower than they.

Coincidentally, nearly every major world religion teaches about heavenly beings similar to angels. These heavenly beings are often depicted in religious writings as spiritual creatures, very close to the deity and to humans, full of wisdom, and able to travel at will. In religious art, they have been illustrated as fantastic creatures that sometimes combine parts of animals, such as lions and eagles, with parts taken from the human form.

The Bible describes the angelic hosts as giving dignity and majesty to God's eternal presence. There are a number of forms angels can take. The seraphim, for example, have six wings and act as emissaries of God to execute divine judgment. The Bible describes cherubim in various ways, sometimes looking human with wings, sometimes having a hybrid human-animal form.

The word *angel* comes from the Greek meaning "messenger." Christian doctrine understands angels as created by God, pure, immortal spirits lacking material bodies or gender, but possessing free will, wisdom, and intelligence. They relate to humans in a personal way, as the *Catechism of the Catholic Church* teaches, "surpassing in perfection all visible creatures, as the splendor of their glory bears witness" (CCC 330).

Jesus Christ is the center of the angelic world; angels exist to do his bidding and are messengers of his saving plan. The nine commonly held choirs, or categories, of angels in the Catholic Tradition are the cherubim, seraphim, thrones, dominations, principalities, powers, virtues, archangels, and angels.

Certain angels have names filled with meaning. Gabriel ("Man of God") announced the births of John the Baptist and Jesus. Raphael ("God heals") guided Tobias on his journey to seek healing for his father, Tobit. Raphael is also one of the seven angels who offer the prayers of God's people and enter the presence of the Holy One. Michael ("Who is like God?") is the protector of God's people and adversary of Satan. Michael drove Satan into hell and is to do battle with him on the Last Day.

The *Catechism* also reminds us that from infancy to death, each human life is surrounded by the watchful care and intercession of angels, whom we traditionally call "guardian angels." Beside each believer stands an angel as protector and shepherd leading him to life (CCC 336). Even so, we must remember that, apart from God's eternal plan, angels have no purpose in our lives. We need to recall that Satan and his spirits were once angels who, through their rebellion, are now adversaries of both God and humanity. Such spirits seek to mislead unsuspecting people and will use every means to disguise their sinister intentions.

Good Angels, Bad Angels

When I was a kid they always depicted angels standing by your shoulder—the good angel would speak in one ear and the bad angel would speak in the other. What is the difference between the good angels and the bad angels? Do they ever associate with one another? What is their relationship?

An Angel Devotee

Dear Devotee,

Some time ago, I read that a mother caught her three-year-old son taking pennies from her purse. She told him not to take things that belong to others. She then asked, "Could you hear your good angel crying when you took those pennies?" After a moment's reflection, the child replied, "No, the bad angel was laughing too loud."

But angels and devils are no joke. Angels, according to the *Catechism of the Catholic Church*, are personal and immortal spiritual beings created by God with intelligence and free will. The word *angel* means "messenger," and throughout Scripture angels are sent by God to care for people. Angels watch over and protect us as members of the Church, and we enjoy their company on life's journey (CCC 325–337).

Devils (also called demons, and personified in Scripture as Satan, Lucifer, or Beelzebub) are fallen angels. They were created good by God, but rebelled against God, becoming evil by their own choice. God does not annihilate creatures when they misuse freedom, and so demons continue to exist, and they try to get people to join their rebellion (CCC 391–395).

The difference between angels and devils, then, is that angels, after their creation by God, freely chose to do God's will, while devils chose to disobey. We don't know the exact nature of this diabolical disobedience, but it may well have been the sin of pride, the refusal to serve God. Because of the extraordinary intelligence of spiritual beings, and because they exist in eternity rather than time, the rebellion of devils against God is permanent and irrevocable.

Just as good people (like Mother Teresa, for example) try to encourage others to serve God, so angels inspire us to obey God. The Book of Tobit pictures the angel Raphael as a friend and companion of the young man, Tobias. Raphael instructs Tobias and guides and protects him. The *Catechism* states that all of us enjoy the watchful care of angels, and quotes Saint Basil's teaching that believers are protected by (guardian) angels who lead us to eternal life (CCC 336).

Just as evil people on earth try to recruit others for evildoing (a drug baron recruits others; gangs recruit others for hatred and violence), so devils try to recruit us into their rebellion against God. The Book of Genesis graphically represents Satan as a serpent who tempts the first human beings with the lie that they can become like God by disobeying God.

The only association between angels and devils pictured in the Bible is that of conflict. Revelation 12:7–12 portrays Michael and the angels battling against the devils and casting them from heaven. We tend to think of battle in terms of weapons, gaining territory, and bodily harm, but angels and devils, as spiritual beings, battle for the souls of human beings, a battle exemplified in the life of Jesus himself.

Angels proclaimed the birth of Jesus (Lk 2:8–14). They ministered to him when he fasted in the desert (Mk 1:13), and an angel appeared to strengthen him during his agony in the garden (Lk 22:43). Conversely, Satan tried to tempt Jesus to abandon God's plan for our salvation. When Jesus rebuked Satan, of course, Jesus conquered him. Jesus drove out evil spirits and exercised complete dominion over them (Mk 1:23–28, 34, 39; Mt 8:28–34).

"Like a roaring lion your adversary the devil prowls around looking for someone to devour" (1 Pet 5:8). But we need not fear Satan. Christ defeated him and sends angels to watch over us. We should stay in touch with our guardian angel, our companion and friend, through daily prayer, and one day our angel will, in the beautiful words of the funeral liturgy, "lead us into paradise."

Who Are the Archangels Michael, David, and Raphael?

Every year we celebrate the feast of the archangels Michael,
Gabriel, and Raphael. What makes them so special among the
millions of angels that exist?

An Angel Admirer

Dear Admirer,

First of all, let me propose a way of "understanding" your question that's a little different from trying to grasp or comprehend angels in simple and logical definitions. Rather, let us imaginatively "stand under" their mystery in stillness, humility, and awe, not unlike our stance before the crucifix or the tabernacle.

The *Catechism of the Catholic Church* says about angels: "The whole life of the Church benefits from the mysterious and powerful help of angels. In her liturgy, the Church joins with the angels to adore the thrice-holy God....Moreover, in the 'Cherubic Hymn' of the Byzantine Liturgy, [the Church] celebrates the memory of certain angels more particularly (Saint Michael, Saint Gabriel, Saint Raphael, and the guardian angels). From its beginning until death, human life is surrounded by their watchful care and intercession" (CCC 334–336).

Each of the angels you mention appears in Sacred Scripture. Interacting dramatically with people like Tobit, Mary, or Daniel, these angels' identities are less important than their roles. They are primarily meant to offer several glimpses into the mystery of the God whose emissaries they are. Then, and now, they stir us to "stand under" the communicating, healing, and protective nearness of God.

Gabriel's marvelous and challenging messages to both Zechariah and Mary, in the Gospel of Luke, dares us to believe that we, too, can know God personally. We can trust God's messages to us, as well as our ability to interpret them.

Raphael, Tobit's guardian and healer, is a promise of our own experiences of God's provident protection. God has power over evil and guides us safely in our travels, illnesses, and encounters with temptation.

Michael is the great protector of the Jewish people in the Book of Daniel and of the Church in the Book of Revelation, particularly in their community encounters with evil. As such, we can be confident that we, too, "stand under" God's personal protection, even amid the often terrifying darkness of our personal and community lives.

Who Is the Devil?

Jesus casts out demons in the gospels. Can the devil still force people to commit sin? Can you sell your soul to the devil, like Faust? Is the devil the same as the demon? Why doesn't God cast out the devil once and for all and stop all evil?

Joey

Dear Joey,

Faust, an epic drama by Goethe, is about a frustrated scholar, Doctor Faust, who sells his soul to a devil named Mephistopheles in return for happiness in this life. The two sign their pact in Faust's blood, but Faust finds no joy, because every wish granted comes at the expense of someone else's happiness. *Faust* is a great piece of literature, but it is not real. Please don't forget that. Don't cross the line from fiction to fact.

Although *Faust* may be fiction, the devil is real. The devil is alive, and we would be imprudent to deny the devil's existence. We first meet the devil in the Book of Genesis and, lastly, in the Book of Revelation.

The devil carries many names. "Satan" is the adversary. "Demon" refers to extraordinary strength. "Lucifer," meaning "Light Bearer," is the leader of the devils. "Beelzebub" is the Lord of the Flies. "Devil," the most common name, is the deceiver. Part of the devil's deceit may be to have us think of a character in red tights, with horns, goatee, and a tail.

It is a mistake to look too easily at the devil as a source of evil outside ourselves. That can often be an escape, running from the real problem we have to deal with, the source of evil within, "original sin." We need to admit that we are sinners, we are weak; and then we must take the time to search out that streak of evil and allow the power and grace of Jesus to replace it.

We should avoid dabbling in things that are dangerous. Don't give the devil power in your life by giving Satan equal time with God. The best way to deal with sin is to treat Satan as a bad temptation, and concentrate on your relationship with God. We should realize just how much we need God in our lives, and not worry about the devil.

The devil is certainly not behind every bush and around every corner, trying to force us into sin. We shouldn't blame the devil for every problem and sickness in the world today, repeating that old line: "The devil made me do it." The devil can never "make" us sin. The devil may lead us to confuse selfishness for fulfillment, but we are the ones who do evil of our own free will.

It is easy to blame the devil, to avoid guilt for our own actions. Adam and Eve were the first to do that, and some of us still do it. When we look to the devil as the source of evil in our lives, we are refusing to take responsibility for our actions. If we give up our responsibility, we also give up our freedom and our hope for forgiveness. Blaming others prevents us from admitting our sinfulness and asking for God's forgiveness, just as quack medicine can lead us to avoid proper medication for what really ails us. Casting out the devil once and for all won't end all evil, because we are the ones who commit sin.

Superstitious belief in the devil can be just as dangerous as ignoring evil in the world. Jesus can cast out devils and has the power to deal with Satan as well as sin. Jesus Christ has conquered sin and Satan, and we need not fear. We are not alone.

The Devil's Power

In many of the books and movies today, it appears that the devil is an all-powerful, can't-be-conquered force. Is this the true image of the devil? What is the Christian response toward the devil?

Seeking the Good

Dear Seeking,

Your questions sound very similar to those of Saint Paul's early community in Thessalonica. Many believers there had become so preoccupied with the power of evil that they had begun to neglect the normal duties of prayer, concern for the poor, and general Christian living. Paul's message was straightforward and clear: "[Do] not...be quickly shaken in mind or alarmed, either by spirit or by word or by letter, as though from us, to the effect that the day of Lord is already here. Let no one deceive you in any way; for that day will not come unless the rebellion comes first and the lawless one is revealed, the one destined for destruction....The coming of the lawless one is apparent in the working of Satan, who uses all power, signs, lying wonders....But the Lord is faithful; he will strengthen you and guard you from the evil one" (2 Thess 2:2–3, 9; 3:3).

That having been said, I must acknowledge that, in my twenty-six years of priesthood, I have encountered situations, however infrequently, in which the presence of evil was palpable. Typically, the settings involved some unconscionable abuse of someone utterly innocent and vulnerable. Indeed, while the incidents haven't paralyzed me, they have brought me to great humility. They have reminded me of my need for both a deeper trust in God and the strength of someone more spiritually wise and mature than I am, if such evil is to be confronted and repelled.

However, the usual way Satan (evil) operates is by seducing us into confusion, complacency, and self-will. Generations of writers, like C. S. Lewis in *The Screwtape Letters* or M. Scott Peck in *People of the Lie*, have depicted the subtle ways that evil can have power in and over us. Indeed, isn't that what's at stake in the Gospel account of Jesus' own temptations in the desert? (Mt 4:1–11).

Led into the desert, Jesus experienced not so much a frontal assault by the devil, but rather the hunger, fear, desperation, and isolation that make all of us vulnerable to the false gods of greed, consumerism, security, power, or self-righteousness. When the devil addressed him in his privation and vulnerability, Jesus, our Savior and model, found ways to call upon God's word and power so that the devil's power was vanquished, at least for the present moment.

Finally, the most telling part of our dealings with the devil is that these encounters will never be finished in our human lifetime. We will always be vulnerable, and the devil will always be watching for "an opportune time" (Lk 4:13). The phrase "one day at a time" can be a suitable summary of our approach to the devil. Each day, one day at a time, we need to rely on God's power to lead us through the maze of human choices to the ones that are of grace. Having succeeded, we will again, the next day, have to seek the same God-bestowed grace of wisdom and courage, calling on God in order to be led to God's ways. In other words, God's grace is sufficient and available if only we daily call upon it.

3
The Bible

INTRODUCTION
Catholics and Sacred Scripture

Within the Catholic Tradition, as in all Christian traditions, Sacred Scripture is always understood as "the word of God" (CCC 104). It is also an essential component of the Catholic Tradition to accept the Scriptures as the word of God, "written down under the inspiration of the Holy Spirit." With this understanding, Catholics believe, along with their brothers and sisters in Christ, that "God is the author of Sacred Scripture" (CCC 105).

Catholics also believe that the Bible teaches that truth which is necessary for salvation (CCC 107). However, and this is where the Catholic Tradition and other Christian traditions are not in agreement, Catholics are not solely people "of the book." Catholics do not believe that Scripture is the only place where we can discover the Word of God (CCC 108).

More often than not, this belief provides a singular point of contrast between the Catholic Tradition and other Christian traditions. This point of contrast can be easily illustrated by recalling conversations when friends and family belonging to other Christian traditions engage in spirited dialogue about faith and religion with a Catholic. People raised in the Protestant tradition frequently quote the Bible, and seem able to easily provide a specific text and reference in order to claim the "authority" that they need to bolster their argument. Catholics, on the other hand, are often frustrated by their inability to quote a particular Scripture reference as they search for the necessary "authoritative resource" to bolster their argument. More often than not, it is a particular dogma or teaching that more easily comes to mind, rather than a Scripture reference.

This inability does not have to be a negative experience, nor does it mean that Catholics do not value or accept the biblical Word of God as essential. Rather, it illustrates the point made by Saint Bernard of Clairvaux (1091–1153) so long ago when he wrote that the Word of God is "not a written and mute word, but incarnate and living" (CCC 108). The Catholic Tradition celebrates God's living and incarnate word, in the Sacred Scripture, in the Apostolic Tradition, in the sacred liturgy, and in the teachings of the magisterium (CCC 11). It should come as no surprise to Catholics that their response to a particular question or challenge would not necessarily be limited to a biblical quotation or reference.

The Bible: God's Last Word?

Why did revelation stop with the last book of the Bible? Does it mean that God cannot reveal more? It appears to limit God, whom I've always thought was limitless.

A Curious Bible Student

Dear Curious,

Yes, it's true; the Church holds that revelation closed with the last book of the Bible. The reason is simple: there was no more to reveal. All truth has been revealed in Jesus Christ. He himself said it: "I am the way, and the truth, and the life" (Jn 14:6). All that would remain after Christ—and this is a monumental task—would be the unfolding, the spreading, and the living of this way, truth, and life for all ages to come.

The fact that revelation stopped with the last book of the Bible does not limit God in any way. Rather, it attests to the fullness of revelation in and through Jesus Christ. Jesus is the definite revelation of God. Up to that point, God had made himself known through the medium of dreams and visions, angelic intermediaries, and specially chosen spokespeople we know as the prophets. And even though these conveyed the word and the will of God, they were clouded and filtered through the peculiar experience of the human agent; the communication was indirect.

In Christ, however, the mystery of God is unveiled, opened, and manifested directly for all to see. John makes this pivotal point in the prologue of his Gospel: "In the beginning was the Word, and the Word was with God, and the Word was God...the Word became flesh and lived among us, full of grace and truth (Jn 1:1; 14). The word used for "flesh," "*sarx*" in Greek, means "full of the human reality of life." The very Word of God, the Son, becomes a person, and can be seen, heard, and touched—experienced as a fellow human traveler. In and through Jesus Christ, the mind and heart, the thoughts, wishes, attitudes, and aspirations (if we can use these human attributes to describe God) of the hidden God are no longer hidden, but visible and tangible. In chapters 10 and 14 of his Gospel, John gets even more explicit when he has Jesus say, "The Father and I are one" (10:30), "If you know me, you will know my Father also" (14:7), and "Whoever has seen me has seen the Father" (14:9). The Letter to the Hebrews adds, "[The Son] is the reflection of God's glory and the exact imprint of God's very being, and he sustains all things by his powerful word...having become as much superior to angels as the name he has inherited is more excellent than theirs" (Heb 1:3, 4).

In Jesus, two worlds meet, the human and the divine. Christ is at one time the face of God and the quintessential human. As the former, he revels the inner core of God. All we need to know of God, especially his love and mercy, is contained and revealed in the person of Jesus. On the other hand, as one of us, he personifies how to respond to God—that is, with total openness and obedience to the Father's will. In the garden Jesus prayed, "Not my will but yours be done." We need only to look to Jesus to know the mind of God as well as to relate back to God in human response.

Even though there is no need for further revelation, there is need for continual unfolding and teaching of God's truth. The Church's task, as well as the Christian's mission, is to mine the rich deposit of revelation in the person and word of Jesus, and to show how it speaks to the ever-changing circumstances of life. This does not constitute new revelation so much as creative applications and responses to new life situations. Jesus continues to be alive and present in our world, challenging us to flesh out his revealed word in all areas of life.

Why Is the Bible So Hard to Understand?

Why is the Bible so hard to understand? The Word of God is critical to our Christian lives, but it can be so difficult to interpret.
A New Student of the Bible

Dear New,

The Bible is a unique piece of literature, perhaps the most unique in the world. In fact, it is not just one piece. The word *Bible* derives from a word meaning "library." The Bible is a library of seventy-two books, to be exact, dating from ancient times, written and edited by any number of authors, some known, some unknown. It contains, as any library would, a vast array of literary forms and expressions. The Bible covers more than three thousand years of history. Reading and understanding the Bible, and living up to its demands, is indeed a formidable task, one that will probably take us all a lifetime to accomplish.

The first key to understanding the Bible is to note that this is not just the work of human authors; it is the Word of God. We acknowledge the human element of the Bible; the authors' lived experience, the historical circumstances that form the background of the revelation. But we hold unequivocally that the truth and meaning of the Bible is the inspiration of God. The Catholic view is that God was able to reveal truth through the work of the sacred writers.

The Scriptures are layered accounts. They begin with historical facts, which are followed by years of oral tradition, and then end with the author's final version.

The best way to familiarize yourself with the Scriptures is to find a good Bible study program or group. This will acquaint you with the history of Israel, the times and culture in which the Bible was lived and written, the rich variety of literary forms in the Bible, and much more. Enjoy your biblical journey.

Why So Many Versions of the Bible?

In the last few years, many new versions of the Bible have appeared on the market. Why this seemingly sudden flood of new translations? Wasn't the older version of the Bible good enough?

William

Dear William,

Your question reflects the feelings of many Christians of all denominations. People are often bewildered by the new translations of the Bible that occupy ever-increasing shelf space in mass-market and religious bookstores alike. For centuries, the *Authorized (King James) Version*—and later the *Revised Standard Version*—served the needs of English-speaking Protestants in church and at home. The *Douay-Rheims-Challoner Version* played a similar role in the lives of English-speaking Catholics.

The purpose of the modern translations of the Bible is most certainly not to deny or belittle the historical importance and beauty of the earliest English-language versions. In fact, if you read the introductions and prefaces to the modern versions, you will discover that the translators take pains to acknowledge the far-reaching influence of earlier versions, which are literary masterpieces. Then the question remains: Why new versions at all? The following considerations may prove helpful.

Accuracy of Translation: Our contemporary knowledge of Hebrew, Aramaic, and Greek (the languages in which the books of the Bible were originally written) is much greater than at any time in the past. Studies of ancient Semitic languages, as well as discoveries of thousands of papyrus fragments written in first-century Greek, have enabled modern linguists to achieve a more thorough understanding of many biblical passages that puzzled earlier translators. Consequently, modern biblical scholarship can attain an unprecedented level of accuracy in its translations of the ancient biblical texts.

Clarity and Readability of Style: When the earliest English-language versions of the Bible began to appear, the translators had no thought of creating a special biblical vocabulary or style of writing (which, after all, was not present in the original languages either). The goal was simply to allow their translation of the Scriptures to communicate in English, as closely as possible, what the original versions had communicated to those whose languages were Hebrew or Greek. To this end, the translators of the sixteenth and seventeenth centuries employed the most vigorous and meaningful style available to them, in the educated literary speech of their own day. Pronouns such as *thee* and *thy* and words such as *peradventure* formed a natural part of their speech and writing. Some people today regard such usage as biblical English, but in reality it is simply archaic. There are, for example, no special forms as *thou* and *thy* in the original Greek and Hebrew. The aim of modern translators is the same as those of earlier centuries: to allow the Scriptures to speak to us in our own current idiom as vividly and clearly as the original languages did to those who spoke them.

Bridging the Denomination Gap: One of the results of the Reformation was that the Bible became a battleground between Christians of different denominations, as Protestants and Catholics alike were warned not to read one another's Bibles. Thanks to the ecumenical movement, which has begun to heal the deep-seated wounds of the Body of Christ, Protestant and Catholic scholars have been able to cooperate in their studies and translations of the Bible. We look for the day when the various denominations will approach reunification as closely as they approach a uniform translation of the Word of God.

How Should I Read the Bible?

The Bible is so large. What is the best way to read it or use it for prayer?

Julie

Dear Julie,

Most people get discouraged when they try reading the Bible, because they approach it like any other book. They begin on page one of Genesis and intend to read the whole Bible through the Book of Revelation. What often happens, though, is that somewhere around the Book of Numbers, readers get bogged down in confusion and boredom. So they give up.

Let me offer you a different approach that will likely make reading the Bible more manageable for you.

Begin with the New Testament: A good place to start is with the Gospel of Luke and follow this with the Acts of the Apostles, which Luke also wrote. Luke's Gospel will tell you the story of Jesus, and Acts will tell you the story of the early Church. Then you will be prepared to handle just about any part of the New Testament. Only after reading the New Testament should you go on to the Old Testament.

Remember that the Bible is a complex work: As important as *what* to read in the Bible is *how* to read it. This really requires study on our part. God is the author of the entire Bible in the sense that its writing was divinely inspired. But the Bible is not one book. It really is a library of books penned by different writers over various centuries and in various kinds of circumstances. You'll find poetry, fiction, history, parody, laws, and even census records in the Bible. Each kind of writing must be read in a different way.

Choose the right Bible: You should have a readable version of the Scriptures—one that is written in contemporary English. For some reason, many people think that the English King James version of the 1600s is more original or holier than the translations we have available today, simply because of all the "thee," "thou," and "art" language.

But this translation is not any holier than today's modern versions. The original texts of the Bible were written in Hebrew and Greek, not "thee" and "thou" English. We should read a version that has understandable language, introductions to the various books, and footnotes explaining the difficult verses. Some excellent Bibles for Catholics are the *New American Bible*, the *Jerusalem Bible*, and the *Christian Community Bible*, to name just a few.

Pray with the Bible: Finally, remember to use the Bible for prayer. Once your study leads you to recognize what a passage of the Bible says, sit down and think about it. What is the religious meaning contained in the passage? The Bible is not guaranteed to be accurate in its history, mathematics, science, or geography—only in its religious meaning. Pray over how that meaning can be applied today.

Reading the Bible is not easy, but it is rewarding, because in it we find the richness of God's truth. Perseverance is a necessary attribute of any Bible reader. Set up a certain time every day when you will look at the Scriptures and use them for prayer.

Saint Jerome said, "Ignorance of the Scriptures is ignorance of Christ." Remember this as you grow in your knowledge of the Scriptures, and you will grow in your knowledge of the Lord.

Is the Bible Just Myth?

Someone told me that the Bible is mostly myth, especially the Old Testament, and since myth is not fact, we don't have to put much stock into it. I've always thought the whole Bible was the revealed Word of God and factual. Would you help me understand?

An Avid Bible Reader

Dear Avid,

You are correct on both counts. The Bible is the Word of God and factual. But whoever told you that the Bible contains myth is also correct.

God's Word in the Bible is based firmly on historical fact. The principal event reflected throughout is God's free intervention in human history and the consequences of this intervention for all people.

The Bible traces the long history of this monumental saving event, from the call and faith response of Abraham to the final victory in the heavenly kingdom. But it does so strictly from a religious point of view. Historical accuracy, as we understand it, did not concern the sacred writers. Instead, their main goal was to express the religious meaning of history. They related salvation history.

After the time of the patriarchs (Adam through Abraham), the Old Testament chronicles the triumphs and defeats of Israel with the stories of Moses, kings like David and Solomon, and the prophets, who call Israel to faithfulness. Prophecy gives way to apocalypse and hope. Finally, in the "fullness of time," Jesus is born. We know the rest.

This all happened. Real people lived real lives in real historical circumstances. The stories and accounts are told in almost every literary style imaginable—saga, epic narrative, storytelling, poetry, song, prophesy, wisdom sayings, and hero stories. Scripture writers also used myth. But don't confuse myth in Scripture with fantasy or fairy tales. Like other literary forms, myth can be a vehicle for conveying God's revealed truth.

Myth gives coherence and meaning to the fundamental truths upon which all revelation is based. In this way, biblical myth is similar to pagan mythology. For example, Aesop's fables convey truths about human nature by using human-like animals as characters. We don't really believe that the animals talk and behave like humans, but these stories do contain truths about how human beings behave or should behave.

Pagan myths and fables have something in common with many biblical stories because they grapple with profound realties that go beyond simple observation or explanation. Jesus' parables do the same thing: while they are not factual stories, they do express truth. Scriptural myth is different from other myths in that it remains true to the Hebrew idea of God as known through divine revelation.

Even though myth can be found throughout Scripture, it is most evident in the first eleven chapters of the Book of Genesis. Here the author explains truths like: From where or whom did creation come? Is creation inherently good or bad? How did evil come to be? What kind of God are we dealing with? What are the origins of God's chosen people? Who are our ancestors and heroes of the past? How did present realities come to be the way they are?

These are fundamental bigger-than-life realities that demand the expression only mythic stories can provide. In summary, yes, there is the element of myth in the Bible, but no, the Bible is not myth.

Can Scripture Set Me Free?

I heard a priest recently say that Scripture should set us free. I wish this could happen to me! I feel so trapped by life. My job, my kids, my aging parents, bills, health insurance. It seems that everywhere I turn I am cornered by responsibilities. How can Scripture be a help?

Melissa

Dear Melissa,

Your question provokes a lot of thoughts in me about the importance of the Scriptures in our Christian lives. We begin with a deep belief that the Scriptures are a gift of God to us. There is power in the Word of God to challenge us, to change us, and to promote genuine spiritual growth. The Scriptures can lead us to freedom, the freedom of the children of God. Yet, for many people, the Scriptures often remain "a treasure hidden in a field."

True to your experience, many of us feel trapped by life. Life is complicated. Life is complicated because often there is too much to do, too many obligations, too much going on. We find ourselves a step or two behind. We feel burdened and many times even guilty that we're not doing more. There is never enough time. People complicate our lives. They do not respond as we hope. People are demanding and sometimes hurt our feelings. We can easily become victims of it all. In order to deal with all this complication, we become defensive or aggressive or overly "people pleasing."

If we read and pray over the Word of God, we can learn another pattern of behavior: "Consider the lilies, how they grow: they neither toil nor spin; ...how much more will he clothe you—you of little faith!" (Lk 12:27, 28); Jesus spoke to Martha saying, "Martha, Martha, you are worried and distracted by many things; there is need of only one thing" (Lk 10:41–42); Jesus invites, "Come to me, all you that are weary and are carrying heavy burdens, and I will give you rest....For my yoke is easy, and my burden is light" (Mt 11:28, 30). After the storm on the lake, Jesus calmed the winds and said to his disciples, "Why are you afraid? Have you still no faith?" (Mk 4:40). These and similar passages challenge us to put our trust in God and become less frantic in our lives.

But the Scriptures work only if we work the Scriptures. I invite you, Melissa, to pray the Scriptures each day. Quiet yourself; open yourself to the movement of the Spirit. The Spirit of God is alive in the Word, and the Spirit of God is alive in you. Read a short passage. Think about it. Put yourself into the scene. Picture yourself listening to Jesus speak. Allow him to use your name. Let yourself be comforted, loved, freed, healed, and challenged to change your hectic pace in life. Instead of trying to control all that happens, may you begin to surrender and trust in God. May you begin to open your eyes to see the beauty around you. May you begin to experience the love of others. The Word of God can lead us to freedom, as you heard, if only we open our hearts to the wisdom it contains. As you meditate on the Word, it will probably lead you to prayer, to ask for God's help, to knock, to seek, and to find. You may find your heart opening to receive the love of God you encounter in the Word. Remember Melissa, "Blessed...are those who hear the word of God and obey it!" (Lk 11:28).

Genesis: What Does It Mean?

I understand that the accepted opinion of Scripture scholars, as well as most scientists, is that God didn't create the world in exactly seven days. That makes sense, but what do the stories in Genesis mean then?

A Genesis Reader

Dear Gen,

I admit it is difficult to think of the familiar creation story other than literally. We grew up with this image of God neatly creating the world in six days, and then slumping in exhaustion on the seventh. Today we know that this is too simplistic a view. Due to the monumental work of Scripture scholars, we now have access to the long-hidden treasures of the Bible. The Bible must be taken in context and seen for what it is: a complex and extraordinary piece of theological literature compiled over centuries, reflecting a mid-Eastern Semitic culture and literary styles far different from our own. For this reason, there exist new attitudes toward the Bible.

Biblical research shows that Genesis is not a single, smooth-flowing narrative, written by one author. There are too many repetitions, inconsistencies, and differences in detail and style to be the work of one individual. It turns out to be a masterful amalgam of four separate traditions woven into one narrative by an unknown but brilliant editor around 358 B.C. In his book, *The Men and the Message of the Old Testament*, Father Peter Ellis explains that the editor's intent was to present the "origins of the Israelite people," along with "profound religious truths which were to be passed on to the world."

The first eleven chapters of Genesis—the first book in the Bible—are called "pre-history." They are the sacred writers' inspired attempts to explain realities that predate recorded history. The world and all in it—from where did it come? How did evil come in the world? Was it from God or from evil spirits? What do the stories of Cain and Abel, the Tower of Babel, and the Flood mean? How did God's chosen people come to be?

The first and primary truth is that God created the earth and everything in it. Creation not only came from God's hand, but it was good, not evil, as Israel's neighboring cultures held. Genesis affirms the special creation of man and woman not only as equal, but more amazingly, as made in the image and likeness of God. Of all creation, only man and woman bear the imprint of the divine in their being; only they represent God. They are to rule the earth and subdue it by making it habitable for human society. Harmony and peace were the original plan of God, symbolized by Adam and Eve innocently naked, strolling serenely and happily in the garden twilight at peace with God, each other, and all of nature.

But evil entered to shatter the serenity of Paradise. The sacred writers had to explain the destructive presence of evil in the world. They did so by boldly placing its origin squarely at the feet of the humans, making it clear that God didn't create evil, neither did the devil. People created evil by their free choice, opting to reject God's plan for them and take things into their own hands. In other words, they wanted to be God, rather than be made in God's image—and so the fall from grace. The stories of a brother killing his brother, the Flood, and the Tower of Babel are inserted by the editor to illustrate how pervasive evil had become and how great was the need for salvation.

A promise of victory appears in Genesis 3:5. Vague as it might be, it sets the stage for what follows: God's saving intervention in history by the selection of Israel as God's people. God establishes an everlasting covenant with them that would later culminate in Jesus: a definitive victory and the irreversible establishment of the kingdom of God.

Simplistic as these stories may appear on the surface, they are profound revelations of fundamental truths on which the rest of the Bible is constructed.

What Does Revelation Really Say?

If the Book of Revelation does not contain gloom-and-doom predictions of the world's end, what does it say? It's some of the strangest stuff I have ever read.

Bible Enthusiast

Dear Enthusiast,

The message that Revelation offers today is exactly the same as it was for the people to whom it was originally written. It continues to deliver a positive, spiritual message to all Christians, especially those in difficult or desperate straits. Revelation says: Don't despair or give up faith in Jesus Christ. By his death and resurrection he has won the definitive victory over any and all forces of evil and darkness, including what you are facing. Someday, through perseverance, you will enjoy the fullness of that victory in the company of Christ himself and all those who followed him to the end.

According to tradition, John of Patmos wrote Revelation around A.D. 95. He directed it to Christians who were not accepted as legitimate citizens in the first-century Roman Empire. Jesus had died and had risen some sixty years earlier, and Christianity had flourished for some years as the numbers of Christians grew. But now they were suspect and intermittently persecuted as possible enemies of the empire. Some say the emperor Nero blamed the burning of Rome on Christians, using this trumped-up charge to mount a bloody campaign to wipe them out. It was dangerous, even deadly, to be known as a Christian. Their citizenship, property, and sometimes their lives were in jeopardy.

Some Christians buckled under the pressure and reverted to old pagan ways. Others wavered and became lax. All wondered: *If Jesus Christ is Lord, why do the oppressive and pervasive evils of the pagan Roman Empire continue to flourish? Why doesn't Jesus return and wipe that out once and for all? Why do we have to undergo harassment, persecution, and loss? Why are we left so helpless in the face of this monster?*

John addressed these questions by reassuring Christians that they were, indeed, on the right track in following Christ. Even though it may appear that Rome, the emperor, and other forces of evil dominate, it is only fleeing and temporary. They will eventually deteriorate, along with all the old enemies of God that have long since disintegrated and have become only footnotes of history.

To effectively and safely convey his message, John used language and imagery almost exclusively from the Hebrew Scriptures. Dipping into Old Testament knowledge by using characters and incidents from Israel's past, John constructed a wildly imaginative, symbol-laden revelation about the cosmic struggle between good and evil. To those unfamiliar with the Scriptures—and that may include us today—Revelation was indeed strange and esoteric. But to those knowledgeable in the Scriptures, Revelation made sense. It not only served as a familiar vehicle for his message, but it also provided a safeguard against the oppressors, since they would be hard pressed to know what it all meant.

Revelation's message of hope will remain current and poignant as long as Christians struggle against evil. Even in the absence of overt persecution, Christians still must live and give witness to their faith in a world that is not always receptive. Revelation allows Jesus' followers to maintain Christian perspective in hostile circumstances. Clinging to hope in Jesus Christ, Christians know that whatever the forces of evil and however powerful they may be, Jesus will overcome. And so will they, if they remain steadfast and true to him.

The Bible and Inclusivity

I've noticed lectors in our church occasionally changing the wording of the readings. Where the text reads "men," they change it to "persons." I personally appreciate that, as it gives me a sense of inclusion, but I do wonder: Is the Bible chauvinistic or anti-female?

A Wondering Woman

Dear Wondering,

I don't think it is accurate to characterize the Scriptures as chauvinistic. The *Random House Dictionary of the English Language* defines chauvinism as "zealous and aggressive patriotism or blind enthusiasm for military glory" and "biased devotion to any group, attitude, or cause." Recently, chauvinism has also come to mean excessive attachment to the masculine and disdain for the feminine. But women are not disdained in the Bible. Scripture use of masculine gender doesn't stem from chauvinism, but rather from patriarchy, which means a "form of social organization in which the father is the supreme authority in the family, clan, or tribe, and descent is reckoned in the male line, with the children belonging to the father's clan or tribe."

In the preface to his *Book on Revelation*, John Tickle notes, "Our Scriptures originated in the living community of the people of the Old Testament and the disciples of the early Christian community." Those communities were profoundly patriarchical.

This, however, is no excuse for containing non-inclusive language. Today we must be acutely sensitive to both chauvinism and possible undertones of patriarchalism in Church functioning and language. Even if it is not overtly chauvinistic in the contemporary negative sense, patriarchalism still remains non-inclusive and, therefore, offensive to many people. Equality of persons is a sacred characteristic of Christ's Church. The Second Vatican Council declared, "In Christ and in the Church there is, then, no inequality arising from race or nationality, social condition or sex" (*Dogmatic Constitution on the*

*Church, §*32). This equality needs to be espoused as principle and expressed in daily life. Inclusive language is a way of putting this into practice.

To this end, in 1989, six bishops, who were members of the pastoral team of the Canadian Conference of Catholic Bishops, issued a statement on inclusive language. It begins with the reminder that, "as Christians, we are called to witness to the fundamental equality and dignity of all people." Along with the cultural signs of our times, most notably the women's movement, they cite significant theological reasons for using and promoting inclusive language. In other words, to believe and live our faith is one thing, but we must also articulate it.

We must make real the "understanding of the Church as a communion," and as "a sacrament or sign of the unity to which the whole of humanity is called." In other words, we need to express equality of persons before God, and one way this can be done is through using inclusive language.

The bishops urge implementation of inclusive language. However, they admit that this will take time because of people's differing opinions on the topic and because Scripture scholars and theologians must be careful to preserve the accurate *meaning* of the Bible and the Sacramentary as they move to implement inclusive language. In the meantime, the bishops wrote, "Action can be taken to introduce inclusive language at home, in social gatherings and on the job. Parishes can commit themselves to using inclusive language in the prayers of the faithful, in hymns, in written material such as parish bulletins, in announcements from the pulpit, at parish gatherings, etc."

By striving to use inclusive language, we heighten our sensitivity, include all people without discrimination, and live the communion we are called to be.

What Is "Private" Revelation?

A member of my parish showed me the back of her Bible where she had written down the names of various saints who have appeared to her and spoken to her. Is she crazy, or is this something that really happens?

A Sane Catholic

Dear Sane One,

Your friend might be experiencing what we call "private" revelations. Most of our recognized saints experienced visions in which Jesus, Mary, or the disciples spoke to them. Many times these revelations were the sparks that caused these future saints to leave whatever they were doing, change their lives, and follow Jesus in a dynamic way. Saint Francis of Assisi is an example of such a visionary. He was a rich young man who had a vision of Christ that radically changed his life. After this "private" revelation, Francis devoted himself to poverty and care of the sick. He founded the religious order we now call the Franciscans to carry on his vision. An example of a recent private revelation is the apparitions and messages at Medjugorje. Even though the Church has not yet formally recognized these messages, many have found a deeper faith because of them.

The *Catechism of the Catholic Church* says this about private revelations: "Throughout the ages, there have been so-called 'private' revelations, some of which have been recognized by the authority of the Church. They do not belong, however, to the deposit of faith. It is not their role to improve or complete Christ's definitive Revelation, but to help live more fully by it in a certain period of history" (CCC 67).

It is important to note whether the private revelation is contrary to the faith or the morals of the Church, and whether a particular revelation brings one closer to God.

4
The Blessed Mother

INTRODUCTION
The Blessed Mother

Catholics believe that Christ is always to be seen at the center of God's plan of redemption. Both the Apostles' Creed and the Nicene Creed declare that our redemption is the mission of Jesus Christ. However, within the Catholic Tradition there has also been a place for the role of the Blessed Mother, not as the center of God's plan or, for that matter, even at the center of Catholic catechesis, but a place of honor nonetheless.

Mary, the Blessed Mother, is seen as the Mother of the Redeemer, the person who fully cooperated with the Holy Spirit and who continued to cooperate throughout her life with God's will for her. At the same time, Mary is the Jewish woman, wholly human, who is Jesus' mother. She is the God-bearer, the mother of a divine and human person, which is the mystery of the Incarnation, the true and singular event of our human history.

In the *Dogmatic Constitution of the Church*, from the Second Vatican Council, the bishops helped us to understand that Mary is "the gracious mother of the divine Redeemer here on earth, and above all others and in a singular way the generous associate and humble handmaid of the Lord" (§61).

The Role of Mary

Recently, there seems to be a lot of discussion concerning Mary and her role in the Church. When Mary appears and reveals different messages, it seems to add more fuel to the question of her position among the angels and saints. What is Mary's primary role, both in history and now?

Pro-Mary

Dear Pro,

There is no doubt that Mary's primary role is that of the mother of Jesus. This allowed the Son of God to enter the world and accomplish our salvation. For this reason, she is called "blessed" through all generations.

Everything else about Mary receives its significance from her primary role as Mother of God. She is known as a woman of faith, because she answered "yes" to the angel's request that she become God's mother. Her obedience to God's will becomes a source of inspiration to us, as we try to love God and be obedient to God's will. Mary's courageous love for her son at the foot of the cross is a model for us when we must face sorrow over the loss of a loved one. She is with the apostles in the upper room, praying for the coming of the Holy Spirit, so we imitate that woman of prayer, particularly in asking for the gift of the Holy Spirit.

The Church has taught us that Mary was conceived without original sin, that she remained a virgin throughout her life, and that upon the completion of her earthly pilgrimage, she was assumed into heaven.

Personal experience assures us that we can ask Mary to join us in our prayers. Many who have lost confidence in their own ability to approach God have found an advocate in Mary. She leads them back to their loving, forgiving, and compassionate Father.

The Church has honored Mary under a multitude of titles and through innumerable works of art and song. For some "Our Mother of Perpetual Help" speaks most warmly to our hearts. For others, the title "Our Lady of Guadalupe" or "Our Lady of Fátima" or "Our

Lady of Lourdes" is favored. In every case, it is the same woman we honor. New apparitions seem to be reported from time to time, and faithful who have put a great deal of confidence in Mary's prayers and love for them readily go off to the site of the apparition, hoping to see this woman who is so important to them. Some of the apparitions are not genuine. People who are deluded, or those with less than honorable intentions, may try to take advantage of the people's love for Mary, but even in those cases, the faithful have a genuine love for the woman they believe is coming to them.

These are a few notions about Mary. They all stem from the primary grace Mary was given in her life: to be the Mother of God. And perhaps, after "Mother of God," the title Mary most appreciates is that of "Mother of the Church"—mother to each of us who struggles to imitate her, to have faith and to act on it.

Are Beliefs About Mary Bible-Based?

Where does devotion to Mary come from? Is it based on Scripture?

Richard

Dear Richard,

Catholics' basic devotion to Mary and understanding of her life are based on Scripture; however, some of our Catholic doctrines about Mary are not.

Scripture-based beliefs about Mary include, most basically, that Mary is the mother of Jesus. Since Jesus is God, we call Mary "Mother of God." That means she was the human mother to God who came to earth as a human being. "The Word became flesh and lived among us, and we have seen his glory, the glory as of a father's only son, full of grace and truth" (Jn 1:14).

Scripture also tells us that Mary was a woman of deep faith. This enabled her to say "yes" when the angel asked her to be the Mother of the Messiah. We also consider Mary to be an example of God giving victory over the lowly. Once Mary found out she would be the

Mother to the Messiah, she sang out: "My soul magnifies the Lord, and my spirit rejoices in God my Savior, for he has looked with favor on the lowliness of his servant" (Lk 1:46–48). Yes, Mary was a "nobody" in the eyes of her society, but through her, Jesus would come to transform the whole human race.

These are just several of our Scripture-based beliefs about Mary. Other things that we believe about her have come to us through oral tradition. That means they are not specifically mentioned in the Bible but, at the same time, do not contradict the Bible. Oral traditions are beliefs handed on to us by previous generations. Among these oral traditions about Mary is the doctrine that she was conceived without sin. This is called her Immaculate Conception. We celebrate Mary's Immaculate Conception on December 8 of each year.

The Church's tradition also teaches that Mary remained a virgin even after the birth of Jesus. The Scriptures themselves declare she was a virgin at the time of Jesus' birth (Mt 1:23–25), but they say nothing either way about her "virginity" afterwards.

We also believe that Mary was "assumed into heaven." That means she was taken into heaven immediately, body and soul, on the day of her death.

With the exception of the Eastern Orthodox and some Anglicans/Episcopalians, our non-Catholic Christian brothers and sisters have not given Mary the same focus or attention that we have.

We will have to arrive at a more profound understanding of "Church" itself before we come to a consensus with non-Catholic Christians on the doctrines pertaining to Mary that we Catholics have received from our forebears. Pope John Paul II has held out a hope that all will join together in honoring Mary. In his 1987 encyclical, *Mother of the Redeemer*, he wrote: "Why should we not all together look to her as our common mother, who prays for the unity of God's family and who 'precedes' us all at the head of the long line of witnesses of faith in the one Lord, the Son of God, who was conceived in her virginal womb by the power of the Holy Spirit" (§20).

Why Is Mary Called the Mother of God?

Why do Catholics call Mary "the Mother of God?" Doesn't this mean that Mary came before God?

Lauren

Dear Lauren,

Catholics do call Mary the "Mother of God," but this does not mean that Mary came before God. Rather, it expresses our belief that Mary is truly the mother of Jesus Christ who, from the first moment of his conception, was both human and divine.

Catholics believe that God is a Trinity of Persons—Father, Son, and Holy Spirit—in one divine nature. We believe that God existed from all eternity and is the source of all created things.

We believe also that, to save us from sin, the second Person of the Trinity, the Son (also called the "Word" in the Gospel of John) took on a human nature. God became one of us in the mystery of the Incarnation (God becoming flesh).

The story of the Incarnation is related in the Infancy narratives of the gospels of Luke and Matthew. Luke 1:26–38 tells us that God sent the angel Gabriel to Mary, a young woman of Nazareth in Galilee. Gabriel announced that Mary would have a child, the Son of God, by the power of the Holy Spirit. Mary consented, and Jesus Christ was conceived in her womb.

In Luke's Gospel, Mary is greeted by Elizabeth as "mother of my Lord." This greeting expresses the reality that the Lord, the God of the Hebrew Scriptures, is present in the womb of Mary. Other passages in the Bible testify to the same fact. Mary is the mother of Jesus Christ. Jesus Christ is God (Jn 20:28). Therefore, Mary is the Mother of God.

Jesus Christ's origins are both divine and human. The miraculous conception of Jesus in the womb of Mary was the moment when the immortal, eternal God took on a mortal body and entered our history. From the moment of his conception, Jesus was both God and human, thus Mary is the Mother of God. Therefore, belief in Mary as

Mother of God is tied to belief in the reality of the Incarnation. This is a mystery that is beyond our understanding and must be accepted in faith.

When we honor Mary as the Mother of God, we are actually professing our belief that Jesus is truly God. We are not saying that Mary came before God. Rather, the second Person of the Trinity, who existed from all eternity, "became flesh and lived among us" (Jn 1:14).

Is Mary an Obstacle to Ecumenism?

During a recent homily, the priest said that we should imitate Mary. I have a lot of non-Catholic friends, and it seems like Mary just gets in the way of ecumenism. If the Church is going to be ecumenical, then we'll just have to give a little. We should concentrate on Christ because all Christians can relate to him. When are priests going to get that point?

Bob

Dear Bob,

I chose your letter because it is so unusual. Many Catholics think that the Church has all but forgotten Mary. Yet you seem to think that she *should* be forgotten. I just cannot agree with that.

Mary is important to me personally, but she is also important to the Church. Mary entered into the consciousness of the Church from the very early centuries. Those early Christians were not concerned with Peter's mother or Paul's mother, but the witness of tradition shows a great interest in Mary.

Was Mary important to the Church because she was the mother of Jesus or because she involved herself in the life of her Son? Perhaps due to both of those factors, Mary has been ever-present in the Church.

The privileges accorded to Mary are granted because she is God's mother. The place of honor she holds among us is due to her exemplary life. Mother of God and perfect disciple earn for Mary the premier place among the saints.

Her feast of the Assumption, celebrated on August 15, for example, celebrates one of the privileges given to Mary. The Church believes that Mary was preserved from the deterioration of the grave. Another privilege given to her was that she was preserved from the stain of original sin. That is what is meant by the Immaculate Conception, celebrated on December 8.

These and other feasts that recount the special privileges given by God to Mary follow from her special place in the scheme of salvation—Mary as the Mother of God.

You may be right when you state that some non-Catholics have a hard time believing these things about Mary. The words used to describe Mary's privileges are difficult to understand. But all Christians can come to appreciate Mary's faithful devotion to her Son's teaching.

It is in this sense that the Church has always presented Mary as one to be imitated. When the early Church looked around for an example of what it meant to be a follower of Jesus, it turned to Mary. Her fidelity, life of charity, and commitment to the values taught by her Son, as well as her deep belief in the divinity of Jesus and her conformity to God's will, made her the best example of the Christian life. If all Christians examined their lives using Mary as the model, they would have a clear indication of the virtues Jesus counseled.

Ask the Virgin Mary to help you attain those attitudes and virtues that will make you holy. Holiness is the best contribution to ecumenism that anyone can make.

What Is Mary's Role Today?

I have been struggling to understand the role of Mary in today's world. In the past, love of Mary was important to me, but now I am not so sure. Does Mary have a place in our world and in my life today?

Joann

Dear Joann,

Mary did live a long time ago, and her world was simple and slow moving compared to ours. We live in a rapidly changing world, a world dominated by computers, television, space exploration, and nuclear arms. It's a world filled with terrorism and unrest. How can Mary possibly fit into such a world?

We must remember that Mary changed the world by her simple "yes." She agreed to do the will of God. She gave Christ to the world, and the world has never been the same since. She challenges us to do the same. Mary's example inspires us to give to our world right now, in our time and in our place.

To do that we must in today's world, we face several challenges—just as Mary did. To give Christ to the world, Mary first challenges us to be willing to take risks. Because she consented to do the will of God and become the Virgin Mother of the Christ Child, Mary risked shame, criticism, misunderstanding, and false accusations. She also risked bearing the brunt of small-town gossip. Living a Christian life today is also risky. We risk being ridiculed by a society that endorses many forms of immorality—a society that often ridicules our notions of God and religion.

To give Christ to the world, Mary also challenges us to be courageous and faithful. It took courage and faith for Mary to do what God was asking of her each day. It takes the same qualities for us to do God's will. It also takes courage and faith to endure suffering and hardship, as Mary did. She was no stranger to suffering. Remember, one of the titles that we give her is the "Sorrowful Mother."

In addition, Mary challenges us to be prayerful people. Prayer is a profound awareness of and response to God's presence in our lives. The great prayer of Mary, her *Magnificat* (Lk 1:46–55), is a prayer that sings gloriously of God's presence in her life.

Mary challenges us to be compassionate and sensitive to the needs of others as a way of giving Christ to our world. That's why she visited her cousin Elizabeth, and that's why she asked her Son to help at the wedding in Cana. She challenges us to see what is needed, and then do something about that need.

Mary also challenges us to be strong in order to give Christ to the world. She showed her strength as she stood beneath the cross. We must be strong and stand by our Christian principles in a world of violence, terrorism, and nuclear threat. Mary's strength challenges us to give to our world the peace her Son came to bring.

Finally, Mary challenges us to know God loves us, and then to give that love to others. Because Mary knew God loved her, she was able to give love to the world in the person of Jesus Christ. Love is the way we, too, can give Christ to our world today.

We can see that Mary was a woman willing to take risks. She was courageous, faithful, and prayerful. She was compassionate and sensitive to the needs of others. She was a woman who knew God loved her and so was able to give love to the world. What Mary did for her world we can and should do for our world today.

What Is "Popular Devotion" to Mary?

I recently went to Medjugorje, where I experienced a great renewal of my faith and devotion to Mary. Someone told me that the reason the Church doesn't make any official statements about Mary's appearances at Medjugorje is because they are "popular devotions." What does this mean?

Angelo

Dear Angelo,

People who read and study theology deal with concepts of the faith about Mary. Some of these concepts include our beliefs that Mary was God's mother, that she was a virgin, that she was immaculately conceived, and that she was assumed body and soul into heaven. When the Church asks us to believe in these concepts, we call them "dogmas of faith." Dogmas are the truths about the faith that we Catholics believe, even though we might not fully understand them.

There is another level of faith that deals with the thoughts and feelings of ordinary Christians toward Jesus, Mary, the saints, the devil, heaven, and hell. This level of faith is usually referred to as "popular faith."

Popular faith relies on physical signs and wonders as proof of the divine. Over the centuries, Catholics have cultivated a faith that promotes pilgrimage to shrines associated with Mary, Jesus, and the saints; statues of Mary and Jesus that cry or smile; divine power issuing from the water of holy places; blessed medals, scapulars, or pictures. Through the centuries, these popular practices have offered a conduit to God for many believers. Mary has always been a favorite of this popular style of devotional life.

Mary became a figure for popular devotion among the first Christian communities. As early as A.D. 150, in the catacombs of Rome, people painted pictures of Mary holding the baby Jesus. This popular devotion of painting Marian pictures evolved into building churches in her honor. Today, almost every Catholic church contains a shrine to Mary.

In the twentieth century, people have formed many organizations in honor of Mary. The Legion of Mary, for example, was formed in 1921, the Word of Mary (or Focolare) movement was formed in 1943, and the Blue Army of Fátima was formed in 1947.

This great amount of popular devotion to Mary has remained consistent throughout the last two thousand years. Here are some examples of how the eyes of popular faith have viewed Mary throughout the centuries:

Mary As a Restorer of Health: Every year, thousands of pilgrims visit Marian shrines for healing. The miraculous cures attributed to Mary number in the thousands, perhaps even in the millions.

Mary As an Intercessor: Mary will intercede with God on our behalf. Many of the apparition messages (Fátima, Lourdes, and Medjugorje, for example) ask us to pray with Mary for certain needs in the world.

Mary As the Mother of Mercy: Mary will always ask God's forgiveness for us. She is the faithful mother who never turns away from us.

The Church usually says nothing official about popular devotions unless a given devotion is injuring the Faith or misleading the people. You can continue, Angelo, in your devotion to Mary and be secure in the knowledge that the Church encourages it. You might also want to make note of some of the more popular Marian apparitions that seem to have occurred continuously over the centuries. These popular apparitions include:

> 1531: Our Lady of Guadalupe, Mexico
> 1858: Our Lady of Lourdes, France
> 1879: Our Lady of Knock, Ireland
> 1917: Our Lady of Fátima, Portugal
> 1981: First apparition of Mary at Medjugorje, Yugoslavia

Mary's Assumption

What is the history behind Mary's Assumption, and what does this feast mean for me?

A Marianist

Dear Marianist,

There is a tradition among some of the tribes in Africa that, when one tribal member gets a good-paying job in the government or in the army, all of the people in that person's clan share in the money earned. The success of one is shared by all.

The feast of the Assumption of Mary carries with it the same dynamics. Mary, because of her special union with her divine Son, gives witness to Jesus' complete victory over death. In Jesus and through Mary, we share in the graces that come from that triumph.

The feast of the Assumption is a very ancient one. It was initiated in the fifth century and was celebrated at the site in Jerusalem where Mary was believed to have rested as she journeyed from Jerusalem to Bethlehem. At that time, the feast was called *Theotokos* (which means "God-bearer") and was celebrated on August 15. Later, the feast was celebrated at the basilica where Mary's tomb was venerated. By the end of the sixth century, the feast came to be called the *Dormition* (Mary's "Falling Asleep"). By the end of the seventh century, the name of the feast was changed to the Assumption. Throughout this time, the celebration of this feast of Mary increased and devotion to her deepened.

In 1950, Pope Pius XII placed the official stamp of recognition and doctrine on the ancient feast. This decree brought a sense of holy sanctioning to the devout belief surrounding Mary that had been celebrated for centuries.

"The Immaculate Conception Doesn't Seem Important"

The Immaculate Conception doesn't seem important. In my affection for Mary, it makes no difference whether or not she was immaculately conceived. In fact, I'd rather believe that Mary started out on the same level as any other woman. To be preserved from original sin has always seemed to me to be an unfair advantage. My admiration for Mary would be much greater if I really felt that she was one with us in the human struggle.

Karen

Dear Karen,

What you are saying about the Immaculate Conception represents what many people today feel about this Catholic doctrine. It's viewed as removing Mary from the human family—placing her on such a high pedestal that she's totally out of touch with real people. How could such a perfect person understand what we ordinary mortals go through?

My response is that just the exact opposite is true. Mary Immaculate is more human, more a woman, and more interested in us than she would have been if God hadn't given her this singular privilege. What are my reasons for saying this?

Consider what we mean by sin. Although the word is used in different ways when we speak of personal sin and original sin, there are some common characteristics. By its nature, sin divides and alienates people. It destroys relationships that we must maintain if we are to be the graced people God intends us to be. Think of all the harm that hatred, violence, deceit, and greed do to the worldwide community, individual nations, communities, families, and persons.

Besides that, sin makes us less human than we were meant to be. It keeps us from becoming the full human beings envisioned by God. Look at some of the ways we describe sin—degrading, unnatural, and animalistic. This is a far cry from what we are called to be—sons and daughters of God and, ultimately, sharers of the divine life itself.

Mary was never under the dominion of sin, personal or original. This means that there is nothing to prevent her from experiencing the closest possible solidarity with other human beings. For Mary, the barriers of sin that we usually erect are missing. There is nothing to keep her heart from going out to all human beings. Mary has a better understanding of redemption than we do. Prevention is better than a cure. She has more to be grateful for than we do, and we owe everything to God. The best way she can show her gratitude is by doing all she can to make sure her Son's blood wasn't shed in vain for even one person.

The gospel account that speaks of Mary doesn't tell a tale of some aloof queen living in regal splendor, unaware of the life of the ordinary person. Rather, we read about "the handmaid of the Lord," a teenage girl who always tried to do whatever God asked of her. When Gabriel addressed her as one "especially favored by God," she was the most surprised person on earth. But that wasn't all. Next came the most incredible invitation ever offered: to become the Mother of God! This time she was ready. She asked herself if this was what God wanted. Assured that it was, her whole being answered, "Yes!" But aside from that one brilliant heaven-touched moment, the record suggests that the Virgin Mother lived a life of faith, just as most of us do.

Mary was immaculately conceived not for her own sake, but because she would give birth to Jesus. This extraordinary grace made her, after her Son, the most human of all persons, and the most loving of mothers.

What Is the History of the Rosary?

I have prayed the rosary ever since I was a child. The other day, my grandchild asked me about the rosary—when it started and what it means. I was sorry that I couldn't give her an answer. What is the history of the rosary?

Praying Grandma

Dear Grandma,

The traditional story of the rosary was that Mary herself appeared to Saint Dominic in the twelfth century. At that time, tradition says, she gave Dominic the rosary and promised that if he spread devotion to the rosary, his religious order would flourish. It is true that Dominic was quite devoted to the Blessed Mother, but no one knows for sure if our Lady herself gave Dominic the rosary. If she did, it is quite certain that she did not give him a rosary that looks like the one we have today.

The complete rosary consists of 150 beads, the same number as there are psalms in the Catholic Bible. In the twelfth century, religious orders recited together the 150 psalms as a way to mark the hours of the day and the days of the week. In order to pray the psalms, though, people had to know how to read. People who didn't know how to read wanted to share in the practice, so the rosary, or praying on beads, began as a parallel to the psalms. It was a way that illiterate persons could remember the Lord and his mother throughout the day.

The first rosaries consisted of a string of 150 beads, and, much as we do now, a person would pass over each bead after saying a prayer, usually the Our Father. The Hail Mary, as we know it, wasn't even around at that time.

Various persons have added other things to the rosary over the centuries. In the fifteenth century, a Carthusian monk divided the rosary into fifteen brackets (or decades), and a Dominican assigned mysteries (events from the lives of Jesus and Mary) to each of the decades. His decades were the same as the ones we use today (until 2002 when Pope John Paul II added five additional mysteries to the rosary) with the exception of the last two. In those two, the Corona-tion and the Assumption together made up the fourteenth decade, and the fifteenth decade was the Last Judgment.

The Hail Mary owes its origin to the rosary. When people prayed the rosary in the twelfth century, the archangel Gabriel's greeting— "Hail Mary, full of Grace, the Lord is with thee"—was often said, along with the Our Father. Later, Elizabeth's prayer—"Blessed art thou among women"—was added. It was not until the sixteenth cen-tury that the words "Holy Mary, Mother of God, pray for us sinners, now and at the hour of our death" were added.

Today's complete rosary is made up of twenty decades of the Hail Mary separated by an Our Father, a Glory Be, and sometimes a prayer in memory of Our Lady of Fátima, "O My Jesus, forgive us our sins, save us from the fires of hell, lead all souls to heaven, especially those who have most need of your mercy." We usually divide the rosary into four sets of five mysteries, and pray a different set of mysteries each day. There are many variations though, such as the rosary re-membering the seven Sorrows of Mary. In countries other than the United States, the rosary varies from this traditional format, and may even have different mysteries.

Despite all the additions and changes, the important core of the rosary has always remained the same. It is a way for God's people to make holy the day and to remember the life of Jesus and his mother. May these humble origins always be with us each time we pray the rosary.

The Rosary: A Meditation on the Scriptures

A few years ago, before my grandmother passed away, she gave me her rosary as a keepsake. I have always cherished it in her memory; but I also know it is supposed to help me to pray. I'm sorry to admit it, but I've never learned how to pray the rosary. Can you tell me know to use the rosary?

Nancy

Dear Nancy,

The rosary is a meditation on New Testament Scripture events in the life of Jesus and Mary, and it uses our basic Catholic prayers as a framework: the Sign of the Cross, the Apostles' Creed, the Our Father, the Hail Mary, and the Glory Be. Just as an Eastern monk might chant a "mantra" while mediating on the truths of the universe, the rosary uses our basic prayers as a kind of repetitive chant while meditating on the Good News of the Bible.

There are four sets of meditations for the rosary, taken from the Bible's account of the lives of Jesus and Mary. These are the Joyful Mysteries, traditionally prayed on Monday and Thursday; the Sorrowful Mysteries, prayed on Tuesday and Friday; the Mysteries of Light, prayed on Wednesday; and the Glorious Mysteries, prayed on Thursday and Sunday. The Joyful Mysteries are: the Annunciation, the Visitation, the Birth of Christ, the Presentation, and the Finding of Jesus in the Temple. The Sorrowful Mysteries are: the Agony in the Garden, the Scourging at the Pillar, the Crowning with Thorns, the Carrying of the Cross, and the Crucifixion. The Mysteries of Light are: Christ's Baptism, Christ's Self-Revelation at the Marriage Feast of Cana, Christ's Announcement of the Kingdom of God, Christ's Transfiguration, Christ's Institution of the Eucharist at the Last Supper. The Glorious Mysteries are: the Resurrection, the Ascension, the Descent of the Holy Spirit at Pentecost, the Assumption of Mary into Heaven, and the Crowning of Mary as Queen of the Universe.

For those times when you want to pray, but find it difficult or impossible to pray in your own words, the rosary gives great consolation by focusing on these scenes from the life of Jesus and Mary. For ease in praying the rosary, it is helpful to memorize the mysteries. Once you've become familiar with the mysteries and the pattern of the prayers, the rosary is very easy. You can take it with you in your purse or pocket, and pray it anytime.

This is how to pray the rosary:

1. Make the Sign of the Cross and pray the Apostles' Creed.
2. Pray the Our Father.
3. Pray three Hail Marys (these are usually said for the intentions of increasing the three virtues of faith, hope, and charity).
4. Pray the Glory Be to the Father.
5. Recall the first mystery and pray the Our Father.
6. Pray ten Hail Marys while meditating on the mystery.
7. Pray the Glory Be to the Father.
8. Recall the second mystery and pray the Our Father.
9. Repeat steps 6, 7, and 8, continuing with the third, fourth, and fifth mysteries.
10. There is an added prayer that is customarily prayed after each decade. It is a prayer requested by the Blessed Virgin Mary at Fátima: "O my Jesus, forgive us our sins, save us from the fires of hell, lead all souls to heaven, especially those who have most need of your mercy."

For your reference and use in your prayer, the biblical references used for each of the mysteries follow:

The Joyful Mysteries
The Annunciation (Lk 1:26–38)
The Visitation (Lk 1:39–45)
The Birth of Jesus (Lk 2:6–14)
The Presentation in the Temple (Lk 2:22–24; 29–32)
The Finding in the Temple (Lk 2:42–50)

The Sorrowful Mysteries

The Agony in the Garden (Jn 18:1; Mt 26:42)
The Scourging at the Pillar (Mt 27:17–22)
The Crowning with Thorns (Mk 15:17–19)
The Carrying of the Cross (Jn 19:16–17)
The Crucifixion (Lk 23:44–47)

The Mysteries of Light

Christ's Baptism in the Jordan River (Mt 3:13–17)
Christ's Self-Revelation at the Wedding Feast at Cana (Jn 2:1–11)
Christ's Announcement of the Kingdom of God (Mk 1:14–15)
Christ's Transfiguration (Mt 17:1–13)
Christ's Institution of the Eucharist at the Last Supper
  (Lk 22:14–28)

The Glorious Mysteries

The Resurrection (Mk 16:1–7)
The Ascension (Lk 24:51)
The Descent of the Holy Spirit on Pentecost (Acts 2:1–4)
The Assumption of Mary into Heaven (Jdt 13:23–31)
The Crowning of Mary as Queen of the Universe (Rev 12)

Mary's Tomb

> *Various writings mention that there is a tomb of Mary. I was taught that Mary was assumed, body and soul, into heaven. My eighty-one-year-old mother agrees with me. So why the tomb?*
>
> Linda

Dear Linda,

The tradition and belief that, upon her death, Mary was assumed, body and soul, into heaven has been a part of Christian teaching from very early times. The oldest known writings we have on the Assumption date from the fourth or fifth centuries. One of these writings,

De Transitu Virginis, the work of Saint Melito of Sardis, contains the legend that Mary died in the presence of the disciples, and they saw her soul rise into heaven. The apostles then laid her body in a tomb and sealed it.

Saint Thomas arrived after the burial, and, when he went to the tomb, he witnessed Mary's body rising. Thomas begged Mary for a sign, and she threw down her belt. He then told the other disciples that Mary wasn't in the tomb, and produced the belt as proof. The astonished apostles reopened the tomb and found it filled with flowers. The traditional icon of Mary's Assumption paints this scene.

Around this legend there arose two traditions of the burial place of Mary: one is in Jerusalem and the other is in the city of Ephesus. In Jerusalem is the Abbey of the Dormition (sleep) of Mary. The Jerusalem tradition asserts that Mary spent her latter years on Mount Zion. The tradition of the Christians in Ephesus is that Saint John (the apostle) built a house for Mary, in which she lived and died. In back of this house is the cave in which Mary's body was placed.

Our current celebration of the feast of Mary's Assumption into heaven is the outcome of centuries of Christian reflection. We believe that Mary is completely with God, body and soul. This enables us to believe that we, too, will one day be completely at home with God.

5
Catholic Beliefs

INTRODUCTION
The Foundations of Catholic Beliefs

The *Catechism of the Catholic Church* teaches that if a Catholic or anyone of any faith or persuasion intends to understand the essential and fundamental content of the Catholic faith, that person needs to look to four sources in order to establish a point of reference:

1. the Sacred Scriptures
2. the Fathers of the Church
3. the liturgy
4. the Church's magisterium (CCC 11)

A study and appreciation of these four sources will then lead to the four "pillars" on which Catholic catechesis is constructed:

1. the baptismal profession of faith (the Creed)
2. the sacraments of faith (the sacraments)
3. the life of faith (the Commandments)
4. the prayer of those who believe (the Lord's Prayer) (CCC 13)

If a Catholic looks to the content of the faith, as it is expressed through the living tradition and practice of the Church, that person will inevitably be led to a firm and life-giving practice of what it means to be a Catholic.

Is Everything We Believe in the Bible?

A non-Catholic coworker of mine recently asked me: "Why do you Catholics hold nonscriptural beliefs?" As examples, he pointed to our belief in the papacy as a divinely willed institution and our beliefs about Mary. How can I respond to my Protestant friend?

Ray

Dear Ray,

When non-Catholics say that a particular belief is "nonscriptural," they are referring to one that is not stated *explicitly* in the Bible. We need to remember that we Catholics look to both Scripture and Tradition as the source of divine revelation, whereas non-Catholics look only to Scripture. *Sola Scriptura* (Scripture alone) was Martin Luther's famous phrase.

For a Catholic, Tradition refers to the whole context out of which the written word of God emerged. Tradition includes the liturgical life of the Church, creedal statements of faith, and the faith as lived by Christians from one generation to another. When a written tradition (the books of the Bible) emerged, it was never meant to replace the oral tradition (Jn 21:25). Both were to continue side by side.

A concrete example of this distinction between what is scriptural and what isn't can be seen in the Catholic belief in the papacy as a divine institution. Protestants do not believe in the papacy because nowhere in Scripture does Jesus state that the successors of Saint Peter should be regarded as head of the Church. Jesus did appoint Peter as leader of the apostles and head of the early Church. When Peter died in Rome, his series of successors (bishops of Rome) were gradually recognized as head of the whole Church. Catholics see this tradition as the will of Christ. We reason that if Jesus clearly wanted his apostles and first disciples to have a leader, surely he would want his Church in future generations to have a particular leader. So the finger of God is recognized by all Catholics in the tradition of the Bishop of Rome being head of the whole Church.

Tradition involves the Church's ongoing meditation on the Scriptures. This meditation gradually led the Church to a fuller understanding of truths that are present in the Scriptures in seed form. This process is called "development of doctrine." Catholic beliefs about Mary, purgatory, the sacraments, and the papacy are implicitly present in the Bible and, through centuries of meditation, have been drawn forth and expressed. You may recall how Jesus, in his last discourse, told his apostles that there were many things they did not yet understand, but "when the Spirit of truth comes, [the Spirit] will guide you into all the truth" (Jn 16:13). Obviously, there was more to come!

If It's Not in the Bible, How Do We Know It's Right?

A Protestant friend of mine is always asking me why Catholics believe things not found in Scripture. Can you explain this to me?

Ted

Dear Ted,

The Catholic Church has always taught that God's revelation is transmitted in two ways: Sacred Scripture and Sacred Tradition. Many Churches, especially those who interpret the Bible in a fundamentalist way, reject this. Members of such churches often challenge Catholics for teaching "things not found in the Bible," yet Catholics' belief in Sacred Tradition is solidly based.

We believe that God continues to interact with us. God did not drop a Bible from the sky and then cease all communication with us. Rather, God continues to speak through the Word, Jesus (Jn 1:1), who speaks through the Church. Jesus sent the Spirit to guide the apostles (and us) to truth. (See John 16:13.)

The Church existed long before the Bible as we know it. The New Testament did not exist until at least twenty years after Christ's Resurrection, and the last book of the New Testament was written about one hundred years after the Resurrection. If revelation could only be found in the Bible, the early Church would have had little to teach.

Decisions about which books to include in the Bible were made by Church councils. Without the living, teaching authority of the Church, without Sacred Tradition, there would be no Bible, for there would be no one to determine which books the Bible would contain. In other words, the Church produced the Bible; the Bible did not produce the Church. Ask, "What is the pillar and foundation of truth?" and some will claim, "The Bible, of course." But according to Scripture, the Church is the "pillar and bulwark of the truth" (1 Tm 3:15).

The Bible itself asserts that all God's truth is not found in Scripture: "There are also many other things that Jesus did; if every one of them were written down, I suppose that the world itself could not contain the books that would be written" (Jn 21:25).

The Bible also implies that God's truth would be "handed on" by preaching as well as by the written word. Jesus said to his disciples, "Whoever listens to you listens to me, and whoever rejects you rejects me, and whoever rejects me rejects the one who sent me" (Lk 10:16), mandating that God's revelation be carried on by the apostles and their successors. In his Second Letter to Timothy, Paul says, "and what you have heard from me through many witnesses entrust to faithful people who will be able to teach others as well" (2:2).

Scripture explicitly acknowledges traditions passed on by the Church. Saint Paul wrote: "So then, brothers and sisters, stand firm and hold fast to the traditions that you were taught by us, either by word of mouth or by our letter" (2 Thess 2:15).

Nowhere do the Scriptures claim the Bible as the only source of revelation. Thus, anyone who says we must believe only what is found in the Bible is asking us to believe something not found in the Bible!

Bible or Church? Which Speaks God's Truth?

An evangelical friend of mine says the Bible is the only source of God's revealed truth. She belongs to a neighboring church that maintains that we Catholics are wrong in relying on "Tradition" to know what God has revealed. Who is correct?

Caught in the Middle

Dear Caught,

Along with other Christians, we Catholics hold that the Bible is the primary source of revelation. We also maintain, however, that it is not the *only* source. Catholics believe the Church's *Tradition* also provides a legitimate, sacred resource for telling God's truth.

Tradition, as a source of revelation, can be seen as indispensable because it comprises the living faith context out of which grew the formulation and dissemination of God's revealed truth. Without it there would be no Bible, and there would be no experience of faith to pass on.

A community or organization lives what it believes and believes what it lives. The first followers of Jesus lived and prayed as a Christian community even before the New Testament was written, clearly living out what they believed to be God's revealed truth. When the New Testament writers were composing and editing their works, they had no notion or intention of writing the New Testament, as we know it. Rather, they were preserving for contemporaries, as well as generations to come, the enduring Good News of Jesus. Eventually, they came to realize that the message proclaimed and the salvation by Jesus were for all people. Of particular concern was passing on the eyewitness testimony of Jesus' friends. It was only much later that the Church determined what writings were true to Christ's authentic tradition and therefore should be included in the compilation of works we now call the New Testament of the Bible.

The New Testament writings were composed years after Christ's death —between A.D. 40 and A.D. 110. How do we account for the years between Christ's life and the first writing? What did those Christians believe? How did they live? Were they waiting for God to dictate what they were to live and believe and write in the Bible? On the contrary. It was during this most critical time, locked in silence, that the embryonic Church was stirring with new life, faith, and hope. This early Christian community gathered together for the breaking of the bread; they told and re-told the stories of Jesus Christ, recalling things he said and did, attitudes he exhibited, and the works of power he performed. Jesus didn't leave a clear-cut plan or blueprint of what to do and how to do it. He didn't specify or dictate what to write down. He left his sayings, teachings, and commands backed up by his words and personal example. In particular, he left his death and astonishing resurrection as vindication and approval of all he had done. Finally, he sent the Holy Spirit to remind his followers of all he said and did to guide their groping journey. He also left his apostles and followers the freedom to allow his living legacy to develop according to the demands and dictates of changing history.

Tradition is the Church's lived practice. It's what the early Christian community instinctively lived before it articulated its belief in written form. What many evangelical Christians do not seem to understand is that the Bible found its existence within the context of a living community. That community's lived beliefs—written down—formed the New Testament. In other words, the Bible did not create the Church; rather, the Church—that early community of believers—created the Bible.

Fundamentals and Fundamentalism: What Is the Difference?

Some people in the Church warn us against fundamentalism, yet these same people don't hesitate to say we need to always be mindful of the fundamentals. What's the difference?

Confused

Dear Confused,

Fundamentalism represents what Catholics believe to be a distortion of God's Word under the appearance of seeking the unvarnished truth of that Word (and accepting *only* that Word) as God's plan for humanity. *Fundamentals*, on the other hand, are the basic foundations of our faith—those pillar truths on which our Christian lives rest.

Fundamentalists assume that God's truth comes from only the Bible. Catholics, on the other hand, believe divine truth is also expressed via the Church of God, the community of faith, and Catholic Tradition, which put us in touch with God through Christ living on and sharing his Holy Spirit with us.

Fundamentalism is a religious stance that claims to have a lock on the truth contained in the Scriptures. Its method for seeking the truth is to take the Word of God more literally than do other Christian denominations. Fundamentalists treat Scripture uncritically, as if it were originally written in English, in our time and culture, and as if God dictated these exact words to our contemporaries. Fundamentalists bypass most accepted norms of literary criticism and biblical scholarship. They do not consider the original biblical context as envisioned by biblical authors for their intended audiences.

To comprehend God's Word, we must understand that Scripture was written centuries ago in lands and cultures vastly different from our own. The biblical authors addressed the immediate situations of their people. In doing so, they employed many literary forms and devices to convey God's message. By not taking this fact into consideration, fundamentalism distorts the Bible's message by removing Scripture from its historical context and treating it as if it were dictated by God to people who simply acted as stenographers.

God appeared to the Israelites in dramatic ways, singling them out to be a people of choice and destiny. God liberated them from tyranny, gave them a land and identity, and promised prosperity and innumerable descendants if they remained faithful to the covenant. This was extraordinary, and nothing like this had happened before. Scripture reflects this tumultuous development and astounding historical reality with all its nuances and implications for God's people then and for all time.

We must use the best modern scholarship to decipher what it is that God, through the sacred writers, intends to communicate. Only then can we apply it to our lives and learn what God is doing, as well as what God asks of us in response. To not accord the Bible this degree of literary respect exposes God's Word to misinterpretation. The Word of God preached by fundamentalism, and the Word that emerges from the best Catholic and Protestant Scripture scholars aren't the same. Catholics are warned about fundamentalism because of its potential for causing serious misinterpretation of Scripture's meaning.

Fundamentals, on the other hand, are those solid, bedrock truths of which our faith and Christian life firmly rest—a loving, caring God; salvation won by Christ; the kingdom of God on earth; the Church where God's people meet; the liturgy and sacraments that celebrate and strengthen our life of faith; and the pursuit of justice, peace, and service to all. We must stay close to these fundamentals or get back to them if we have strayed.

Are You Saved?

Someone recently rang my doorbell and asked if I was "saved." He seemed to know that he was saved. Are we supposed to have some inside knowledge of who will be saved and who won't? What do we Catholics say about this?

Looking for the Truth

Dear Looking,

It can be puzzling for a Catholic to be approached by someone who asks, "Are you saved?" or "Are you absolutely sure you will be with Jesus in heaven?" From a Catholic point of view, this is like asking about the state of one's conscience: "Have you committed a serious sin for which you have not repented and received absolution?" However, for many Christians, this merely means: "Have you, as an adult, turned your life over to Jesus and been baptized?" If the question were asked that way, we would simply say: "Yes, I am baptized and saved, and I continue to live as Jesus taught, asking for forgiveness when I fail. I trust in God's grace to support me until the end of my life, and I trust that the process of salvation will be completed when I am happy with God in heaven."

Does that mean that the person speaking to me believes that he can do anything against God and still remain saved? I doubt it. This theology often mentions "backsliding," which means that someone who is saved falls back into sinful ways and so changes his or her relationship with God. This is, in effect, saying the same thing that Catholics say: until we have died, the process of salvation is not complete. The reason it is not complete is that God created us with the ability to determine our lives through the gift of intelligence and free will. Catholic theology says that the process of salvation goes on until we die, because we remain free until we die. If we are free, then we have to choose over and over again between good and evil. For that reason, we say: "Yes, I have been saved by God, but I continue to work out my salvation in cooperation with God's grace, trusting that God will help me remain faithful and so be with God forever in heaven."

The person at the door may quote Scriptures, such as "If you confess with your lips that Jesus is Lord and believe in your heart that God raised him from the dead, you will be saved" (Rom 10:9). However, Saint Paul, who wrote the Letter to the Romans, speaks in another way in his First Letter to the Corinthians. Certainly Paul confessed Jesus with his lips and believed in his heart, so he could be sure that he was saved. However, he says: "I punish my body and enslave it, so that after proclaiming to others I myself should not be disqualified" (1 Cor 9:27). In other words, in spite of all he has done, Paul does not take his salvation for granted. Rather, he has a healthy fear of human weakness and the power of evil. We are saved in baptism, but we need to continue on the journey, following the Lord all our lives.

Have You Been Saved?

In today's Gospel, Jesus seems to ask the Samaritan woman to accept him as her personal Savior. Doesn't this sound like the evangelical denominations that demand you accept Jesus as your personal Savior before you can receive baptism?

A Good Catholic

Dear Good Catholic,

Catholics are sometimes asked, "Have you accepted Jesus as your personal Savior?" or "Have you been saved?" People who believe that baptism is merely a ceremony affirming one's personal acceptance of Jesus may ask such questions. "We are not saved by baptism," they claim, "but by a profession of faith in Jesus." They contend that only adults may receive baptism, and that baptism has no power to bestow grace.

Jesus does not ask the Samaritan woman to accept him as her personal Savior. That expression, in fact, is not found anywhere in the Bible. Jesus leads the woman and many other Samaritans to faith, but he does so in the context of baptism (Jn 4:1–2). He speaks of "living water," a reference to baptism: "The water that I will give will become in them a spring of water gushing up to eternal life" (Jn 4:10, 14). He offers salvation to the woman not only as "personal Savior" but also within the framework of community. Jesus is "the Savior of the world" (Jn 4:42).

The expression "I accept Jesus as my personal Savior" is incomplete because it gives the impression that salvation is only a personal matter. We put faith in Christ not only to get to heaven but also to build up the Church as Christ's Body. The *Catechism of the Catholic Church* states that God saves people "not as individuals without any bond or link between them, but rather to make them into a people who might acknowledge him and serve him in holiness" (CCC 781).

Do the Unbaptized Go to Heaven?

It seems to me that when I was younger the stance of the Catholic Church was that if you were not baptized, you did not get into heaven. Is this still the case or have the heavenly gates widened a bit?

Baptized and Saved

Dear Baptized and Saved,

The Gospels present to us various passages that, when looked at together, give us a sense of whether or not baptism is necessary for salvation. In one passage, Jesus says, "No one can enter the kingdom of God without being born of water and Spirit" (Jn 3:5). A second passage is Jesus' words at his Ascension: "The one who believes and is baptized will be saved; but the one who does not believe will be condemned" (Mk 16:16). From these two passages we can see that salvation is the combination of baptism and believing. Those who learn of Christ's gospel and purposely reject it are rejecting eternal life.

In the early Church, some catechumens were martyred before they could be baptized. Others desired baptism but died before they could receive it. Still others sincerely tried to do what is right but had no opportunity to learn about Christ. Salvation is available to these groups. The Church identified these as baptisms of blood, of explicit desire, and implicit desire.

The First Letter of John 4:7 tells us that "everyone who loves is born of God and knows God." Here the gift of salvation comes to us in loving. Also, in Matthew 25, we have the great scene of the Last Judgment, where people are saved because they ministered to Christ in the poor and the hungry, even though they might not even have been aware of Christ's presence. Salvation here comes because of kind action. It seems, then, that we can say that baptism combined with believing is certainly one of the means to salvation, but not the only means. In God's goodness, there are other roads that can lead us into the kingdom. God's mercy and goodness are not limited to the sacrament of baptism. If you wish to read more about this issue of the baptized and the unbaptized, refer to the *Catechism of the Catholic Church* (CCC 1257–1260).

Praying for the Dead

How do our prayers actually help people who are deceased? I keep thinking it should be the other way around: the deceased should pray for us! After all, they have it made—and we don't.
       Lookin' for Prayers

Dear Lookin',

Perhaps you should think about how you would feel if tonight you were called home to God. Would you be looking for prayers from those you left behind? I know I would! I think the reality is that we all need prayers, and a wonderful thing about our Church is that we are a part of a family of faith that assures us we'll have those prayers. That is the meaning behind the words we say in the creed every Sunday: "I believe in the communion of saints." When we were baptized, we became part of the body of Christ, joined with all those who have ever been, are, and will be "in Christ."

From the early days of the Church, there has been the tradition of remembering those who have died. In the fourth century, Bishop Cyril of Jerusalem noted in his catechetical instructions how, in the eucharistic prayer, we remember in two different ways those who have died. First, we remember those special ones who have fallen asleep, the fathers and mothers of our faith, the prophets, the apostles, and the martyrs; and we ask that God enables us to share in their inheritance, thanks to their prayers and intercessions for us. And this is still the case. At every Mass, we remind God that we rely on Mary and the saints to intercede for us.

But also at every Eucharist, since the early days of the Church, we have prayed for those who have died. We pray that God will welcome into the kingdom those we knew as our brothers and sisters in our lifetime, and "all who have left this world in your friendship."

What good do our prayers do? I don't know how to answer that in a precise way. But I do think that God hears our prayers as a proud parent, seeing in them that we have learned the lesson Jesus taught in John's Gospel: "And this is the will of him who sent me, that I should lose nothing of all that he has given me, but raise it up on the last day. This is indeed the will of my Father, that all who see the Son and believe in him may have eternal life; and I will raise them up on the last day" (6:39–40). When we pray for the dead, that they have eternal life, it is another way of praying "Thy will be done."

Also when we pray for those who have died, we are reminded that love lasts more than a lifetime. It reaches out across time and space, and even across the divide of death. When we have loved, we yearn for the beloved to live on, not just in memory but in a place that is beyond suffering and tears; and we yearn to see that loved one again. I think this is one of the most telling reasons that we pray for the dead. It tells us something about ourselves, as men and women made in the image of God, God's children who wish what God wishes: that no one be lost, that all be redeemed. For this purpose, the Word became flesh—that we might see his glory, full of grace and truth. And for this purpose, the Spirit continues to pray—through us—for all those who die.

6
Catholic Practices

INTRODUCTION
Uniquely Catholic

In addition to the firm foundations and pillars of our Catholic faith (refer to the introduction of section five) there are recognizable practices that most Catholics appreciate and understand as "outward expressions" of piety and faith. In the traditional practice of Catholicism, many of these practices form a discernable expression of spiritual practice and piety. Some are lifelong expressions of faith, while others seem to be a part of a particular liturgical season of the year or perhaps an important expression of faith at certain times in our spiritual journey. Still other practices can best be understood not so much as personal expression of faith or piety, but rather expressions of deeply held perceptions and judgments about the world in which we live and how our Catholic faith impacts that world, both now and in the world that is to come.

Stations of the Cross

As long as I can remember, our parish has offered the Stations of the Cross as a special devotion during the Lenten season. How ancient is this practice?

Belinda

Dear Belinda,

Over the centuries, many pilgrims would visit the Holy Land and try to retrace the steps of Jesus. When they returned to their home churches, many of these pilgrims paid for shrines to be built that represented the holy places they visited. In 1342, the Franciscans became the official guardians of the holy places, and they would guide pilgrims along the Way of the Cross. In 1668, Pope Innocent XI gave permission to the Franciscans to place Stations of the Cross in all of their churches. The number of these early stations varied, from as few as seven to as many as thirty-seven. Finally, in 1731, Pope Clement XII defined fourteen stations as the official devotion.

In recent years, two modifications of the Stations of the Cross have become fairly common. Some churches have a fifteenth station representing Jesus' Resurrection. Other churches have scriptural accounts that are not in the traditional station devotion. In more recent years, a popular Lenten devotion is the "Living Stations of the Cross." This is a play with music, singing, and dramatic speaking parts.

Regardless of their format or the liturgical season of the year during which they are celebrated, the Stations of the Cross are a gentle reminder that we journey with Jesus on his way to Calvary.

The Poor Souls

When I was young, we always prayed for "the poor souls in purgatory." Is this because some go to hell and some go to heaven? Does the language used have anything to do with what happens in purgatory?

Praying for the Souls

Dear Praying,

On the feast of All Souls' Day, we remember all of our faithful departed. Most of them are already with God in heaven. But some of them might still be in need of some purification. Those in need of purification from the temporal punishment still due to their sins are in purgatory. These people are not the damned. They are the elect and are friends of God. They are already saved, assured of salvation. There is no going to hell from purgatory. There is only upward movement to heaven.

There has always been an ancient tradition in the Church that there exists a strong bond between the faithful who have died and those of us that are still alive. The Church especially emphasizes the mutual help that Christians on earth and in purgatory give to one another by their prayer. It is the belief of the Church that our prayers lessen the amount of time a person could spend in purgatory. Our prayers speed their journey into the fullness of God's love.

Saint Thomas Aquinas, the famous theologian of the Middle Ages, wrote that the Holy Spirit unites the Church and communicates the goods of one member to another. So in the communion of saints, we all, those in purgatory included, share in the graces of the saints in heaven and the virtuous people on earth. Here is a beautiful quote from Saint Cyprian: "A great number of loved ones await us in heaven. An enormous host is filled with longing for us. Their concern is only for us. To be in their presence, to be embraced by their arms—what immeasurable joy it will be for them and for us" (Sermon on Death, 26).

On this All Saints' Day and All Souls' Day we are invited to unite with all the faithful Christians, living and dead. These feast days are our opportunities to pray for and with them and to receive the benefits of their prayers in return.

Is Incense Out of Style?

I am an "old" parishioner. I used to enjoy the pleasant smell of incense used in church. But I can't remember incense being used for a long time. Is it out of style, or is it forbidden? Can you also say something about its meaning?

Faithful One

Dear Faithful One,

Incense is not out of style nor is it forbidden. Incense is still burned to signify that Christ's sacrifice ascends to God as an odor of sweetness. It is also used to signify the people's pleasing and acceptable prayers rising to the throne of God.

In Revelation 8:3–4 we read that an "angel with a golden censer came and stood at the altar; he was given a great quantity of incense to offer with the prayers of all the saints on the golden altar that is before the throne. And the smoke of the incense, with the prayers of the saints, rose before God from the hand of the angel."

Incense is a resinous substance obtained by cutting into the bark of a fir or pine tree. Frankincense, a specific type of incense, was one of the gifts that the Magi brought to the Christ Child: "Then, opening their treasure chests, they offered him gifts of gold, frankincense, and myrrh" (Mt 2:11). Frankincense is white and expertly prepared from equal portions of fragrant gum resins, spices of resin, and aromatic shell. These are mixed, salted, and ground into fine powder. When the bright grains are put on glowing coals, they burn and exude perfume.

The Hebrew word's original meaning for incense was "fragrant smoke." Ancient Jews burned incense as an act of worship in the tabernacle and in the Temple. From this came the old expression, "sweet smelling sacrifice." Scripture mentions incense in many places: "...live in love, as Christ loved us and gave himself up for us, a fragrant offering and sacrifice to God" (Eph 5:2); and "I am fully satisfied, now that I have received from Epaphroditus the gifts you sent, a fragrant offering, a sacrifice acceptable and pleasing to God" (Phil 4:18).

During biblical times, people were forbidden to used sacred incense for ordinary purposes. The penalty for doing such a thing was severe: "Whoever makes any like it to use as perfume shall be cut off from the people" (Ex 30:38). Most likely, wealthy people regularly burned incense in their homes to produce pleasing odors, but sacred incense was burned on a special altar or in a censer. The ancient Jews burned incense twice a day, and this was exclusively a priestly function. These men decided by lot who would get the privilege of burning the incense: "...[Zechariah] was chosen by lot, according to the custom of the priesthood, to enter the sanctuary of the Lord and offer incense" (Lk 1:9).

Today, incense is often used at Benediction of the Blessed Sacrament, at funerals, and during other special liturgical celebrations to highlight the festivity of a particular occasion. Celebrants can also use incense in any liturgy to bless the congregation, the altar, the Lectionary, and the gifts of bread and wine.

No, the use of incense is not out of style. It continues to endure as a tradition that symbolizes our Catholic beliefs.

What Does Holy Water Do?

A non-Catholic friend recently went to church with me. While there, she saw a grandmother lift her little grandchild up to the holy water font near the door. The little girl put her hand into the water and then made a cross over herself. My friend asked me why Catholics do this and seemed to think it was superstitious. Is it?

Fred

Dear Fred,

Blessed water is a sacramental. *Sacramentals* are signs of spiritual effects and favors from God. There is nothing superstitious about this. An ordained man prays over a material thing—water in this case—and asks God to accept the prayers of the Church for those who reverently use the blessed object. There is no magic power. The Church admonishes us to use sacramentals, like holy water, crucifixes, and rosaries, with reverence and respect.

Water is full of mystery. Water, although material, can express something spiritual. Water cleanses us from filth and impurities; therefore, water is an apt symbol of interior cleansing and purifying.

Water is also an apt symbol of life. The scarcity of water in many parts of the world, including the Holy Land, lends it a special value. What's more, water is necessary for the existence of plants, animals, and people all around the world.

The practice of using water for sacred purposes stretches across many times, places, and cultures. The ancient Egyptians, for example, performed ritual washings before entering a holy place. In the Old Testament, we read about people using water to remove legal uncleanness. Aaron purified himself with water before entering the tabernacle: "The Lord spoke to Moses: You shall make a bronze basin with a bronze stand for washing. You shall put it between the tent of meeting and the altar, and you shall put water in it; with the water Aaron and his sons shall wash their hands and their feet. When they go into the tent of meeting, or when they come near the altar to minister, to make an offering by fire to the LORD, they shall wash with water" (Ex 30:17–20). In the New Testament, John the Baptist baptized with water as an outward sign of inner sorrow for personal sins. In the sacrament of baptism instituted by Christ, we are washed completely and born again of water and the Spirit. Water here symbolizes the washing away of sin, inner purification, and receiving and rising to new life in Christ.

The custom of placing holy water in a font near the doors of a church is quite old. We make the sign of the cross with blessed water to renew us in the spirit of our baptism. It signifies our purification before we approach the presence of God in the church. Holy water also reminds us to pray for health of soul, body, and spirit. We also pray that the devil may depart from any place in which the holy water is used. Sometimes people think that blessed water is a spiritual rabbit's foot; this is not true. Rather, using holy water begs of God a blessing upon those who use it with reverence and devotion. The prayer also asks for protection from the powers of darkness.

Remember to bless yourself devoutly with holy water. It is not superstitious, but a sacramental. Remember that, as you enter a Catholic church, this action reminds you of your baptism and of cleansing yourself before you approach the presence of God. As you leave, bless yourself again and recall that baptism has marked you for eternal life. When we bless ourselves with holy water, we must always remember that we do it "in the name of the Father and of the Son and of the Holy Spirit. Amen."

Divine Mercy Sunday

Our bishop has declared the Sunday after Easter as "Divine Mercy Sunday." The bishop encouraged everyone to partake of God's mercy by going to confession and having a special devotion to the Sacred Heart of Jesus. Is this "Divine Mercy" a new feast in the Church?

Francis

Dear Francis,

Your bishop is most likely responding to the canonization of Sister Faustina Kowalska. She is a disciple of God's divine mercy for the twentieth century. Pope John Paul II declared Sister Faustina a saint of the Church on April 30, 2000.

Saint Faustina was born in 1905 and spent most of her life in Poland, in the Congregation of the Virgin Mary of Mercy. Her life concealed an extraordinary union with God. She received exceptional graces, revelations, visions, hidden stigmata, the ability to read souls, and the gift of prophecy. One of the images that was revealed to Faustina was that of the merciful Jesus, touching his Sacred Heart, from which beams of red and white light came forth. This image and her devotion to the divine mercies gathered thousands of supporters throughout the world. We still see the traditional image of the Sacred Heart of Jesus in many of our churches today. In some churches, we might see the newer image, inspired by the saint. Saint Faustina Kowalska died at the age of thirty-three, leaving an impressive mystical legacy.

The feast of Divine Mercy can be celebrated by the local church at the discretion of the bishop on the first Sunday after Easter. It is usually celebrated with an emphasis on the merciful forgiveness of God and the sacrament of the Eucharist.

What Is an Indulgence?

What is an indulgence and how do I obtain one?

Curious

Dear Curious,

The Church's practice of granting indulgences must be understood in the context of the sacrament of penance. When we sin, a temporal punishment is connected to that sin. The sin is forgiven through the sacrament of penance, but the temporal punishment still remains. This temporal punishment can be taken away on earth through works of mercy and love, as well as through prayer and penance. After death, whatever temporal punishment remains is taken away through a process called *purgatory*.

The Church has traditionally offered *plenary indulgences* that take away all temporal punishment, or *partial indulgences*, which only lessen the temporal punishment. The indulgence, once obtained, can be used for yourself or applied to the souls of the deceased.

What Is Infallibility?

I have been a Catholic all my life, but I am still fuzzy about infallibility. What do I answer a Christian of another denomination when the question arises about who can make infallible declarations of doctrines? People I have talked to say the pope and only the pope has the gift of infallibility. I'd like to be able to give a clear answer.

Cyril

Dear Cyril,

First of all, the Church's belief in the gift of infallibility comes from Jesus himself. On one occasion, Jesus asked the apostles what people were saying about him. They replied that some thought he was John the Baptist, others Elijah, others Jeremiah or one of the prophets. Then Jesus inquired, "'But who do you say that I am?' Simon Peter answered, 'You are the Messiah, the Son of the living God.' And Jesus answered him, 'Blessed are you, Simon son of Jonah! For flesh and blood has not revealed this to you, but my Father in heaven. And I tell you, you are Peter, and on this rock I will build my church, and the gates of Hades will not prevail against it" (Mt 16:13–18). This passage shows that Jesus intended to establish a Church, that Peter would have a special place in it, and that the powers of evil (the gates of Hades) would never overcome the Church. The promise of Jesus surely means that he would not allow the Church to be misled in essential matters of faith or morals. In these matters, Jesus grants the gift of infallibility...not only to the pope, but to the bishops and faithful in union with the pope.

The Second Vatican Council explained that the "whole body of the faithful who have an anointing that comes from the holy one (cf. 1 Jn 2:20, 27) cannot err in matters of belief...when, 'from the bishops to the last of the faithful,' they manifest a universal consent in matters of faith and morals" *(Dogmatic Constitution on the Church,* §12). This does not mean that believers can create some new doctrine. On the contrary, it affirms that the truths we have always believed (such as the doctrines of the Creed) are infallible because the whole Church has always professed and believed them. Here is an example of how this "universal" belief can come up in a real situation: Before Pope Pius XII made (in 1950) the official declaration of the Assumption of Mary, he concluded that the Holy Spirit had guided the Church's belief in the Assumption, and he declared that it was part of our official doctrine.

The council stated that bishops have this gift of infallibility when they, in agreement among themselves and with the pope, teach authentically on a matter of faith or morals which they concur is to be held conclusively. An example would be the Councils of Nicea and Constantinople, where the bishops, with the approval of the pope, made definitive statements of the Church's belief regarding the humanity and divinity of Jesus.

The pope speaks infallibly when he teaches *ex cathedra*, as the leader of the whole Church, on the matter of faith or morals, expressly defining doctrine as a matter of faith or morals (*Dogmatic Constitution on the Church*, §25). The pope has done this only once in the past one hundred years, when he declared the dogma of the Assumption.

The Church's understanding of infallibility reflects our Catholic belief that God will not allow evil to lead the Church astray. It helps us to distinguish what is essential from what is not. A clear understanding of infallibility and its limits may be seen as a safeguard against the misuse of authority. Understood in this manner, infallibility is another gift given to the Church by the Lord.

Can the Pope Retire?

Some months ago our local bishop retired and a new bishop was appointed to take his place. Some of us were wondering about the pope. Can he also retire?

A Retired Catholic

Dear Retired,

Church law does offer bishops the opportunity to resign from their office as shepherd of a diocese and retire at the age of seventy-five. In the 1980s, the Holy Father approved a revision to the Church's Canon Law to provide for papal retirement. Because medical science can certainly maintain our lives for so much longer these days, many Church leaders worried about a pope who might eventually rule from a hospital bed. It is especially worrisome in this age, when the pope is required to travel to many countries, speak in various languages, write numerous letters, and be a diplomat as well as a religious leader. Should a pope have a lingering illness, the Church might suggest that he retire from his position and allow a healthier person to take up the arduous task of leading the Church. This new addition to Canon Law now allows such a scenario to happen.

Most Church politicians agree that a pope's retirement is a highly unlikely event. It would be too confusing to have two living popes. The obvious worry is what would happen if they gave different opinions about a certain topic or theological issue. Whom would we listen to? Who would hold the most authority?

Interestingly, a research firm recently polled the Italian people concerning the retirement of a pope, and 90 percent of respondents said that a pope should not retire. The last pope to actually resign the papal office was Pope Celestine V in 1294. Dante, the great writer and poet of that time, was so angry at the pope's resignation that, when he wrote his classical work on heaven and hell, he placed this pope in the realm of hell.

Regardless, you should certainly continue to pray for the good health and strong leadership of our Holy Father.

Is Exorcism Back in Vogue?

I see that the Church is promoting a revised Rite of Exorcism. Is the devil coming back with a vengeance, or does Rome know something we don't?

Robert

Dear Robert,

Most people received their information about the Rite of Exorcism from the series of movies and books dating back to the 1970s. These dramas always depicted a lone priest outgunned and outnumbered by the power and force of the devil. The priest won, but usually either went crazy or lost his life in the process.

It is true that the struggle between good and evil has pervaded the whole of human history. This struggle was central to the mission of Jesus in his constant victories over the devil's power. Christ gave this power to expel evil spirits to the apostles. Many forms of exorcism continue in the Church to this day. The Church prays a small prayer of exorcism over catechumens. The Rite of Baptism even includes a prayer of exorcism.

In January 1999, the Church issued a decree revising the Rite of Major Exorcism. This Rite of Exorcism is regulated solely by the bishop, who may appoint a priest-exorcist (a man of piety, knowledge, prudence, and holiness of life) to act in the bishop's name. All other avenues of helping the seemingly possessed person must be explored before engaging in the Rite of Exorcism.

The occurrence of diabolic possession is very difficult to understand. In exorcising evil spirits, the Church acts not in its own name but in the name of Christ the Lord, to whom even the devil and the demons must be obedient in all things. This Rite of Exorcism is therefore not new. It is very ancient. The Church obviously wishes to keep this rite current, polished, and ready in its struggle against evil.

Excommunication

Doesn't the idea of excommunication go contrary to the image of the pope as the servant of all and the supreme shepherd?
                                                    A Democratic Catholic

Dear Democratic,

As the supreme shepherd, the pope has the responsibility to guide and protect the Church. Certainly, of the many tools available to the pope for handling conflict within the Church, excommunication is the most grave. Excommunication of serious offenders from Christian communities is associated with the power of binding and loosing conferred upon Peter (Mt 16:19; 18:18). Saint Paul was probably the first apostle to actually exercise this power (1 Cor 5:1–5).

The pope or bishops can impose the penalty of excommunication on those whose thinking and actions come into conflict with the way of life contained in the gospel and taught by the Church. This situation usually involves public scandal and the refusal of the offender to yield to the teaching authority of the Church. The decree of excommunication deprives the person of his or her rights of membership in the Church, such as reception of the sacraments and Christian burial. It is the hope of the bishops that the excommunicant would then repent, acknowledge the authority of the Church, and be reconciled with the community of the faithful.

In history, the two most famous "examples" of excommunication

were Martin Luther and Henry VIII. Martin Luther was excommunicated in 1521, after he refused to recant his teachings (he also burned
the papal decree and the book of church law). Henry VIII was excommunicated when he remarried without papal permission and set
himself up as the head of the Church of England. In recent history,
Monsignor Marcel Lefebvre was excommunicated July 1, 1988, when
he illicitly ordained four priests as bishops without the pope's permission.

It is always the Christian hope and way that encourages dialogue
and charity before punishment.

7
Christian Living

INTRODUCTION
What Is a Christian?

From a historical perspective, *Christian* is the name applied to those persons who, in the city of Antioch (the capital of ancient Syria), were identified as followers of Jesus Christ in A.D. 43. That designation may well be the earliest and perhaps even the simplest designation, but it certainly is in no way definitive or even inclusive of those people who acknowledge Jesus Christ as God, the third Person of the Blessed Trinity, or the Incarnate Word of God. It would not suffice as an accurate and complete description of what we might understand as "Christian" today.

At the same time, however, we need to acknowledge that there may well be more points of disagreement than there are points of agreement among the various communities of people who would identify themselves as Christian, as followers of Christ, in our present day and age. Such communities would readily identify with the designation as it was once used long ago, but the actual lived experience of each community, rooted in the experience of their identity with Jesus Christ as they understand it, may well be very different.

That being said, there are nevertheless certain kinds of questions that concern all Christians, regardless of their particular denomination or practice.

Gifts of the Spirit

*I know that there are many gifts given by the Spirit, but I have a
hard time understanding the gift of "speaking in tongues." What
is the significance of this gift?*

Puzzled

Dear Puzzled,

You are probably speaking from the experience of a "charismatic"
prayer service, in which an individual suddenly enters into an ecstatic
state and begins speaking what sounds to others like gibberish.

Sacred Scriptures offer us some examples of this phenomenon. On
the day of Pentecost, for example, the apostles were overtaken by the
Holy Spirit and were understood by people of many nations, each in
his or her own tongue (Acts 2:3–4, 6). The phenomenon occurred
again when the first Gentiles were converted to the faith: Peter heard
them "speaking in tongues and extolling God" (Acts 10:46). Paul,
too, saw the ecstatic condition of the people he confirmed (Acts 19:6).

Saint Paul reminds us that speaking in tongues is one of many gifts
the Spirit may bestow upon a person (1 Cor 12:10, 28, 30), but that,
above all of them, there is love (1 Cor 13:8). He tells us that, like the
gifts of prophecy and knowledge, so too will the gift of speaking in
tongues come to an end. But love will prevail.

We must remember Paul's words as we contemplate all the gifts of
the Spirit: "So, my friends, be eager to prophesy, and do not forbid
speaking in tongues; but all things should be done decently and in
order" (1 Cor 14:39–40).

Anger and Lust

*My thoughts are my worst enemy. Sometimes they turn to lust
and anger. When I recognize what I am thinking, I pray to Jesus
and Mary, but I still struggle. What else can I do?*

Struggling

Dear Struggling,

Bad thoughts, hateful or lustful ideas and images, cross the minds of many, if not most, of us. Unless we want them or deliberately keep them in our consciousness, they are not sins, but temptations. What really matters is not that these thoughts come to us, but what we do about them.

When angry and lustful thoughts enter our consciousness, we should say a prayer and turn our mind to something else. Such thoughts or temptations become sins only when we deliberately encourage them or when we make plans to commit the sin. Again, what counts is what we do after the thought or temptation crosses our mind.

You wrote that when you realize you are thinking the wrong things, you pray to Jesus and Mary. This tells me that you are not choosing sin, because you don't want the thoughts and you are trying to get rid of them. The thoughts are temptations, not sins. I would recommend that you put your trust in Jesus and Mary, and try to focus on what is good and peaceful. But do so without excessive anxiety or worry.

A good thing to turn your attention to is God's Word in Scripture. You might want to memorize all or part of the following New Testament verse: "Whatever is true, whatever is honorable, whatever is just, whatever is pure, whatever is pleasing, whatever is commendable, if there is any excellence and if there is anything worthy of praise, think about these things" (Phil 4:8). Peacefully reflect on these words when troubled by temptation.

Suffering

I have a friend who is suffering greatly. She is very spiritual about her suffering and seems to have found a truly Christian way to embrace it. How can we best understand suffering?

A Sympathetic Christian

Dear Sympathetic,

Mother Teresa tells us this about suffering: Suffering will never be completely absent from our lives. If we accept it with faith, we are given the opportunity to share the passion of Jesus and show him our love. She tells this story: "One day I went to visit a lady who had terminal cancer. Her pain was tremendous. I told her, 'This is nothing but Jesus' kiss, a sign that you are so close to him on the cross that he can kiss you.' She joined her hands and said, 'Mother, ask Jesus not to stop kissing me.'"

The Book of Job in the Hebrew Scriptures gives us the classic approach to suffering. Job was inflicted with great suffering. He was able to find meaning in his suffering only when he stopped scolding God and complaining to God. Job suddenly started to see the beauty and mystery of all the life that surrounded him. He began to see that every part of God's creation was marvelous. He found that knowing and accepting God was more important than finding the answers to why he suffered. Job testified, "By his light I walked through darkness" (Job 29:3).

Jesus brought a new notion to suffering: for Jesus, suffering is redemptive. When we suffer, we can link our experience with the Lord's. Our sufferings then have a redeeming place in the salvation of the world. They can bring a miraculous presence into the life of another. In times of trial, Jesus is the companion and the guide who can lead us through.

Any Sense in Suffering?

Can anyone make any sense out of suffering? A friend of mine is in great pain, and I find myself thinking that she should not have to suffer so much. No one should!

Anti-Suffering

Dear Anti-Suffering,

The most popular book of devotion in the history of the Catholic Church is *The Imitation of Christ*, written by Thomas á Kempis. It was first published in 1471 and has gone through six thousand separate editions in dozens of languages. Thomas wrote this book as he watched his best friends and fellow members of his religious community suffer and die from the plague. Much of the book revolves around the issue of suffering. Thomas wrote that it was not deep words that made a person holy and upright, but a good life, lived in God's presence. Thomas believed that God walked with the simple and revealed God's very self to the humble. For Thomas á Kempis, there is no solution to suffering except to put your faith in the person of Jesus Christ.

The Book of Job, in the Bible, explores the mystery of innocent people experiencing misery and evil. In this book, Job suffers great pains and hardships, but comes to the conclusion that faith in God must transcend personal pain and suffering.

Jesus advises his followers to take up their cross and follow him (Mt 10:38; 16:24; Mk 8:34; Lk 9:23; 14:27). Saint Paul reminds us that we suffer with Christ so that we may also be glorified with him (Rom 8:17). The Letter of James even goes so far as to challenge Christians to consider trials of any kind as nothing but a great joy (Jas 1:2).

There is no doubt that we will all suffer; suffering is part of being alive. Our faith in Jesus is the bridge that can lead us over the chasm of suffering to the place of peace that so many of the early martyrs and great saints found.

Sexual Freedom and the Catholic Church

I am a family man who is struggling to raise my children with an understanding that sexuality must stay within marriage. This is really an uphill battle. Our society and media seem to give the impression that marriage is out and sex is in. What about this sexual freedom and what's a parent to do?

Kyle

Dear Kyle,

A national evening news program recently announced some startling statistics. It seems that one out of every four college-age young adults has cohabited ("lived with" someone) for varying lengths of time. Another statistic reported that in the United States alone the teenage pregnancy rate exceeded one million. Both these statistics point to the trend that separates sexuality from commitment. Actually, we don't have to hear statistics to realize this. Our television shows, movies, magazines, billboards, and music bombard our senses daily with the idea that sex is only for pleasure. You can partake of sex much like a summer weekend on the beach. These sources want us to believe it's always enjoyable, there are no responsibilities connected with it, and you can walk away whenever you want.

Many times parents have come to me disgusted and helpless over the sexual freedom of their young adult children. One mother told me that her son and his girlfriend purchased a home. The mother called it "the house of sin," and she refused to visit them. Another couple told me about visiting their daughter in college to find her living with a young man. The daughter's comment was, "It's no big deal!" However, it was a big deal to the parents.

A recent survey pointed out the contradiction that, although most parents think they should be the primary providers of sex education for their children, these same parents are afraid or embarrassed to talk about sex as their children become teenagers or young adults.

The Catholic Church has maintained a countercultural stand regarding sexuality. The Church promotes the understanding that sexuality and commitment must go hand in hand. The Church encourages us to make the marriage commitment first and then engage in the sexuality. Pope John Paul II addressed much of his encyclical *Familiaris Consortio* ("On the Family") to this issue of commitment. This document emphasizes that sexuality must be interwoven into the fabric of spouse, family, and marital commitment. The dedication to loving and respecting the unique power and pleasure of sexuality has the best chance of occurring inside a healthy marriage and family structure.

If you are just starting your family, you have an excellent chance of instilling these Catholic values of marriage, family, and individual worth in each of your children. You do this by telling your children how important marriage and commitment are to you and by living this value through your own relationship with your spouse and family.

Sunday worship as a family, openness to talk with your children about sexuality and its place in marriage, telling the story of your own love and marriage—these are important building blocks of family sexual values.

What can you do if you find your children are developing sexual attitudes or practices contrary to your values? Some simple rules are

- Do not encourage them in any lifestyle that is not a value you hold about marriage or family. This might mean some parental control over television, movies, and records.
- Remind them of your love for them and speak to them of your own commitment to marriage and family.
- Offer them help whenever they might need it.
- If the conflict between you and a child creates anger and distance, agree to talk together with a priest or counselor.

Many people believe that the sexual freedom promoted by our society is on the rise. This demands a strong stance by Catholic families to balance this trend by instilling healthy sexual values in their children. The family values in the twenty-first century are planted by your actions and works today.

What Is a Covenant?

I have read your bulletins and have often seen the word covenant. I understand it as the relationship God had with Israel, but I recently heard the word used to describe Christian marriage. I find this intriguing. How are marriage and covenant related?

Struggling to Understand

Dear Struggling,

Covenant, indeed, is the word of choice that the Church employs to define and describe Christian marriage and the sacrament of matrimony. It is clearly based on the idea of covenant contained in Scripture. In contrast, society uses the related word *contract* as in the "marriage contract." However, these two words do not mean the same thing.

Contract is too limited a word to contain the full commitment of Christian marriage. When you sign a contract, you are legally bound only to the terms, large or small, of the contract. You need not do more or less than what is stipulated in its wording. The transaction is cold, impersonal, and businesslike. With a contract there is generally not much warmth or concern for the well-being of the other party, and you're not required to enter into an interpersonal relationship with the other party to the contract.

Covenant, on the other hand, is uniquely different. Although it may contain some aspects of contract, it establishes a personal relationship of closeness, affection, and warmth. It locks the parties in to a mutual commitment of exclusive love and unswerving loyalty.

As God freely chose Israel from all the nations possible, so a woman and a man choose each other from all the other people in life. It is a free choice that starts with a mutual attraction but, with the development of friendship and affection, leads to love. As God declared, "I will take you as my people, and I will be your God" (Ex 6:7) so a husband and wife pledge to be totally for each other in a committed and exclusive way. But this exclusivity does not preclude love for others. Indeed, God loves all people equally but elected to manifest that love through the mediation of his specially chosen people. Jesus does the same in his high priestly prayer when he says: "I ask not only on behalf of these, but also on behalf of those who will believe in me through their word, that they may all be one. As you, Father, are in me and I am in you, may they also be in us" (Jn 17:20–21). In this passage, Jesus prayed first for his close friends and companions, and only later for all others. Likewise, a husband and a wife do not cease loving other people. In fact, they should become an oasis of love and compassion for others. But their first love is for each other, and from that emanates love for all others.

Throughout the covenant relationship, God remained faithful and true. Even as Israel wandered from her commitment, reverting to former pagan ways and renouncing Yahweh in favor of false gods,

God remained steadfast, waiting patiently for Israel's return. God sent prophets—personal emissaries—to call the people back to faithfulness. This persevering facet of God's forgiving and healing love is personified in the prophet Hosea.

Hosea witnessed the utter deterioration of Israel into powerlessness, chaos, and finally exile. It had abandoned fidelity to God in favor of alluring pagan cults, and destruction was the punishment. The prophet's own marriage is used to illustrate this collapse. His unfaithful wife, the symbol of an unfaithful people, wanders wantonly from her commitment to him. She strays into adultery. But Hosea, who represents God, is always there to take her back. There is reconciliation.

This story is not intended to condone unfaithfulness or suggest that spouses be pushovers for similar behavior. Rather, it's meant to illustrate that no matter what Israel did, God never wavered from love for the chosen people. God is the faithful and forgiving spouse, true to commitment. Husbands and wives are to be the same to each other.

It's clear from this comparison that the married love of husband and wife closely parallels the love relationship God initiated with the people through divine covenant. Christian marriage bears the same characteristics of covenant commitment—the personal relationship of caring, loyalty, intimacy, exclusivity, permanency, and, above all, love; hence the use of *covenant* to define Christian marriage.

What Is a Vocation?

I hear people saying, "I have found my vocation in life and I am really happy!" How do I know what my vocation is?

Nicholas

Dear Nicholas,

Our Catholic understanding of *vocation* is traditionally understood as "a call from God to a particular state in life." By "state in life" we usually mean single, married, priest, or religious. As such, we believe that when we live out this call from God, we are entering into a especially blessed relationship with God. God calls, and we respond.

When you hear people speaking about finding their "vocation in life," it is possible that this is what they have in mind. On the other hand, it is also quite possible that they be referring simply to a particular occupation, business, or profession that they feel comfortable with and may wish to pursue.

Although what you do or may do in the future has something to do with vocation and is important to discern, the root understanding of *vocation* is really the understanding of God's call and our response. This is an important distinction. Vocation has not so much to do with what we do, but is rather reflective of what we believe about our relationship with God.

Vocation assumes that we believe that God is active in our own unique history, and is actively involved in our decision-making process; that God desires to manifest God's will to us; and that God does in fact communicate with us in a very personal way.

Now, that sounds like an earful, doesn't it, but it is in fact part of the lived everyday experience of people like you and me. I cannot begin to relate to you the experiences of people I personally know who have entered into a process of really trying to understand God's will for themselves, who have chosen to do something that is entirely the opposite of what they might feel inclined to do. All this because they have come to believe and to trust that God truly has a plan, a preference for them. Coming to such a understanding is difficult and usually demands many little changes in personal choices. The end result, however, is a real peace in knowing that you are following the will of God.

The next time you hear or read something from Pope John Paul II, think of this distinction, this deeper understanding of vocation, as a call, and not just as an occupation. When the Holy Father is speaking about vocation, when he is speaking about the need for our human society to heed and to listen to the voice of God, he is talking about this type of vocation process. He is assuming that all people truly desire to know God's will in their lives, and are willing to follow God's will as they understand it.

If you are truly open to the will of God in your own life, if you are willing to listen to God's call and make your decisions and choices based on this experience, you too will discover the true happiness that a real vocation can bring.

Christians and Ecology

Every time I pick up a Catholic newspaper or magazine, I read articles about taking care of the earth, the atmosphere, the animals, and the trees. Shouldn't Christians be more concerned with the big problems in the world—such as war, hunger, and sickness?

Christopher

Dear Christopher,

When visitors asked Mother Teresa about why her followers spend so much of their energy with the dying when there are so many other great issues of the world to be dealt with, she replied, "We are not here to do great deeds but to do small deeds with great love." The same words could be spoken to any Christians confronted with the task of directing their love.

Most of us are not in a position to solve the problems of hunger, war, sickness, and pollution on a global level. But each of us can take small steps by doing things like giving bread to persons who are hungry, visiting people who are sick, planting one tree, or protesting the amount of our tax dollars that goes to building weapons for destruction.

When people asked Jesus about how to obtain eternal happiness, he answered them in very individual terms. He emphasized that we must act lovingly toward someone who needs love (Lk 10:25–37). The criterion for eternal life in this parable of the Good Samaritan involves action directed toward an individual who needed help.

In Matthew 25:31–46, we find the classic story involving the separation of the sheep from the goats at the final judgment. In this story, Jesus forewarns us that people will be judged on the basis of how they helped or neglected the "least" of their brothers and sisters. If we truly are Christian, we are obliged to act.

Why should we act in a loving manner toward the earth? Because all creation leads us back to God. The spiritual side of ecology challenges us to reclaim the presence of God in the physical world.

Have you ever looked closely at a spider web sparkling with morning dew, and then wondered about the God who first laid the genetic pattern in the spider to create this miracle? People have told me how they have driven through the Rocky Mountains at sunset and felt connected to the power and majesty of God. Others have mentioned how they love to sit by a lake or the ocean in the early morning. The quiet and calm of the dawning day fills them with a sense of the God who manages all things rightly. Many of the astronauts who have seen the earth hanging like a solitary ball on the end of a cosmic thread tell of a God who is endless and eternal. I imagine that everyone has a special place outdoors that speaks to them about God.

For a Christian, reclaiming the presence of God in the physical world must mean more than just reflecting on it. We are a people of action. So we must act upon the physical world in a way that respects its relationship to God. If nature leads us back to God, then we must act in a godly way toward nature.

If you are a Christian, you are challenged to act with love toward all creation. You cannot feed a hungry person, then turn around and dump toxins on the ground and claim you have love for God's creation. You cannot visit a sick person, then throw aluminum cans out your car window and claim you are blessed. Love demands that you act with care toward all creation. This is a new revelation to many Christians today, and, like all new learning, it will take time to redirect our efforts to care for the planet with as much energy as we care for one another.

We cannot sever creation from the Creator. If you respect the earth, the atmosphere, the animals, and the trees, you will find it easy to revere the hungry, the sick, and the war-torn. Let us praise the Lord from whom *all* blessings flow.

Gossip

*Please clarify for me what the Church considers as "gossip."
This question is prompted by a recent emphatic statement made
in church, that "when you say anything about another who is
not present, whether good or bad, this is gossip."*

Amanda

Dear Amanda,

Human beings have the great gift of speech. We continually talk *to*
one another and we talk *about* one another. Gossip, at its most basic
level, is just idle talk. It is neither good nor bad. But it is a tool we can
use to build up another human being or tear that person down.

Ephesians 4:29 tells us to say only the good things that people
need to hear. In Colossians 3:12–13a, Paul tells us: "As God's chosen
ones, holy and beloved, clothe yourselves with compassion, kindness,
humility, meekness, and patience. Bear with one another and, if anyone has a complaint against another, forgive each other."

Gossip becomes evil when we use our words to unjustly hurt the
reputation of another, or to judge another person rashly. The two
words that the Church uses to describe this evil side of gossip are
detraction and *calumny*. The *Catechism of the Catholic Church* tells
us that detraction is "without objectively valid reason, disclosing
another's faults and failings to persons who did not know them."
Calumny occurs when a person, "by remarks contrary to the truth,
harms the reputation of others and gives occasion for false judgments
concerning them" (CCC 2477).

To judge whether your own gossip is good or evil, simply ask yourself: *Do the words that I am saying help others or hurt others? Am I
building them up or tearing them down?* Hopefully, as a Christian,
you are committed to the gospel of love, and to using your words for
the good of others (Phil 2:2–5).

What Is the Gospel of Prosperity?

Is there such a thing as a "gospel of prosperity"? I heard a televangelist say that it was the Lord's will that all people share in the cars in the driveway and the money in the bank. What do you say to this?

Wondering About Riches

Dear Wondering,

If there is such a thing as a "gospel of prosperity," Matthew, Mark, Luke, or John didn't write it, and it isn't about Jesus of Nazareth. If anything, the true gospels of Jesus would be called "gospels of poverty." Jesus himself was born in poverty. Had he wished to extol riches and prosperity as a gospel way of life, he could have been born in the lap of luxury, amid the pomp and circumstances of wealth. But God chose the poverty of a stable and not-well-to-do parents. And this was no accident; Scripture scholars tell us that the first ones to hear of the Messiah's birth were poor shepherds in the field.

Early in his public ministry, Jesus declared himself for the poor. Luke recounts how Jesus, in the midst of growing adulation and popularity, went home to Nazareth. He went into the synagogue, as was his custom. They handed him the scroll and he read from it. Nothing was written about God's favor on the rich. Instead, Jesus said, "The Spirit of the Lord is upon me, / because he has anointed me / to bring good news to the poor" (Lk 4:18)

In chapter 6 of Luke and chapter 5 of Matthew, we have Jesus' great sermon. In some translations of Luke, it is called the Sermon on the Plain; in Matthew, it is called the Sermon on the Mount. Both begin with the beatitudes, the first of which is to the poor. "Blessed are you who are poor," says Jesus in Luke (6:20); "blessed are the poor in spirit," he says in Matthew (5:3), "for theirs is the kingdom of heaven. "But woe to you who are rich, for you have received your consolation" (Lk 6:24) warns Jesus after he states the beatitudes.

Can there be any doubt about Jesus' leanings? Mary's too. Her *Magnificent* (Lk 1:46–55) acknowledges that God has chosen her, a lowly maiden, and made her great in the eyes of history. In her, and in her son Jesus, God has exalted the lowly "and sent the rich away empty" (Lk 1:53).

Although the subject of riches and poverty appears in all the Gospels, Luke deals with it more than the other evangelists. It is thought that Luke was concerned because he was of, and dealt with, upper-class people, people of means. Luke sees money and this world's goods as clearly dangerous to a person's salvation. Although not impossible, because "nothing will be impossible with God" (Lk 1:37), it is difficult for a rich person to enter into the kingdom. Luke uses the image of a camel passing through the eye of a needle (18:25). It's easier for that to happen than for a rich person to enter the kingdom. Scary words.

A harrowing example of this is the story of the rich man and Lazarus (Lk 16:19–31). The rich man enjoyed all that money could buy, living opulently. Lazarus was poor and needy. The rich man ignored the destitute Lazarus. When they both died, there was a dramatic reversal of fortune. We should use our wealth to help our less fortunate brothers and sisters in this life—for only then can we be numbered among the sons and daughters of Abraham in the next.

Yet, for all this emphasis on the poor, poverty itself is not hailed as good. Nor are riches and possessions condemned in themselves. It's what wealth does to people—why they accumulate and preserve it. When attention is focused solely on riches and worldly possessions, we risk turning away from God, growing deaf and callous to the cries of our poorer, hurting brothers and sisters. Possessions and wealth are to be shared, not hoarded.

It sounds suspiciously like the televangelist may have written the so-called "gospel of prosperity" himself, perhaps to justify his own gains. I hope not, because getting rich off the message of Jesus Christ is also contrary to the gospel.

Sunday: Work or Rest?

When I was growing up, we were taught that Sunday was a day of rest. You don't hear or see much that emphasizes this teaching today. Has there been a change in thinking?

Tom

Dear Tom,

The teaching you refer to reflects directly on the third commandment, "Keep holy the Sabbath day." This commandment has deep roots in the Jewish belief that the seventh day of the week was to receive special reverence. It was the Jews' day of worship and spiritual renewal. This came, in part, on their reflection of the creation account in Scripture where God rested on the seventh day from all the work undertaken. God blessed this day and made it holy (see Gen 2:2–3).

It is on Sunday, the first day of the week, that the Christian community comes together for the celebration of Mass. Vatican II states its place as follows: "On this day Christ's faithful are bound to come together in one place. They should listen to the word of God and take part in the Eucharist, thus calling to mind the passion, resurrection, and glory of the Lord Jesus, and giving thanks to God" (*Constitution on the Sacred Liturgy*, §106).

While the law against work is in some ways connected with the Jewish "Sabbath rest," it is also based on other important premises. First, there is a religious reason. There should be a day, if at all possible, when the spirit is freed from material preoccupations. Without such an opportunity, spirituality is easily crowded out by materialism.

Second, there is a family reason. The observance of Sunday helps to promote family togetherness. The family cannot be strengthened without members spending some time together. Granted, not every Sunday will be an occasion for the whole family to gather together, but at least the possibility is there.

Third, there is a human need for rest and relaxation. In an age when the world moves at an ever-greater speed, we need time to pause and reflect on our relationship to God, to others, and to ourselves.

Because the Lord's Day is a feast day, and because these values are so precious, the present law of the Church states that all servile, judicial, and commercial work is forbidden on Sundays. Ordinary work is allowed. In reflecting on this obligation of Sunday rest, however, two extremes are to be avoided.

We should avoid a negative, legalistic attitude. Jesus said, "The Sabbath was made for humankind, not humankind for the Sabbath" (Mk 2:27). On the other hand, we should avoid a careless and completely secular attitude toward the Lord's Day with the result that it becomes "just another day."

One moral theologian has suggested the following norm for making decisions in this regard. "If possible, one should avoid those works and activities which are not compatible with the worship of God or which deprive one of rest and renewal of body and soul. Or, to put it positively, if we celebrate the eucharistic liturgy with reverence and love, if we avoid unnecessary work and business and shopping, if we seek wholesome recreation and fun (especially with our family members), and if we look out for the needs of others (for example, visiting the sick), then we can be quite sure that we are keeping holy the Lord's Day."

8

The Church

INTRODUCTION
The Church Is a Sign of the Presence of God

Catholics believe that one of the ways we may encounter Christ in our world today is through the Church. In the Gospel of Matthew, Jesus promises his disciples, and by extension each of us, that he will be with us "always, until the end of the age" (Mt 28:20). In John's Gospel (14:15–16) and in the Acts of the Apostles (1:4–5), Jesus promises us that he would send the Holy Spirit to help build up the Church, and Saint Paul, in his letter to the Christian community at Ephesus, proclaims, "the Church is the Body of Christ" (Eph 1:22–23).

But perhaps the most powerful statement supporting the fact that we encounter the Body of Christ within the Church can be found in 1 Corinthians 12:12–13: "For just as the body is one and has many members, and all the members of the body, though many, are one body, so it is with Christ. For in the one Spirit we were all baptized into one body—Jews or Greeks, slaves or free—and we were all made to drink of one Spirit."

The Church, which is the Body of Christ, demonstrates that it is filled with the Spirit of God, just as Jesus was filled with the Spirit, when it preaches the word of justice, calls upon the people of God to open their hearts and minds to conversion, and celebrates the healing, forgiving, and saving ministry of the Lord.

When Jesus walked among us, it was his words and his saving

actions that demonstrated to those who were willing to "see and believe" that the Spirit of God was active in him. After his death and resurrection, and the experience of Pentecost, the same Spirit of God was alive and active in his apostles and disciples. Again, for those who were willing to "see and believe," the "spirit-filled" lives and activity of the followers of Jesus reminded them of the person of Jesus and the kingdom that he preached.

Another way of coming to an appreciation of this perspective is to understand that, just as people came to recognize that Jesus was a sign of the presence of God in the world, people also came to comprehend that the community of believers, the Church, was also the sign of the presence of God in the world. It is this understanding and appreciation of the activity of the Spirit of God that prompted Saint Paul to clearly identify the Church as the Body of Christ.

Whenever the Church, or any individual member of the Body of Christ, acts in the spirit of Christ, it continues the saving ministry of the Lord in the world. When people love as Jesus loved, when they forgive as Jesus forgave, or when they reach out to one another, especially to those who are poor, alienated, or marginalized, they become the sign—and indeed the presence—of God in the world.

The Second Vatican Council, in the *Dogmatic Constitution on the Church* (§48), taught that whenever the saving message of Jesus was proclaimed, whenever people experienced the truth and love of God in the myriad number of ways that this has been manifested in our lives and in our choices, the Church became a sign and instrument of the presence of God in their lives and a sign of the kingdom that has been promised (CCC 779–780).

Do I Have to Join?

Just last week, my parish ran a "join up" campaign at all the Masses. I felt guilty because I didn't sign up for anything. Do I have an obligation to join any of the parish organizations?

A Quiet Parishioner

Dear Quiet,

When you join any of your parish organizations, you will experience a network of people dedicated to building up the Body of Christ through the various parish ministries.

The Canon Law of the Church does lay down certain obligations and rights that you have as a parish member. These obligations can be found in the Code of Canon Law (209–212). They are as follows: to maintain communion with the Church; to fulfill your particular duties to the universal Church and your parish church; to live a holy life and promote the growth of the Church; to work to spread the gospel; to follow what the pastor and bishop declare as teachers of the faith and the leaders of the Church.

The various organized ministries of the parish offer ways that you, as a parishioner, can fulfill some of the above obligations without having to go it alone.

Of course, you also have certain rights as a parishioner. These are also outlined in the Code of Canon Law (213–218). They include: the right to make your spiritual needs known to your pastor; the right to receive assistance from your pastor out of the spiritual goods of the Church, especially the Word of God and the sacraments; the right to promote apostolic action; and the right to receive a Christian education. Perhaps you will rethink your decision to not sign up for anything. It is never too late to become a parish volunteer!

The Heart of Vatican II

What was the principal change brought about by the Second Vatican Council? I realize this may be difficult to pinpoint with so many changes, yet there must have been one or two upon which the others decided. What is at the heart of today's Vatican II Church?

An Avid Reader

Dear Reader,

Your assessment of the Council is right on target; there were, in fact, several major shifts from which many other no less important changes flowed. For the record, the Second Vatican Council issued sixteen documents on a wide variety of topics, touching almost every conceivable aspect of Church and Christian life. Four of the documents bear the title of *Constitution* and contain the core formulations of the Council's teachings.

According to most observers of the changes, the critical innovation was the redefining of the Church. This one central doctrinal shift triggered an almost complete Church facelift.

Prior to the Council, the Church's self-concept was that of a hierarchical structure, strong on authority, and unbending in its positions. It was seen as a status system, with pope and bishops at the top, followed by priests and religious, with the laity at the bottom. Directives came from on high, and nothing was to be questioned or disputed. The man and woman in the pew were to be like the proverbial child, seen but not heard.

Vatican II changed this by redefining the Church as the "people of God." In this vision, all members are equal; all are called to holiness in service to one another and the world; and all are called to share their life and gifts in the community of God's faithful. Baptism admits all onto the same journey of faith, initiating each person with differing talents and abilities into the mission of the Church. The hierarchy continues, but it is to hear and serve God's people; "servant leadership" is the way to exercise authority in the Church of Vatican II.

Other prominent features in the Church's Vatican II self-understanding can be seen in the strong emphasis on lay ministry: pastoral councils, finance committees, education and liturgy boards. Laypeople are assuming responsibility, along with clergy, for the care of the Church and the spread of God's word. Today, many laypeople, both salaried and volunteer, are actively engaged in the ministry of the Church.

Historically speaking, we are Vatican II babes in the woods, the Council being little more than forty years old. It is considered the most monumental religious happening in the last four centuries. It has spawned any number of additional decrees and statements, from Rome as well as from national and local synods of bishops, all clarifying and developing positions originally contained in the Council documents. Avery Dulles quotes Pope John Paul II as saying that the Council "remains the fundamental event in the contemporary Church" and "the constant reference point of every pastoral action." All of this is due to the Church's simple yet profound rediscovery and redefining of itself as the "people of God."

What Happened to My Neighborhood Parish?

My neighbor used to belong to my parish, but now she drives thirty miles every Sunday to go to Mass in another church. The reason, she says, is that the liturgy in the other parish is "more meaningful." She says she is now a registered member in that parish. Doesn't the Church require geographical boundaries for parish membership?

Curious

Dear Curious,

A 1981 document from the United States Catholic bishops titled "The Parish: A People, a Mission, a Structure" states that the parish is, for most Catholics, the single most important part of Church. This is where, for them, the mission of Christ continues. This is where they publicly express their faith, joining with others to give proof of their communion with God and with one another.

The Church touches most Catholics through the parish. This was true of the pre-Vatican II Church, and it is still true today. However, lately there seems to be a slightly different emphasis in Church law regarding the parish. The old Code of Canon Law described parish in judicial terms. The parish was a "territorial section of the diocese" with a "proper church edifice" to which "a Catholic population was assigned" under a "proper pastor" who was responsible for the "care of souls."

Canon 518 of the new Code of Canon Law begins: "As a general rule, a parish is to be territorial, that is, one which includes all the Christian faithful of a certain territory." It then goes on to talk about the establishment by the bishop of personal parishes based on rite, language, nationality, "or even some other determining factor."

Perhaps as a result of this—and even more, Vatican II's shifting of the idea of parish in the direction of "community" and away from organization and institution—there have risen some new ways of looking at parish affiliation. Some people say that, although the territorial principle for parish alignment makes for good order, the varied needs and expanding styles of commitment of modern Christians dictate the need for a new approach.

We must always remember that parishes exist to provide pastoral care to the Christian faithful by teaching, sanctifying, and governing their members in such a way that they see themselves as part of the diocese and indeed of the universal Church. It may happen occasionally that an individual (such as your neighbor) feels his or her personal spiritual needs are not sufficiently met in one parish, at least not as well as in another. If that person would respectfully present this problem to the pastor, it is likely that he—as would most pastors today—would understand and allow a transfer to another parish that would answer this person's needs and concerns.

The Deacons

In our parish the deacons seem to run everything. When and how were deacons established in the Church?

Wondering

Dear Wondering,

You are fortunate to have the services of deacons in your parish. The *Catechism of the Catholic Church* calls the restoration of the diaconate by the Second Vatican Council "an important enrichment for the Church's mission" (CCC 1571).

The history of the diaconate goes all the way back to the first years of the Church. Saint Paul greets the deacons in the first verse of his letter to the Philippians. In the letters to Timothy (1 Tim 3:8) and Titus (1:7), their role is clearer, and the qualities they should possess are specified. The Acts of the Apostles (6:1–7) actually describes the establishment of the deacons.

Pope Paul VI's letter of August 1972 describes the ministry of deacons in the early Church. They served the whole people of God, taking care of the sick and the poor, bringing the Eucharist to those confined to their homes, baptizing people, and preaching the Word of God. The diaconate remained a constantly exercised ministry in the Eastern Church, but was not exercised in the Western Church, except as a transitional stage for candidates to the priesthood.

In the sixteenth century, the Council of Trent spoke of the possibility of renewing the diaconate in the Latin Church, and in 1957, Pope Pius XII briefly alluded to it. It was not until Vatican II and Pope Paul VI, however, that the diaconate was restored. The ministry of deacons is flourishing today, as your parish testifies.

Deacons: Part Time or Full Time?

We have a permanent deacon at our parish, but he also has a full-time job in the business community. Why doesn't the Church encourage these men to become full-time ministers, like the priests, whose only job is the care of the parish?

Against Job-Splitting

Dear Against Job-Splitting,

In the years before the Second Vatican Council, there was a movement in Western Europe called the Worker Priest Movement. These "worker priests" were clergy assigned to live in neighborhoods and work alongside laypeople in various factories and businesses. It was hoped that these "worker priests" could encourage people, by example, to take their faith more seriously—not just on Sunday and not just in the church, but in the home, in the factory, in the office, in the store, and in the neighborhood. With the return of the permanent diaconate and the new emphasis on lay formation, this movement of "worker priests" slowly died out.

Retired Archbishop Weakland of Milwaukee, Wisconsin, described permanent deacons as "living in both worlds," the world of the Church and the world of the workplace. Deacons, in fact, tie God to the marketplace. Even though some deacons are employed as chaplains in jails, schools, military bases, and hospitals, many others bring their spiritual influence unofficially to their businesses and neighborhoods. It is hoped that deacons will be leaven in the marketplace for the reign of God.

Of course, one need not be ordained to engage in marketplace ministry. The source of this call to minister in the marketplace goes back to our baptism, where all of us enter the priesthood of the laity. Ordination to the permanent diaconate, however, gives a special emphasis and seal to this call to ministry, both in the Church and in the world. What you lose in full-time work in your parish, you gain in the evangelization of the workplace. Remember, Jesus directed us to "go therefore and make disciples of all nations" (Mt 28:19).

What's the Church Calendar?

One Sunday a priest started his homily by showing this huge poster. He said it showed the Church calendar for the whole year. There were several different colors to represent different seasons and celebrations. Would you please explain this further?

Janet

Dear Janet,

The liturgical calendar gives a full picture of the Church year. It shows the liturgical seasons of Advent, Christmas, Ordinary Time, Lent, and Easter, each highlighted in its appropriate color. It gives the days and dates of these principal celebrations. It's the Church year at a glance.

The Church calendar is particularly useful to parish staffs needing to plan for the year. For liturgy committees, the calendar is a must, since it serves as the frame on which people carefully plan for the entire year's liturgies.

Advent: The Church year starts with the First Sunday of Advent. The recommended color is a deep bluish purple or violet, symbolizing the dark and cold of night that only the warm rays of the dawning sun can dispel. This season lasts four weeks, and its mood is one of waiting, longing, yearning for the coming of the Daystar, the Son of Justice who is the Lord, the object of our hope.

Christmas: Advent is followed by Christmas, which celebrates what Advent points to and prepares for: the dawning of the Son. The *Word*, as Christ is called, pierces the darkness of sin, ignorance, and injustice. The Word is made flesh and comes to dwell among us. The Christmas season includes the related celebrations of the Holy Family; Mary, Mother of God; Epiphany; and the Baptism of Jesus. The themes are joy, peace, and wonder that the Lord has arrived and is present among us even now. The colors for this festive season are white or gold.

Lent and Easter: The next major season is Lent, the preamble to Easter. Lent begins on Ash Wednesday, when we're marked on our foreheads with a cross of ashes. This gesture dramatically ushers in our special season of penance, fasting, and heightened prayer that prepares us to renew our baptismal commitment at Easter. Lent and the following Easter season are the high points of the Church year. They redefine Christians and celebrate a people reborn in the waters of baptism and risen with Christ to live a new life. The color for Lent is penitential purple, while the colors for Easter are white or gold.

Ordinary Time: Ordinary Time comprises the longest season of the Church year. This is the season when the great mysteries of salvation unfold in all their depth and richness. At this time, we explore, nuance by nuance, virtue by virtue, the facets of belonging to Jesus' kingdom. The God who sent Jesus to save all from darkness and death is revealed in splendor. During Ordinary Time, noted by the color green, a number of feasts celebrate specific aspects of Jesus. Other feasts honor Mary and the saints.

The Church has a vigorous life—past, present, and future. We celebrate this life in liturgy. The Church calendar guides us through the year, taking us from season to season in an ongoing effort to form us into God's kingdom here on earth, and to lead us to that kingdom in heaven.

What Is Appropriate Music for a Funeral?

My father recently passed away. I wanted to have his favorite song played at the funeral Mass, but our pastor refused to allow it. He said it was not liturgical. What does "liturgical" mean, and what does it have to do with my father?

Paul

Dear Paul,

Webster's dictionary defines liturgy as "a rite or series of rites, observances, or procedures prescribed for public worship in the Christian church in accordance with authorized or standard form." The introduction to the *Constitution on the Sacred Liturgy* expands on this: "It is the liturgy through which…'the work of our redemption is accomplished,' and it is through the liturgy, especially, that the faithful are enabled to express in their lives and manifest to others the mystery of Christ and the real nature of the true Church" (§2).

Throughout the ages, the Christian faithful have gathered to worship God and call upon the saints. These gatherings have taken the form of eucharistic celebrations (the Mass), the celebration of the other sacraments, and other prayer occasions.

The purpose of each of these gatherings is ultimately to worship God for God's goodness, and to call upon that goodness for the benefit of all creation. Worship is expressed through words, music, gesture, and format. Although we may not be aware of it, much of our liturgy is rooted in Jewish liturgy, which is thousands of years old. Since the time of Christ, we have continued to build upon that foundation (cultic action) as our understanding of God and community has grown. The liturgy we have today is a carefully developed expression of faith as expressed throughout the ages until this very moment.

We sometimes forget that the focus of liturgy is God and God's saving action in all creation. It is a public act. Often, without realizing it, we attempt to make liturgy our own private act rather than the Church's act. Because it is easy to fall into this misunderstanding, there are liturgists who assist us—through study and research—in the proper planning and use of liturgy. These individuals help us focus on the purpose and practice of prayer in the Church.

When your father passed away, you wanted to plan a liturgy that reflected his life and what that life meant to the people he had touched. Although you don't mention the name of the song you requested, you were told it was not liturgical. This means that it did not fall within the norms that have been determined to be proper to the funeral Mass liturgy. This is often the case with music that, while beautiful or meaningful, may have no connection with the religious nature of the occasion.

The Church has carefully studied the funeral rite, and, in 1989, promulgated some revisions in the rite. Some words from the instruction that accompany this new rite may be helpful.

> *Music is integral to the funeral rites. It allows the community to express convictions and feelings that words alone may fail to convey. It has the power to console and uplift the mourners and to strengthen the unity of the assembly in faith and love. The texts of the songs chosen for a particular celebration should express the Paschal Mystery of the Lord's suffering, death, and triumph over death, and should be related to the readings from Scripture.*
>
> *Since music can evoke strong feelings, the music for the celebration of the funeral rites should be chosen with great care. The music at funerals should support, console, and uplift the participants and should help to create in them a spirit of hope in Christ's victory over death and in the Christian's share in that victory.*
>
> Order of Christian Funerals, §§30, 31

The fact that the Church has regulations for liturgies, such as your father's funeral Mass, should not be interpreted as meaning the Church is merely legalistic. The Church grieves with you in losing a most significant person in your life and in the life of the Christian community.

Through its liturgy, the Church wishes to also express its faith that Christ's saving action has touched your father for all eternity. It is a message that we all need to sing out about.

What About Anti-Catholic Literature?

For some time now, I have been troubled by a "Christian" publisher who produces religious "tracts," some of which have a strong anti-Catholic message. How should I respond to people who give me this literature?

Travis

Dear Travis,

I know how you feel. I discovered an anti-Catholic brochure on my windshield after Mass one Sunday morning. My reaction was to tear it up in disgust and throw it away. Unfortunately, because I found it so upsetting, I thought about it all the way home, and let some drivers know how I felt about their driving!

My advice (which I should have followed myself) is try to ignore the message and concentrate on the messenger. People who produce or distribute material that is anti-anything or anti-anyone usually do so for one dominant reason: they feel personally threatened and fear the person or group they despise.

What these people have in common is that they fixate on an idea or experience—in this case, our Church. They do so in a vain belief that by fixing, changing, or challenging what they fear, they will no longer feel threatened. This is seldom the case.

The only remedy for fear is found not outside of oneself but within. To invest emotional energy and physical resources on anyone other than self often does not produce the result for which the energy is used. Many people don't understand this truth. Other people understand it yet choose to ignore it.

People who distribute anti-Catholic tracts don't understand this dynamic of fear. They believe that the Catholic Church is not a Christian church. This belief triggers a sense of feeling threatened. Why do they feel threatened and also find it necessary to propagate their beliefs?

Unfortunately, I believe the answer is that some Christian traditions find it necessary to be the messengers of anti-Catholic literature. They believe that by propagating their own fears and opinions they are serving God.

Before we react too strongly to this, we might reflect that we too sometimes act unjustly, and sometimes do so in the false belief that we are serving God. Each of us can recall events and experiences in which we might have spread our fears and opinions, confident that we were doing the right thing.

Many people who believe that the Catholic Church is not a Christian church have no experience of Catholicism. Still others do so because they have been taught to do so, and such teaching has not been challenged. People who fall into these categories are often good people. At the same time, however, they are misinformed and fearful of the truth.

Still others who hold such a position, if they are honest with themselves, will discover through personal reflection that they are not just anti-Catholic; rather, they are intolerant of anyone and anything that is not within the realm of what they believe to be acceptable. Such people suffer from ignorance.

When you add up all of these reasons, I think you can understand why you should concentrate on the messenger and try not to let the message bother you. The most appropriate and healthy response to such a situation might be to simply learn how to accept the person demonstrating intolerance. This response is truly the most effective witness to the gospel.

Who Are the "Old Catholics?"

I recently came across a church that offered a traditional Catholic Mass. The church called itself an "Old Catholic Church." Is that a legitimate Catholic Church?

Jenny

Dear Jenny,

The "Old Catholic Church" is a sect that broke away from the Catholic Church, beginning in Holland in the seventeenth century. Following the First Vatican Council, in 1870, considerable dissent among Catholics, especially in Germany, Austria, and Switzerland, arose over the teaching of the Church in regard to papal infallibility. The dissenters could not accept the proposition that the pope, acting in matters of faith and morals, is empowered with infallibility through the divine assistance of Christ and conferred on his Church through Peter. Many formed independent communities that joined the "Old Catholic Church." They are called "Old Catholics" because they adhere to the beliefs and practices of the Catholic Church of apostolic times. Currently, there are approximately two hundred fifty thousand Old Catholics throughout the world.

In this country, the Old Catholics have numerous tiny sects with self-appointed bishops and minuscule congregations. Old Catholics conduct services in the vernacular, and there is inter-communion with the Church of England. They differ from the Catholic Church in their view of clerical celibacy. For example, married men may be ordained and clergy may, with the bishop's consent, contract marriage after ordination. They do not accept the doctrine of papal infallibility as it was determined at Vatican Council I. The sacrament of reconciliation in the Old Catholic Church is optional. Finally, the Old Catholic Church is not in union with Rome, and so would not be considered "legitimate."

9
Confession and Sin

INTRODUCTION
Jesus and Forgiveness

Even people who do not believe that Jesus is the Son of God are nevertheless left with the impression that he was a person with an unusual capacity for forgiveness. He was able not only to forgive sinners, but to forgive those who had sinned against him (Lk 23:34). The gospels are filled with illustrations of his forgiveness in action: the story of the Sinful Woman (Lk 7:36–50), forgiveness of his crucifiers (Lk 23:34), and his words to Peter (Mt 18:21–22) are some obvious examples.

The message that Jesus preached—a message preached by John the Baptist ("repent and believe") but completed by Jesus ("because the kingdom of God is among you")—was a message that called people to *metanoia*, the Greek word that means to "change your life and your heart." It was more than a message of calling people to repentance, which means to be sorry for what you have done. Rather, Jesus called people to go beyond being sorry; he also desired that people be fundamentally changed by their sorrow and their personal experience of forgiveness. This fundamental change, the reordering of their life and their decisions, was to be understood as *gospel* (good news) because it would usher in a new way of living, which he called the kingdom of God.

Jesus was insistent on *metanoia* and the ramifications of this life-changing decision. When Peter asked him for further clarification—

"Lord, if another member of the church sins against me, how often should I forgive?"—Jesus answered, "Not seven times, but, I tell you, seventy-seven times" (Mt 18:21–22). In other words, in the kingdom of God, there was no limit to what can be forgiven and no limit to what needs to be forgiven: "Forgive us our sins, as we forgive those who sin against us" (see Lk 11:4).

After his Resurrection, Jesus appeared to his disciples and spoke to them in the words that have traditionally been understood as the words that instituted the sacrament of penance: "If you forgive the sins of any, they are forgiven them; if you retain the sins of any, they are retained" (Jn 20:23). Within the context of Jesus' life and ministry, it can be understood that although the power to "bind someone" is certainly a prerogative, the intention of Jesus was not to bind but rather to loose, to free people from that which held them fast and set them firmly on the path to the kingdom of God.

How Does the Bible Define Sin?

The word "sin" gets used in lots of ways. What does the Bible actually say about it?

Curious

Dear Curious,

I'm sure your question does not come out of nowhere, and that you're "curious" for a reason. Here are some of the notions about sin that the Bible gives us. You can apply then to your own situation.

The Hebrews believed that human beings have two inclinations: "good" and "evil"—and when evil wins out, we sin. Sin was viewed as an arrow being aimed at the center of a target but missing its mark—*hed* in Hebrew. The act of "atonement" sought to hold our evil inclination in check.

So when we sin, we "miss the mark." The oldest biblical references to sin begins with the Genesis story of Adam and Eve. It is interesting that when Saint Paul talks about the sin of Adam and Eve (Rom 5:12), he uses a Greek word, *hamartia*, which also means "missing the mark." This word has a meaning beyond that of mere moral fault.

John says that God is love (1 Jn 4:8), therefore we were created to be "love-centered" people. When we try to make ourselves the center of the universe, however, we attempt to live out a lie: we become self-centered people, and our universe is knocked out of kilter.

Imitating original sin, every sin is an act of disobedience and of self-centered pride. As Thomas Merton said, "I am born self-centered. And this is original sin."

There is nothing arbitrary about sin or the commandments of God. The Ten Commandments were given to us by the Author of the World (Ex 20:1–7 and Deut 5:6–21). The first three commandments were meant to guide us in our relationship with God; the remaining seven commandments have to do with our relationships with other people. When we live according to these precepts, the world becomes integral and balanced. When we neglect their guidance, we become disorientated.

Sinfulness is a condition shared by all of humanity (except for Jesus and Mary, his mother). But, thanks be to God, we have Christ to restore us to balance (Rom 7:24–25).

Christ came into the world to announce the love of the Father. Knowing the Father's love, we are drawn to love the Father in return. We become again "God-centered" people, and the universe is put back on track (Rev 21). As Saint John said, "If we confess our sins, he who is faithful and just will forgive us our sins and cleanse us from all unrighteousness" (1 Jn 1:9).

Jesus gives us a new motivation for keeping the commandments—the motivation of love. He gives a double commandment: love of God and love of neighbor (Mk 12:28–34). Paul says these commands fulfill those of the Old Law (Rom 13:8–10); and John says that keeping the commandments simply out of fear of punishment is not enough: love must be the driving force (1 Jn 4:18).

While we need to be aware of the reality of sin, we must be even more aware of the reality of grace. As Saint Paul said, "Where sin increased, grace abounded all the more" (Rom 5:20).

Is Evil for Real?

So many movies seem to be centered on hell, the devil, or Satan taking over someone's body. Is this stuff for real? Does the Church still expel demons as in days of old?

Scott

Dear Scott,

Yes, Scott. Evil is very much for real, but maybe not in the way it is popularly portrayed in a Hollywood movie. Many such movies, in an attempt to sell tickets, exaggerate the truth. Unfortunately, when the exaggeration becomes obvious, people have a tendency to dismiss the subject as "just so much fiction." In the process of dismissing the fiction, they then forget the truth of that which is portrayed. Vatican II's document titled the *Pastoral Constitution on the Church in the Modern World* states, "The whole of man's history has been the story of dour combat with the powers of evil, stretching, so our Lord tells us, from the very dawn of history" (§37).

Although evil is very much present to us and sometimes personified with reference to the devil or Satan, we are not as inclined to attribute evil to a personal force as we once were. Rather, in our time, we have a tendency to associate that which confuses or frightens us to a lack of knowledge rather than the presence of an evil person or force. Things were very much different in biblical times.

In those days, when faced with mystery or anything that seemed out of the ordinary, the ancient mind often attributed the experience to the spirit world. What today we might explain as a naturally occurring phenomenon, or as some sort of psychological condition or manifestation, our ancestors might have attributed to the presence of a good or a bad spirit.

When you look at the presence of evil in this light, I think you might discover that it is sometimes a matter of perception rather than the presence or absence of something or someone. Perception also plays an important role in the matter of expelling demons. This, too, is something that still occurs, but not with the regularity that it once did. It's not that people are no longer possessed; rather, we understand the human person in a different way.

In the ancient world, the operative perception—and, as such, the first conclusion that would be reached when faced with what seemed to be unnatural or unacceptable behavior—was to assume that the person was possessed. Today, our perception and our first conclusion would be to wonder if some type of psychological condition is present. Only after this possibility has been fully explored do we think of possession by a spirit, if at all.

Notice how perception works. The New Testament perception assumes possession as the primary consideration. In our present experience, psychological sickness is considered as the first possibility, and only later is "possession" explored.

The Church takes seriously the presence of evil and does not easily dismiss the power of evil. At the same time, the Church takes seriously the insights offered to us by our contemporary understanding of sickness and disease.

What Is Original Sin?

A visiting priest comes to our parish every weekend. His homilies are wonderful. But he often uses phrases like "That's because of original sin" or "We shouldn't forget about original sin." I'm not sure what he means. What is original sin?

Melvin

Dear Melvin,

Letters like yours give the Padre gray hair! In the long course of Christian history, there have been whole volumes written on the meaning of *original sin*. In this short space I can give only a basic answer to your question.

The Second Vatican Council states: "Although set by God in a state of rectitude [holiness], man, enticed by the evil one, abused his freedom from the very start of history. He lifted himself up against God, and sought to attain his goal apart from him" (*Pastoral Constitution on the Church in the Modern World*, §13). This is a concise description of original sin, the sin that occurred at the origins of the human race.

The Book of Genesis tells the story of that original sin in striking detail. The first two chapters tell how God created all things, including man and woman, and saw that they were "very good." In chapter 3, however, Adam rejects God and separates himself from God. Adam tries to hide from God, blames Eve for his sin, and experiences the pangs of guilt.

From the original sin of Adam, a host of evils came into the world. Chapters 4 through 11 of Genesis describe in narrative form how the first sin brought a mushroom cloud of evil into the world. For example, Cain murders his brother Abel in cold blood. Sin is so rampant, in fact, that God sends a great flood (from which only Noah and his family are spared). The flood highlights the chaos and destruction sin brought into the beauty of creation.

Yet, even this does not open the people's eyes. In chapter 11 of Genesis we see human beings still defying God and wanting to be God's equal by building a tower that will reach the heavens. The story of the Tower of Babel, as it is called, speaks eloquently about the effects of sin: human beings not only reject God but also reject and despise one another. There is now division and hatred among nations.

According to Genesis, a world of beauty was deformed by sin. The ongoing result has been division, pain, bloodshed, loneliness, and death. This tragic narrative has a familiar feel to it. The reality it points to is a basic part of human experience. It is no surprise that this reality—the fact of original sin and its effect in us all—is a teaching of the Church.

It is the teaching of the Church that every mortal born into this world, except the Virgin Mary, is affected by original sin. This is not a personal sin committed by each individual (such as lying or stealing); rather, in the words of Pope Paul VI, "It is human nature so fallen, stripped of the grace that clothed it, injured in its own natural powers and subjected to the dominion of death, that is transmitted to all men, and it is in this sense that every man is born in sin" (*Credo of the People of God,* §21).

Original sin means that each "descendant of Adam" (including us) is created without sanctifying grace and is subject to concupiscence (the inclination to sin) and to death. Each of us needs redemption through the saving death and resurrection of Jesus Christ.

Is There Really an Unforgivable Sin?

Did Jesus really say there is one sin, the "sin against the Holy Spirit," that can never be forgiven? How does this fit with our belief in an all-loving, all-forgiving God?

Puzzled

Dear Puzzled,

The gospels written by Matthew, Mark, and Luke record, with slight variations, a saying of Jesus about an "unforgivable sin." In the Gospel of Matthew, Jesus says, "People will be forgiven for every sin and blasphemy, but blasphemy against the Spirit will not be forgiven. Whoever speaks a word against the Son of Man will be forgiven, but whoever speaks against the Holy Spirit will not be forgiven, either in this age or in the age to come" (Mt 12:31–32). Mark quotes Jesus as follows: "Truly I tell you, people will be forgiven for their sins and whatever blasphemies they utter; but whoever blasphemes against the Holy Spirit can never have forgiveness, but is guilty of an eternal sin" (Mk 3:28–29). And in the Gospel of Luke, Jesus says, "Everyone who speaks a word against the Son of man will be forgiven; but whoever blasphemes against the Holy Spirit will not be forgiven" (Lk 12:10).

On first reading, this saying of Jesus can be quite unsettling, seeming to imply the existence of sin—"blasphemy against the Holy Spirit"—that God either cannot or will not forgive. Yet, in contrast to this saying, we have the overwhelming testimony of the Scriptures and Church teaching that God's mercy and forgiveness are more powerful than any sin, no matter how serious or frequent it might be. This apparent contradiction disappears when we consider carefully the context of Jesus' teaching on the "unforgivable sin."

Jesus' statements regarding "blasphemy against the Holy Spirit" occurred as part of his ongoing dispute with the scribes and Pharisees. These men witnessed Jesus' exorcisms but attributed them to the power of Satan: "It is only by Beelzebul, the ruler of the demons, that this man casts out demons" (Mt 12:24). In response, Jesus points out the absurdity of this claim: "No city or house divided against itself will stand" (Mt 12:25). If it was by the power of Satan that Jesus cast out Satan, then the latter's kingdom would be hopelessly divided against itself and headed for utter ruin.

It is in this context of his opponents' stubbornness and disbelief that we must understand Jesus' reference to the "blasphemy against the Holy Spirit" that "can never be forgiven." Jesus' miracles, worked by the power of the Spirit who is the source of all goodness, are maliciously attributed by the scribes and Pharisees to Satan, who is Prince of Darkness and the source of evil. Jesus' enemies thus deny the evidence of the Spirit's saving action in Jesus' work and teaching. And this denial is not simply a misunderstanding of his teaching due merely to human error or prejudice. Rather, it is willful, malicious, deliberate, and unrepentant. For such a one, there truly can be no forgiveness, not because God is unwilling or unable to forgive, but because the person will not recognize the need for repentance, and refuses to ask for forgiveness.

The "unforgivable sin" is not an action so horrible that even God's patience and power of forgiveness are exhausted. Rather, it is the attitude of a person who would deny that the Holy Spirit is the source of Jesus' miracles and preaching, attributing them instead to the power of the evil one. Those who maliciously persist in this attitude reject the Lord's presence in their lives and cut themselves off from God.

God's offer of forgiveness is still universal. We need only respond to God's grace, undergo a conversion from our former attitude, and repent and seek forgiveness. Forgiveness certainly will be granted by the Lord who does "not want any to perish, but all to come to repentance" (2 Pet 3:9).

What Is the Difference Between Temptation and Sin?

We seem to be always talking about turning away from sin. What about temptation? When do we cross the line between temptation and sin?

A Penitent

Dear Penitent,

The temptations of Jesus, as they are recorded in the gospels (Mk 1:12, Lk 4:1, and Mt 4:1), give us the proper direction with regard to sin and temptation. Jesus was tempted three times, but he did not sin. More than that, Jesus put his trust in God during the temptations. Jesus' message is clear: if you feel tempted, call out to God!

The Church has always taught that sin is a deliberative process. If you have to wonder about whether or not you have sinned, then you didn't sin. For temptation to become a sin, you have to think about the action, plan it, do it, and then you've done it! In fact, the *Catechism of the Catholic Church* even uses the words, "full knowledge and deliberate consent" (CCC 1857) when looking at what is sinful.

Although the sacrament of penance is available throughout the year, we place a special emphasis on it at certain times (which are penitential in nature, such as Advent and Lent). Your parish will more than likely offer a reconciliation service during these times. Why not make it your personal obligation to participate in the service? Like Jesus in the Gospel, you would then be choosing God over evil. You would be asking God to strengthen your weakness, especially in the face of temptation. Like the Lord, you can then proclaim: "Worship the Lord your God, and serve only him" (Lk 4:8).

I Don't Like Confession!

Why does the Church stress the sacrament of penance so much?
I never liked going to confession as a kid and I like it even less
now! What would the Church say to hardheads like myself?

Uncomfortable

Dear Uncomfortable,

Over the years, unlike you, I have enjoyed going to confession, or receiving the sacrament of penance, and have gone frequently during my life. One thing I like about it is that I am able to receive forgiveness for my sins and feedback about my life from the priest. This feedback and forgiveness has given me courage to lead a better life. I have noticed that those who confess more frequently not only seem to be clearer on what is right and what is wrong in their lives but also are able to actually live that vision.

The Church directs that we should confess at least once a year. This sacrament helps us, says the Council of Trent and echoed in the *Catechism of the Catholic Church*, to have "peace and serenity of conscience with strong spiritual consolation" (CCC 1468). This means standing up for what is right and trusting in the Lord that we will be happy doing good as Jesus did.

Penance is one of the seven sacraments. The sacraments are the pillars that make up a healthy and holy Christian life. Deciding not to partake of a sacrament is like deciding to take one of the main support beams out of your home, and hoping that your home will still stand through the next big storm.

Saint Gerard, a Redemptorist brother, used to travel with the mission preachers. He was a holy man, and, during the mission, the people would usually consult him before going to confession. You might pray to Saint Gerard to give you a greater love for this sacrament.

Too Young for Confession?

My son is expected to make his first confession soon. He seems too young to have sinned in any serious way. What is the point of making a child anxious about such things?

Worried

Dear Worried,

"Confession," or the sacrament of penance, is not meant to make anyone anxious. In fact, its purpose is just the opposite.

This sacrament provides us the opportunity to reflect on our failures toward God and other people, to express sorrow for those failures, and to be assured of God's forgiveness for them. We shouldn't be too hasty in assuming that young children are unaware of wrongdoing and the need to say, "I'm sorry." Even very young children can be deliberately mean, cruel, or selfish.

Before children experience the sacrament of reconciliation for the first time, they should be able to distinguish between deliberate and accidental actions (breaking a plate may be an accident; breaking it over your sister's head is probably deliberate). They should also be able to express their faults in their own words, and they should have some understanding that their sins affect their relationship with God, who loves them unconditionally but is hurt by their wrong decisions and actions.

In general, children are able to fulfill these conditions between the ages of seven and eight. If a child's moral awareness develops more slowly, parents can request that the reception of the sacrament be postponed.

Guilt and Forgiveness

At the beginning of Mass, the celebrant says: "Let us call to mind our sins." I thought that once sins are forgiven, we shouldn't call them to mind again. This could really lead to a guilt complex!

David

Dear David,

The official name for the part of the Mass you describe is the penitential rite. Penitence is our recognition that we need God. It reminds us that our lives and the lives of others are one in God.

A guilt complex is altogether different from penitence. A guilt complex carries with it a feeling of shame. A person in the throes of a guilt complex thinks, *I am bad. What I have done makes me unlovable to God and to the significant people in my life.* People with guilt complexes feel degraded, hopeless, and worthless. Penitence, on the other hand, is a form of mature guilt.

Mature guilt is a healthy form of self-respect. It helps us recognize that we occasionally go against our own values, but with God's help we can do something constructive about these failings. When we respect ourselves in this way, we set realistic standards for personal behavior, admitting that it is important for us to live up to those standards. We "call to mind our sins" at the beginning of Mass to remind ourselves that none of us is perfect—we all need God's love.

True morality comes out of free choice, enlightened by faith, and put into action with the help of grace; guilt complexes do not. They merely pressure people and make them feel worse about themselves. True morality comes from a healthy self-respect that helps us respect and love God and others as we are respected and loved by God. Guilt complexes only fill people with impossible demands for personal perfection. True morality puts the spotlight on God's love and mercy and on our dignity as children of God.

The penitential rite of Mass is meant to focus our attention on divine love and mercy. The responses "Lord have mercy" and "Christ have mercy" reflect a sense of gratitude for the gift of the Eucharist and the opportunity to gather together around the table of the Lord. At times, it is appropriate to call to mind our sins that keep us apart from one another. As Christians, we have chosen love as our primary value, but there are times when we do not love as fully as we want to. These are the times when it makes sense to petition for God's help.

When we ask for mercy, however, we are not focusing on our unworthiness. Rather, we are focusing on God's love. To ask for forgiveness is to recognize that being human means that we must constantly turn to God. Only God can heal the hurt and calm the fear that is the source of sin.

The penitential rite is not meant to be a list of faults. It is meant to be a prayer of thanksgiving for the mercy that has already been given to us as a gift. God's love in not something we win or lose. Rather, it is a gift we receive even when we do not live up to our values. It is merciful because God recognizes that we are human and loves us just as we are.

The Christian dream—the hope that we ask God to nurture every time we stand together around the altar—is that once we have received mercy we will be merciful. We receive God's gifts so that we can give them away, and when we give away God's gifts, they become ours even more deeply.

10
The Eucharist/Mass

INTRODUCTION
The Second Vatican Council and the Eucharist

The first document issued by the Second Vatican Council was the *Constitution on the Sacred Liturgy*. This document mandated significant change in the liturgy and called for a return to what many believed were the basics of Catholic eucharistic worship. The central thrust of the document was to again situate the people of God, not as a type of spectator, but rather as an assembly of the faithful, active and integral to the liturgical celebration of Word and Eucharist.

Without changing the belief and the dogmas about the Eucharist that had been defined for previous generations of Catholics, the Second Vatican Council nevertheless chose to emphasize different truths from the richness of the eucharistic tradition. This emphasis included an understanding of the Eucharist as an opportunity to offer thanks and praise to the Father, as the sacrificial memorial of Christ and his body, and as the presence of Christ by the power of his word and the power of the Holy Spirit.

Thanks and praise to the Father: The primary meaning of *eucharist* is "thanksgiving," and, as such, the Eucharist is humankind's opportunity to thank God the Father for all we have and for all that has been accomplished through creation, redemption, and sanctification. This prayer of thanksgiving is offered to the Father through Christ, with Christ, and in Christ (CCC 1359–1361).

A sacrificial memorial: The Eucharist is a memorial of Christ's Pass-over—not in the sense of a mere recollection of what happened long ago, but rather in a sense that is both present and real for the people of God today. This memorial is a living sacrifice of the Church, united with the offering and intercession of Christ, for the benefit of those here on earth as well as for all of the faithful departed "who have died in Christ" (CCC 1367–1371).

Christ is present in Word and Spirit: As the Scriptures tell us, Christ is present whenever "two or three are gathered in my name" (Mt 18:20) and in the poor, the sick, and the imprisoned (Mt 25:31–46); but Christ is present in the fullest possible way in the Blessed Sacrament of the Eucharist, "the body and blood, together with the soul and divinity, of our Lord Jesus Christ and, therefore, the whole Christ is truly, really, and substantially contained" (CCC 1374).

Why Do We Call It *"Mass"*?

Most of my life as a Catholic, I have referred to our Sunday celebration of Eucharist as the "Mass." My children, who go to Catholic school, refer to it as the "Eucharist." I know that they are probably right, but why?

A True Believer

Dear Believer,

The word *eucharist* comes from the Greek word *eucharistein*. This word simply means "to give thanks." In Eucharist, we give thanks to God for giving us Jesus. We also give thanks to Jesus, who shares his body and blood with us. The word *eucharist* was used to describe the early church's gathering, where the people repeated the stories of the Lord and shared the bread and wine, as the Lord commanded them to do.

The word *mass* comes from the Latin word *missio*, which means "the sending." This refers to the words of dismissal at the end of Mass. The priest or deacon invites us to "go in peace to love and serve the Lord." In the Latin Mass, this phrase is "*ite missa est.*" No one quite knows why the Eucharist came to be known as the "missa" or "mass." Some think it is because of the way monastic prayers were conducted in the early Middle Ages. When the monks gathered for prayers, they often concluded with a short eucharistic celebration. These celebrations sometimes lasted only ten minutes or so, and as they marked the end of the whole set of prayers, they signaled the end of the service. This, it is suggested, is why the Eucharist came to be known as the "dismissal," or the "Mass."

Why Is Mass So Important?

Why does the Church put so much emphasis on Mass? All I heard while growing up was "Mass on Sunday, Mass on Sunday." It's like you're not Catholic if you don't go to Mass every Sunday. I'm still Catholic, but I'd like to see what else is out there.

A Searching College Student

Dear Searching,

Even though being Catholic means much more than going to Mass on Sunday, you are correct in identifying "Catholic" with going to Mass. They are virtually synonymous, since the very roots of Catholicism can be traced to the early community's gatherings after the Ascension of Jesus Christ. There is irrefutable evidence that the disciples met regularly to "do this in memory of me" by celebrating the Eucharist.

In Luke's Gospel we read the touching story of the two crest-fallen disciples, symbolic of the saddened early Church, on the road to Emmaus after Jesus' death. They are joined by a mysterious traveler whom they eventually recognize as Jesus in the "breaking of the bread"—the term first used for Eucharist. The story clearly says that Jesus is risen and is alive in the Church, particularly in the celebration of the Eucharist. Long before the evangelists wrote the gospels in their final form, before the Mass as we know it took stable shape, Christians gathered together on Sunday (the day of the Resurrection) to commemorate in the Eucharist the salvation Jesus won on the cross.

From the beginning, the Catholic Church has placed strong emphasis on the Mass because it considered Mass the ultimate act of worship—the perfect sacrifice. The Church believes that the Mass commemorates and relives the offering of Jesus Christ to God. Through celebration of the Eucharist, not only is Christ's sacrifice remembered as a historical event of the past, it also comes alive for us in the here and now so that we, centuries removed, can get in touch with it and receive its saving effects. No other event is celebrated in quite the same way. Not only is Christ's giving of himself recalled, it also is reenacted. God can't help but be perfectly pleased at the remembrance of this supreme gift—Jesus Christ.

The Mass is critical, too, in that it forms worshipers into God's people, the living Body of Christ. As liturgists put it, if we keep the liturgy, the liturgy will keep us. By that they mean we are continually being formed and molded into God's people as we regularly celebrate the Liturgy of the Eucharist. The readings, which are an integral part of the Mass, remind us of the wonderful, powerful things the Lord has done and continues to do for us. They exhort us to respond generously with lives of love, justice, peace, honesty, and truth, as we hear over and over what kind of people God wants us to be. In communion with the Lord and one another, we are nourished and strengthened to live Christian lives and to bring God's kingdom to life wherever we go.

The Mass is the single most powerful force in creating the Church and assuring its growth and vitality. It is the center of Catholic Christian life as well as the highest expression of that life. The whole dynamic of the Church's life gets its power from the Eucharist. The diversity and unity of the Church are never more graphically and concretely expressed than when Catholic people gather for their worship.

I would bet that, after your time of experimentation and searching, you'll get back to the Mass. There's truly nothing "out there" quite like it.

How Is the Mass a "Sacrifice"?

Most of us in our parish view the Eucharist as a community celebration or a family meal. Yet, it is still called the "sacrifice of the Mass" or described as the "perfect sacrifice." Please explain this aspect of the Mass.

A Bewildered Believer

Dear Bewildered,

The Mass as a meal and a community celebration is easy to grasp, since so many of our festivities center on food. In the United States, Thanksgiving almost totally focuses on the lavish turkey dinner we enjoy. Weddings, anniversaries, and birthday parties all include food and drink. Since the Second Vatican Council redefined the Church as "people of God," the Mass is easily perceived as a family meal.

By design, the setting for the first Eucharist was a meal. On the eve of passing through death, Jesus and his friends gathered for the ritual Passover meal—a familiar part of their lives. Only this time, Jesus turned the meal into something more than it originally was. Jesus identified himself intimately with the elements of the meal—the bread and the wine. He charged his disciples with the new, deeper meaning of his death and resurrection. By saying "Do this in memory of me," Jesus made this action and this gathering the way Christians for all ages could remember his saving actions and claim them for their own. Even though the context was a meal, the first Eucharist foreshadowed Christ's sacrificial offering of himself on the cross for the salvation of all people. We do the same at Mass: we gather for a meal, but offer the sacrifice of Jesus Christ.

Religious sacrifice dates back to the dawn of human consciousness. All cultures and religions, even the most primitive ones, have practiced sacrificial rites. Belief in gods or God made people instinctively want to do something for the beings they worshiped. Therefore, people developed rituals for pleasing or placating the gods, including various sacrificial rites. In fact, there have even been instances of human sacrifices. But whatever was sacrificed, it represented the people who usually changed the sacrificed object in some significant way. Such change could happen by burning, breaking, or eating to symbolize the people's dependence on and fidelity to the deity.

Through sacrifice, we affirm our role as creatures that have limited powers and abilities—creatures that must rely on God. Even Lenten fasting and "giving up" things foster spiritual renewal via sacrifice. Sacrifice is an integral part of life, and nothing of importance or meaning is accomplished without it.

The eucharistic prayers of the liturgy leave no doubt that the Mass is a sacrifice. These prayers commemorate and "re-present" bread and wine in honor of Jesus' long-ago offering of himself in obedience to God. The prayer of consecration says, "This is my body which is given up for you." The third eucharistic prayer says, "We offer you in thanksgiving this holy and living sacrifice," and further on it prays, "May this sacrifice which has made our peace with you, advance the peace and salvation of all the world." The fourth prayer speaks of the "acceptable sacrifice, which brings salvation to all."

Mass is the perfect sacrifice because the gift offered is perfect— Jesus Christ offering himself to God. The sacrificial aspect of the Mass applies to us as well. As Christ was broken on the cross for our salvation, so we are to be "broken" in service to one another. Christ died for us, but we are to live for one another. "Let us go in peace to love and serve the Lord" sends us out into the world to live our Eucharist and be in life what we just celebrated in ritual.

Sunday Mass: Obligatory or Optional?

My teenager came home from school the other day and announced that his religion teacher told the class that Catholics no longer had to attend Mass on Sunday. This upset me very much. How could a teacher possibly say this in a Catholic school?

Shocked

Dear Shocked,

I bet you were shocked indeed! That is a pretty bold statement for anyone to make. If I were you, I would make an appointment to discuss this statement with your child's teacher. It has been my experience, both as a high-school religion teacher and a college professor, that students often condense lengthy in-depth discussions into one-liners—sometimes losing accuracy in the process. I once heard a rather lengthy and profound discussion on sexuality summed up as "Father said that premarital sex is all right." Father, of course, was shocked!

The subject of Sunday obligation is worth discussing. No good Catholic teacher would say that there is no serious obligation in regard to Sunday Mass. Today's teacher, however, would have a different approach than those who taught us.

It is not good catechesis to approach Sunday Mass on the basis of naked duty. The Eucharist is an incredible gift. Because it embodies Jesus at the moment of his greatest courage and love—the moment in which he faced death for us in faithfulness to his Father—it is a privilege for us to be able to join him. When we participate with Jesus in the Eucharist, we extend in time and space the sacrifice by which he is saving the world. We also grow strong as his pilgrim people by sharing in the one banquet of his body and blood. The Eucharist is the source and the summit of all celebration. It is at the heart of the universe.

In the past, there was an awful stress on naked duty. The wonderful gift of the Mass was wreathed in the smoke of fire and brimstone. We were taught that we could go to hell for missing one Sunday Mass because of human weakness.

Father Bernard Häring, a contemporary theologian, writes: "The Church would fail greatly if she were to present the Eucharist *primarily* as a law surrounded by threats of brimstone and fire....The Church rightly prescribes regular attendance at Mass each Sunday and feast day unless proportionate reason excuses the individual. But since the absolute regularity is by no means a divine law, it seems out of proportion to threaten eternal damnation each time someone exceptionally neglects Mass."

Father Häring concludes that it is right to speak of a serious obligation to participate in Sunday Mass, but for a more positive reason than the fear of mortal sin. Any good Catholic who understands the faith and the invitation of Jesus would be shaken if he or she were to begin to miss Mass because of laziness or human weakness. A good Catholic knows that it is a serious choice to make and that there is danger in leaving the path of salvation. The person who does not understand the gift of the Eucharist will not be drawn to "taste and see the goodness of the Lord" if it is presented as the stumbling block over which one could trip and plunge into the fiery abyss of hell.

The Church's authentic vision of Sunday implies that it be a time of joy; that Christians should gather in Jesus to worship the Father with him, to ask for help, to give thanks for life, and to offer praise for his goodness. It demands that these attitudes overflow into weekday life to make each day holy. A people gathered in fear cannot truly celebrate. Fear strikes at the heart of Sunday worship, destroying the warmth, the sense of family, and the joy.

I am sure your son's teacher did not mean to do away with the obligation to participate in Sunday Mass. The intention was probably to change some of the attitudes that frustrate the true significance of Sunday worship.

Is Missing Sunday Mass Wrong?

If I miss Mass on a Sunday through my own fault, am I committing a sin? I used to think it was a mortal sin to miss Mass willingly on Sunday. Now I see that many of my good Catholic friends miss every once in a while and don't seem to think much of it. When I asked them if they thought it was a sin to miss Mass, they said no. Who is right? This really bothers me.

M.P.B.

Dear M.P.B.,

The Church teaches that we have a serious obligation to attend
Sunday Mass. This obligation can only be set aside for a serious reason, such as illness, conditions associated with aging, or being physi-
cally unable to get to a church. No, it's not a sin to miss Mass if it
happens for these reasons; however, missing Mass is sinful if you miss
regularly and willfully, because regularly skipping Mass shows contempt for an important law of the Church.

When we attend Mass, we're not simply being present to an action
taking place within a church. Rather, we are worshiping God and
acknowledging our dependence on God. Sunday Mass is also a splen-
did opportunity to thank God for past favors and ask for future graces.

A number of people have told me that they can pray to God anywhere (such as on a golf course), and that they don't have to attend
Mass to pray. This, of course, is true. But it misses the point.

Christ established the eucharistic celebration as a special way for
us to express our love and adoration for him. Even more importantly,
God has things to say to us in Mass that we will not hear outside of
Mass. At Mass, we hear the voice of God in a very personal and
direct way in the prayers themselves, in the readings from Sacred Scripture, and in the homily. If someone is intentionally absent, these holy
messages of inspirations and support will not be heard.

The voice of the Church is a voice of God. When the Church spoke
in the Second Vatican Council it said the Mass provides "a supper of
brotherly fellowship and a foretaste of the heavenly banquet" (*Pastoral Constitution on the Church in the Modern World,* §38). That's
why Mass should be the focus of the whole life of the Christian community.

The Mass is so fantastically important in the lives of Catholics
because it presents an opportunity to receive the body and blood of
our Savior in a holy and reverential setting. There is nothing in this
world that can equal the Eucharist. It is the rock and foundation of
strength for living and coping with life. It is love exemplified in a most
perfect manner—through Jesus' union with us. The Eucharist provides
a series of doors to sacred truth and the mysterious reality of God.

Many people think that missing Sunday Mass is not a sin, and others think it's a waste of time. I have often asked people like this what they would put in place of Mass. That's because I believe we must do *something* to acknowledge the life and love that God gives us.

Yes, some Catholics are making up their own minds about what is sin and what is not. That can be good at times, but when it involves attendance at Sunday Mass, no one can err by following the Church's teaching.

I Haven't Been to Mass in Twenty-Five Years

Twenty-five years ago, when my wife died from a brain aneurysm, I blamed God and stopped going to church. After years of living alone and feeling sorry for myself, I recently met a wonderful person who has brought joy back into my life and who has convinced me to return to Mass. So much has changed since I last attended Mass. Can you help me better understand the Mass?

Bob

Dear Bob,

Welcome back to the Church and to the land of the living! You must feel like a new person after all those lonely years. To learn more about the Mass and the teachings of today's Catholic Church, you might consider participating in the Rite of Christian Initiation (RCIA) in your parish. Through a series of instructions, discussions, and religious experiences, the RCIA process helps people deepen their faith. While intended primarily for people who are thinking about joining the Catholic Church, RCIA can help people like you who simply want to learn more about Catholic beliefs and practices.

Another suggestion is to read a short booklet explaining the Mass, or take a missalette home from church and familiarize yourself with the parts of the Mass.

Rather than trying to explain each prayer or action that takes place during Mass, I think I can help you and many other Catholics by

pointing out some basic attitudes and ideas that form the foundation
for all that happens at Mass.

1. *Participation rather than passive attendance:* To occupy a
   space within the church for forty-five minutes, alternately
   watching the priest say Mass and the seconds ticking on
   your watch, might fulfill the letter of the law, but it is not
   what is intended when the Church obliges its members to
   participate in the Eucharist. The key word is *participate.*
   Weekend Mass should be a time of great activity—singing,
   listening intently, praying fervently, reflecting quietly, worshiping joyfully.

2. *Less talk of sin and more awareness of forgiveness:* A few
   generations ago, sermons often were filled with talk of hell
   and damnation. Today's homily is usually centered on the
   mercy, love, and strength that come from friendship with
   Jesus the Savior. At the same time, there are several occasions during Mass when the people are called to acknowledge their need for mercy and forgiveness.

3. *A balance of Word and sacrament:* A generation ago, Catholics focused their primary attention on the offertory, the
   consecration, and Communion. Today's liturgy strikes a
   greater balance between the Liturgy of the Word (penitential rite, Scripture readings, and the homily) and the Liturgy
   of the Eucharist (presentation of gifts, eucharistic prayer,
   and Communion rite).

4. *More than bread and wine:* While the presence of Christ
   under the forms of bread and wine retains a prominent place
   in the Mass, it is also important to realize that Christ is
   present in the words of the Bible, in the prayerful presence
   of the presiding priest, and in the faith-filled assembly. The
   Mass fulfills the Scriptures: "The Word became flesh," "The
   one who hears you hears me," and "Where two or three or
   gathered."

5. *A celebration of family and community:* Jesus fostered a sense of family among his disciples and his first faithful followers. Weekend parish liturgies should be a time when young and old, rich and poor, families and single people, join together to experience their unity in Christ. Friendship, fellowship, warmth, and welcome should be just as much in evidence as collection baskets and parish bulletins.

I hope these few general ideas can help you understand the Mass a little better, and that you will make a real effort to learn more about this central celebration of faith.

What Is the Catholic Belief in the Real Presence?

Could you explain the Catholic belief in the Real Presence of the Eucharist?

A Worshiper

Dear Worshiper,

Our belief in the Real Presence goes back to Jesus himself. Saint Paul describes the Last Supper. Jesus took bread and said, "This is my body." He took a cup of wine and said, "This cup is the new covenant in my blood."

The Catholic Church has always believed that Jesus meant exactly what he said. For the Jews of Jesus' time, *body* meant the person and *blood* was the source of life identifiable with the person. So Jesus was saying over the bread and wine, "This is my very self." He used bread and wine to make himself really present to followers of every age. This seems almost too good to be true, and from the very beginning, some have not been able to believe Jesus.

The Gospel of John records that Jesus, in an instruction at Capernaum, said, "I am the living bread that came down from heaven. Whoever eats of this bread will live forever; and the bread that I will give for the life of the world is my flesh" (Jn 6:51). Many listeners objected, so Jesus declared: "Very truly, I tell you, unless you eat the flesh of the Son of Man and drink his blood, you have no life in you" (Jn 6:53).

These words shocked his followers. "This teaching is difficult," they said; "who can accept it?" (Jn 6:60) Many turned back and no longer went about with him (Jn 6:66). Jesus did not run after them and shout, "Don't go away. You misunderstood. I didn't mean that the bread is my body, but only that it represents my body." Instead, Jesus asked his apostles, "Do you also wish to go away?" Peter answered, "Lord, to whom can we go? You have the words of eternal life" (Jn 6:67–68).

Jesus, when confronted with the difficulty of what he was saying, did not water down his statements, even though they were, indeed, difficult to accept and beyond human understanding. Even Peter did not claim to understand them. He simply accepted them on the authority of Jesus, who had "the words of eternal life."

Saint Paul believed that Jesus meant what he said. He stated, "Whoever, therefore, eats the bread or drinks the cup of the Lord in an unworthy manner will be answerable for the body and blood of the Lord" (1 Cor 11:27).

We Catholics have always believed in the Real Presence of Jesus. The traditional term for this miracle has been *transubstantiation*. The term means that the "substance" of the bread and wine becomes the "substance" of Christ's body and blood, while the appearances of bread and wine remain. When we receive holy Communion, we truly receive the body and blood, soul and divinity, of the Lord Jesus Christ, under the appearance of bread and wine (*Catechism of the Catholic Church*, 1373–1381).

Not all Christians believe in the Eucharist as Catholics do. Some believe that Christ is present along with the bread and wine. They assert that, in taking communion, they are receiving bread and wine in which Jesus is present. Some maintain that Christ is present, not as a result of his power but as a result of their personal belief. Some say that Christ is present only through the faith of the community and that Christ does not remain after the worship service. Some deny that Christ is present at all; they contend that the bread and wine only symbolize the spirit and teachings of Jesus. There are many variations on these themes, and Catholics should carefully distinguish our Church's teaching from other opinions.

Catholic belief in the Real Presence fits into our pattern of accepting the goodness of God's creation, and of knowing that God uses material things to give us divine grace. Bread and wine are changed by Christ into himself in a miracle of love we Catholics call, with awe and affection, the *Blessed Sacrament*.

Eucharistic Adoration

Our parish just recently started eucharistic adoration. My mother told me that when she was growing up in the 1930s, eucharistic adoration was very popular, with huge processions and churches overflowing with people. How far back does this devotion go?

A Eucharistic Devotee

Dear Eucharistic Devotee,

The practice of eucharistic adoration was very popular in the first sixty-five years of the twentieth century. The devotion included prayer and adoration in the presence of a consecrated host, processions, benedictions, the Forty Hours devotions, and perpetual adoration. This practice has returned in recent years, when Pope John Paul II promoted the year 2000 as a eucharistic year.

The practice of adoring the consecrated host goes back seven hundred years, and reached its high point in the Middle Ages. At that time, people felt unworthy to receive Communion. Only the anointed hands of the priest could touch the sacred host. The ultimate moment of the Mass became the elevation of the host. The bells were rung to notify the people that this sacred moment was now happening. Some people dashed from church to church to witness the elevation more than once. Some even paid priests to repeat the elevation. The host became an untouchable sacred object of worship. The solemnity of the Body and Blood of Christ, which your mother probably remembers as the feast of Corpus Christi, was declared in 1264 in response to this movement. Monstrances were designed to display the sacred host, and processions evolved full of pomp and grandeur.

Eucharistic adoration has been praised by saints and popes alike as a genuine source of spirituality for faithful Catholics. Pope Paul VI, in his 1965 encyclical *Mysterium Fidei* ("Mystery of Faith"), wrote that there is nothing more consoling on earth and nothing more efficacious for advancing along the road to holiness than this devotion to the Eucharist. Only Holy Thursday 1980, Pope John Paul II wrote to all the bishops, in which he prayed that eucharistic devotion would never cease.

Hopefully, this devotion in your parish will bring you to a deeper sense of Christ's closeness to you.

Dancing Before the Lord

While visiting my daughter, I attended Mass at her parish. I was shocked when four young girls came out and danced around the altar. My daughter said that they were "liturgical dancers." She finds it beautiful, but I think it is sacrilegious. Does the Church approve of this kind of thing?

Michelle

Dear Michelle,

For a past generation, dancing in general (square dancing was probably an exception) was frowned upon by official and self-appointed guardians of morality. Dancing was considered an occasion of sin, and many pastors denounced members of their flock who indulged in it. For those steeped in this tradition, to view dancing as an expression of worship is difficult.

But new insights come with new times, and good pastors and good Christians today are less inclined to condemn dancing outright. As with all human activities, there are abuses; some dancing does indeed border on the edge of indecency. One does not have to be a prude to disapprove of such excesses. Putting this aside, we are more inclined today to view most popular dancing as a healthy activity. Even the Old Testament states that there is "a time to mourn, and a time to dance" (Eccl 3:4).

But dancing in the liturgy? Isn't that a sacred time, to be kept free of frivolity—such as dancing?

Actually, the roots of liturgical dance reach far back in time. Sacred dance is found in all primitive rituals. By dance and drum and chant, people expressed their need to unite soul and body in worship. A classic ancient instance of sacred dance is found in the Second Book of Samuel. The Ark of the Covenant was being brought in solemn processions from the house of Obed, to be enthroned in Jerusalem. Along the way, there were frequent stops for liturgical sacrifice. "David danced before the LORD with all his might; David was girded with a linen ephod. So David and all the house of Israel brought up the ark of the LORD with shouting, and with the sound of the trumpet" (2 Sam 6:14–15).

Saint Ambrose, fourth-century bishop of Milan and a Father of the Church, admonished his flock against indecent dances, but added: "The dance should be conducted as did David, for everything is right which springs from the fear of the God…The dance is an ally of faith and an honoring of grace."

Seen in this light, liturgical dance can play a healing and prophetic role. It can help shake us from the lethargy that prevents us from being open to the joy God wants us to experience. It can call us to respond to the anguish of a suffering world with a healing reaffirmation of the enduring human spirit. As we see the harmony of the dance, we can deepen our resolve to do our small part in restoring the harmony of our bruised and hurting world.

As difficult as it may be for you, try to be open to this new (but ancient) development in the Church. With the writer of Psalm 149, be glad you can praise the Lord in song: "Praise the LORD! / Sing to the LORD a new song, / his praise in the assembly of the faithful. / Let Israel be glad in its Maker; / let the children of Zion rejoice in their King. / Let them praise his name with dancing, / making melody to him with tambourine and lyre" (Ps 149:1–3).

Perhaps you can even encourage your own parish to consider using a liturgical dance that is both reverent and exuberant to the glory of God.

11
Faith

INTRODUCTION
What Is Faith?

*F*aith is often defined as one of the three God-given and God-directed virtues (faith, hope, and love), infused into the soul with sanctifying grace. In the words of the First Vatican Council, "a person is enabled to believe that what God has revealed is true—not because its intrinsic worth is seen with the rational light of reason, but because of the authority of God who reveals it, that God who can neither deceive or be deceived." We might not be completely comfortable with the language of the First Vatican Council, but we certainly understand the truth of what it teaches: faith comes to us as a gift from God.

The Second Vatican Council, building on the work of the first council, teaches in the *Dogmatic Constitution on Divine Revelation*, that "'the obedience of faith' (Rom 16:26; cf Rom 1:5; 2 Cor 10:5–6) must be given to God as he reveals himself. By faith man freely commits his entire self to God, making 'the full submission of his intellect and will to God who reveals,' and willingly assenting to the revelation given by him" (§5, also see CCC 1814–1816). Again, the language of the teaching might not be the language that we are accustomed to using, but it captures the sentiment—faith is the gift from God that enables us to see the world, the events, and the circumstances of our life in the way that God sees them.

Does God Love Me?

Sometimes I become pretty disgusted with my life and myself. I wonder if anyone really loves me, especially God. Is there any way I can know that God really loves me?

Looking for Love

Dear Looking,

Every human person is made in the image of God. This means that your life is infinitely precious in God's eyes. God values and loves you beyond anything you could ever imagine.

God has also placed into our hearts a yearning for love and happiness that cannot be satisfied by anything less than God. True love will not be found in riches or well-being, in fame or power. True happiness will be found in God alone, the source of all life and all love.

In New Testament times, many people believed that wealth and success were signs of favor and love from God. If disaster struck you or any member of your family, you would assume that God was angry with you, or that you had done something wrong. Ill fortune was a "sign" that God's love had been withdrawn from you.

Jesus turned this sort of thinking on its head. Jesus taught that God truly loves all people, especially those who are down on their luck or outcasts from society. God's love is not based on wealth, fortune, or success of any kind. Rather, God loves you because you are God's own creation, God's child and heir to God's own kingdom.

The prophecies in Isaiah 43 tell us how God has formed us and how precious we are to God: Even should a mother forget the child of her womb, God will never forget us (see Is 49:15).

My Faith, My Children!

I am a very dedicated Catholic mother. Sometimes I worry that I am cramming too much of me and my devotions down the throats of my children. Should my children have more freedom to choose the faith on their own?

Faithful

Dear Faithful,

None of us remember the moment of our physical birth, but many of us can recall moments of rebirth. One of the moments of rebirth in my life is the time my mother took me to Sunday night benediction at our parish church. My recollection of this moment is clear. I am eight years old, and I am sitting in the church with my mother. The church lights are ablaze and the air smells heavily of incense. Even at that early age, I loved the smell of incense. The music of an ancient Latin hymn was pouring from the huge old organ. And even though I was from a family of seven, in this particular memory, only my mother and I are there in church at that moment.

This is a rebirthing moment for me. It speaks to me of how much I love the things of the Church—and that love has continued over my many years of seminary training and priesthood. I believe that I received most of that love from my mother. It is her, in my memory, who sits beside me, lending her mature devotion to my budding wonder.

I think that many of us can connect our faith to our mothers. It was most likely their constancy, love, and devotion that gave us the first hints that faith is very important in one's life. When a women chooses to be a mother, she commits to handing on to her children that which is most powerful and most profound in her own life. Over the years, the children will take all that is given, sift through it, and finally add it in some way to their own personalities. But the gift first has to be given, and the commitment of motherhood is giving that gift.

Mary, who is the patron of the Church and of mothers all around

the world, is first represented in the Gospels as the one "who believed" (Lk 1:45). It was this deep capacity for faith that became the
well which cradled and fed Jesus. As mothers, you model yourselves
after Mary when you become women "who believe" and then cradle
your children in that belief.

It is self-serving to regard children as puppets that can be turned
into copies of one's own person. Each human being is a new creation
of God, different from all others. The mother's task is to believe in
and explain the God in whose hand all life is held and loved. The
Catechism of the Catholic Church points this out in its section on the
duties of the parents: "Education in the faith by the parents should
begin in the child's earliest years. This already happens when family
members help one another to grow in faith by the witness of a Christian life in keeping with the Gospel" (CCC 2226).

The sincerity and reverence of a mother's faith can become a foun-
tain of living water for her children. It will naturally overflow, and
her children can choose to drink of it. I would encourage you to renew your commitment to handing on your faith to your children freely
and without limits.

They Won't Get the Baby Baptized

*My daughter and son-in-law refuse to have their newborn
baptized. Can my husband and I baptize the baby ourselves?
Can we secretly take the baby to a priest to be baptized? What if
the baby isn't baptized and dies? Won't he be shut out of heaven
forever? What a terrible burden for an innocent child!*

Rose

Dear Rose,

Let's look at your concerns one by one. First, the idea that one
must be baptized in order to gain salvation comes from John's Gospel. In it Jesus says, "Very truly, I tell you, no one an enter the kingdom of God without being born of water and Spirit" (Jn 3:5).

This gospel passage, like every other passage in Scripture, must be interpreted in context. The context of this passage is that Jesus is talking to Nicodemus, a member of the Sanhedrin. The statement was actually meant to be overheard by the early Christian community. They were wondering why baptism was necessary for adult Jews, like themselves, who had been faithful to God all their lives. With his command to be born of water and the Spirit, Jesus was saying that people's approach to religion must be motivated by love rather than purely formalistic observance. In other words, Jesus was talking about adult baptism, especially as a commitment to conversion.

The first Christians, however, also believed in infant baptism. In the Acts of the Apostles there are several examples of whole families being baptized, which would have included infants and small children. Some say Jesus' reference to "let the little children come to me" (Mk 10:14) was included precisely as a recommendation in favor of infant baptism.

Still, it would be unthinkable that God would be so indifferent as to punish some infants by denying them heaven because their parents did not have them baptized. That's why our predecessors in the faith believed in limbo (sometimes defined as "a place or state of natural happiness"). Theologians came up with the term *limbo* as an opinion that described what happened to the souls of unbaptized persons.

Today, such an explanation is not necessary. It is enough to recall Jesus' promise that God is love, and to know that when good people die without baptism, God enfolds them in love and carries them into heavenly eternity. So, do not fret for the baby.

Of more concern, however, is the issue of why your daughter and son-in-law don't want the baby baptized. Realistically, you can do nothing without the parent's consent. But do try and explore with your daughter and son-in-law the reason for their reluctance about baptism. Pray for the parents and for your grandchild—and remember to pray for yourself. Pray that you may accept God's will and know that God's ways are not always our ways.

Regardless of how this situation turns out, remember that God would not send a baby to hell simply because the infant's parents decided against baptism.

I Feel Spiritually Empty

My wife and I are in our mid fifties; we are more than comfortable materially, our children are grown and on their own. We enjoy good health. We still have our jobs and our home of many years; we have lots of "toys" that keep us busy. We go to church regularly, pray, and generally consider ourselves good Christians. So what' wrong? We feel empty, hollow, and strangely unfulfilled.

Searching for More

Dear Searching,

It sounds to me that, barring any other unnamed problem, you and your wife are at a spiritual crossroad in your life. You have hit a wall. And the choices you make are critical to your future life, fulfillment, and happiness.

The feeling of hollowness comes over adults in midlife or beyond, when they come to the shocking realization that many of their earlier pursuits, goals, values, acquisitions, activities, accomplishments, and relationships, though good, did not (could not) bring genuine, lasting fulfillment or happiness. There is a mysterious longing for more.

An accident, tragedy, or sudden loss can trigger the same result, throwing a placid life into unexpected chaos. All that people work for is gone in a flash, leaving them empty, disillusioned, questioning, and longing for a new meaningful direction in their lives.

I believe you've come to the disturbing but provocative realization that Saint Augustine voiced when he said, "Our hearts are restless until they rest in thee, O Lord."

It's a bold and profound statement about life and the human spirit. It means that nothing will satisfy the human heart except God. It says we are made by God and for God, and nothing temporal or time-bound will ultimately satisfy.

To seek lasting value from something we do, as creative as it may be, is to court disillusionment and grave disappointment. A stroke of ill luck, an accident, a downturn in business, can suddenly end a career and dash a person to the rocks below. Even a close relationship, as uplifting and life-giving as it is, cannot fulfill all our longings. No one person, loving and trusting though he/she may be, can satisfy the longing of the human heart and spirit for complete meaning. There's a well deep within us that only God can reach and fill.

At stake here is: What is life really about? Up to this point, like many people, you thought it was about success, money, possessions, good health, a nice home and car, a good job, material prosperity, a grown family, and regular church attendance. But when these prove unable to give lasting happiness, you learn that true meaning must be sought elsewhere. You realize it has to be found in the source of all longing, in God. It is God who subtly but persistently invades our comfort zones. It is God who made us and knows we will find authentic fulfillment and happiness only and exclusively in God. It is no longer a matter of knowing *about* God, but of connecting *with* God in close, personal, intimate relationship.

It is time to leave your comfort zone and find a way to attach yourself to God in a deeper and more challenging fashion. You could join a prayer group or work at a soup kitchen. You could learn about meditation practices or help your parish in projects for the poor. You could read more about the saint that you are named after and imitate him or her more fully. You could spend one hour a week before the Blessed Sacrament. These are just a few suggestions. I'm sure your parish priest can supply a hundred more.

How Can I Deepen My Faith?

How can I deepen my faith? The years seem to go by and I don't experience myself developing a more profound belief or becoming any holier. Can you help me?

Motionless

Dear Motionless,

There is a plaque outside my office that reads, "Faith is not belief without proof, but rather trust without reservations." There seems to be some real wisdom in this little saying.

It would seem that at the heart of all experiences of faith is a central component of trust. Trust is necessary because it speaks to us of relationship, and the experience of faith is primarily an experience of entering into relationship with the Lord. Our own life experience profoundly illustrates this point.

Trust is central to a spousal relationship, to a relationship with a significant friend, and to a relationship with the Lord. For example, it is necessary to know that one's spouse is faithful, honest, and willing to commit. On the other hand, trust is helpful but not necessary in those everyday casual relationships that we all experience. I trust, for example, that the letter carrier will deliver my mail, but if it doesn't happen, I am usually just inconvenienced. There is a big difference between being inconvenienced and having an expectation of trust violated.

You state that you believe you are not growing in faith or in holiness. Don't concentrate so much on faith, but look to the development of trust in your own life experience. Do you find yourself trusting in the Lord and in his promises to you? Do you trust that only in Jesus may you discover the way, the truth, and the life, or do your choices in lifestyle and direction seem to indicate something other?

To help in your self-examination, look at your attitude toward money and the Christian virtue of stewardship. Do you share your time, talent, and treasure generously with the Church, your local community, and those whom the Lord has identified as brothers and sisters? There is nothing quite like the experience of simply being generous—without expecting some immediate return—to help an individual understand what it means to trust.

Another place to look at is your commitment to and attitude about personal prayer. Are you willing to "waste time" with the Lord? Do you spend quality time each day reading the Scriptures or some other book that can help your spiritual growth and development? For a relationship to grow, and for trust to deepen, commitment to the other person in the relationship is very important.

I cannot prove to you that the time you spend in self-examination will make you feel better about your own faith and belief. I can, however, suggest that if you honestly enter into such a self-examination, and have the courage to make the choices and decisions that flow from that, your experience of faith and belief will most certainly be enriched.

How Can I Renew My Faith?

When I was younger, my faith was a very important part of my life. Lately, however, I seem to have lost all those feelings of closeness to God. Am I experiencing a crisis of faith? Is there any way I can renew the faith that I had in my youth?

                                                                    Kit

Dear Kit,

My answer might sound a little aggressive, but please have patience with me as we sort out the issues.

Begin by asking yourself these questions: *What are some of the other ways that my life has changed since my youth? Do I feel, react, and appreciate in the same way today as I did even ten years ago?*

It might sound like I am avoiding answering you when I begin to answer your question with another question. However, it is necessary to do so because it is not possible to answer your query in isolation from your lived experience. Spirituality and the spiritual journey are part of the ordinary experience of human life, and so the answers you give to the above questions are important and necessary to answer your question about faith.

As you come to an understanding and clarity in your answers, hopefully you will begin to make some connections. In particular, I would hope that you might discover that the God of your youth, although remembered fondly, is not the God of your adult experience.

You see, many people discover that their lives, their education, their choices, and their decision-making processes have all expanded and matured as they grow older. In the interplay of the demands of our society and our culture, we are forced, in a very real sense, to grow and develop—or suffer the consequences. What worked for us as a child of five is not usually the choice we would make as an adult. Adults who do so are many times judged as immature and selfish.

In the spiritual journey, we are not so much forced, but rather invited to grow and mature. Some people miss the invitation and, in the process, get stuck in a rut. What's more, consequences are not easily recognized until moments of crisis or dramatic change. In such moments, the consequence of not growing and maturing in faith is often reflected by the question, "Where was God when I needed help?"

To avoid this experience, ask yourself, *Have my "human skills" grown, developed, and matured, while I still cling to childlike images of God and somehow expect such images to serve me well today?*

Do you see what I am getting at? It's not so much a crisis of faith that you have described, but a realization, a beginning rediscovery of the desire to pursue the spiritual journey in your life. As this realization deepens, you may come to realize that your image of God must also begin to grow and mature. Don't expect that the God of your childhood is going to fill the needs of your adult experience. You do not make those demands on any other part of your lived experience; why would you expect it to be operable in your spiritual journey.

Begin to relate to God as an adult. Speak to the Lord as an adult, share with the Lord adult problems and concerns. Use the skills that you have learned as an adult in your other important relationships to build a relationship with God, the Church, and the community of believers. In this way, you will discover a living faith, an experience of God, that is important for you today, in the present moment.

If you take up this challenge, I think you might discover some of the feelings of your youth. Maybe you will recall a renewal of hope, a certain enthusiasm, and a belief that all things are possible. The good news will be that these are not just feelings of nostalgia, but rather the lived experience of a mature faith.

I Want to Come Back to My Church!

I have been away from the Catholic Church for a very long time. I would like to return, but I don't quite know how. Is there some kind of program that the Church offers for those "fallen-away-but-wanting-to-return"?

Hoping for Rebirth

Dear Hoping,

Welcome back to the Church. The seeds of faith once sown in baptism are now taking root and bearing fruit for everlasting life.

Many parishes offer opportunities for returning Catholics to share some of the experiences and questions that may have contributed to their leaving the practice of the faith for a time.

Whatever caused you to separate from the Church, whether for a matter of weeks or for decades, it is something God certainly understands, and most clergy and pastoral associates are eager to hear about. It is important to tell your story to begin the healing process and to help folks understand the impact of similar experiences on others.

As you feel more comfortable becoming reintroduced into the life of the Church community, ongoing adult education should be an indispensable part of your formation as a mature Catholic. Bible-sharing groups and adult discussion programs conducted in your local parish may be good places to begin. Prayer meetings may also be worthwhile opportunities to grow in faith, to hear others' witness of faith, to deepen your prayer relationship with Jesus, and to find inner peace and healing.

Perhaps such programs are not available to you. There are several steps you can take on your own.

First, view your past life as part of a larger process that God is using to draw you closer to God. Rather than regret the past, draw the good from it with God's grace.

Second, begin to discuss your experiences with a priest, deacon, or pastoral associate trained to listen with confidentiality. Entrusting your story to another may bring you a new sense of freedom and acceptance.

Third, when ready, celebrate the sacrament of penance as Jesus' own "program of re-entry" and means for inner healing and forgiveness.

Fourth, read and reflect on sacred Scripture. The Bible is inspired by God and tells of many men and women whom God used to do God's will in spite of their weaknesses.

Fifth, develop a daily time for quiet prayer. Prayer is at the heart of spirituality, nourishing our relationship with Jesus and the Church. Prayer can refocus your energies on what is of ultimate value and worth.

Sixth, read and study the *Catechism of the Catholic Church* and spiritual authors who can challenge and renew your mind and heart.

Seventh, celebrate the Eucharist every Sunday and holy day to remain in intimate relationship with the risen Jesus and his Body, the Church.

Eighth, spend time each week volunteering for the needy or in a parish program of service. Positive feelings follow positive actions.

Welcome back to active participation in the Church. We have been incomplete without you.

What Is True Worship?

What is true worship? Some say it is going to Mass, some say it is reciting prayers, others say it is just living a "good" life. What do you say?

A Faithful Worshiper

Dear Worshiper,

I would like to give you a very simple answer. It would be very easy for me to reply to your question by stating my belief firmly and with no elaboration. However, to do so might not satisfy you. I sense that you are searching, and that you don't want a quick answer. Rather, I think you would prefer an informed answer. For this reason, I will take the risk of giving you a more detailed response.

You may at first perceive my reply to your question as an attempt to avoid giving you a firm answer. That is not, however, my intention. My reluctance to answer quickly is because I don't think it is a good idea to single out any one activity and hold it up as the "best" or the "truest." I believe that when we answer an important question by zeroing in on only one part of the question, we find that our answer reduces the importance of what we are talking about. To follow such a route does not provide a helpful service. Remember the old question: "What part of Mass do I have to be sure to attend in order to make sure it counts?" I don't think we want to go down that path again in our pursuit of the truth.

The most honest answer I can give you begins with the assumption that worship is more than just one particular action. At the same time, my answer assumes that worship, because it does embrace ritual action, is more than just an attitude or an opinion. Place and time also enter into the equation, as the woman at the well understood: "Our ancestors worshiped on this mountain, but you say that the place where people must worship is in Jerusalem" (Jn 4:20). To round out the mix, we could also recall the admonition from the Hebrew Scriptures, "For I desire steadfast love and not sacrifice" (Hos 6:6). Taken together, all of these understandings contribute to an informed answer to your question.

If we recall that worship can best be understood as that which "sets man free from turning in on himself, from the slavery of sin and the idolatry of the world," as the *Catechism of the Catholic Church* teaches (see CCC 2097), we might then recall a traditional definition. In the traditional understanding, worship is seen as having three principle acts. The first is the individual recognition of God's infinite perfection; the second is prayer or petitioning for divine help; and the third is to offer as sacrifice to God something that is precious. Within the Catholic tradition, it is the holy sacrifice of the Mass that perfectly fits this definition of worship. From my perspective, the Mass would therefore be the best and truest form of worship. My perspective, however, is not the only perspective. There are literally billions of people who never participate in the Mass. Truly, they, too, worship God and would seem to be faithful to the admonition found in Hosea.

A young Buddhist in Thailand, faithful to the traditions that she has been taught, offers true and fitting worship to God. A Shinto in Japan, burning incense before a local shrine, imploring God's help, offers fitting and true worship. A Muslim, participating in the daily call to prayer, is also someone who is worshiping God in a true and faithful manner. Finally, your own neighbor, attending the local synagogue, is also truly worshiping God.

With all that we have just reviewed fresh in our minds, we can come to the point of your question: true worship includes going to Mass and, for us as Catholics, it would be the preferred response. For those who are not Catholic, however, true worship would include reciting prayers and living a good life. In short, there are as many different types of worship as there are people.

Five Facets of Holiness

You once made the point that all Catholics, not just priests and religious, are called to holiness by virtue of their baptism and confirmation. What are the principal means of lay holiness?

A Searching Layperson

Dear Searching,

Excluding the ministerial duties of a priest and the structured community life of the religious, the means of holiness are the same for all the baptized. They are public and private prayer; love of God expressed in love of neighbor; living out one's vocational commitments; practicing penance and discipline; and, finally, reaching out in discipleship to all around us. Priests and religious do the same but in the context of their vocational calling.

Prayer: Prayer is the most essential ingredient of holiness no matter the vocation. In liturgy (public prayer), we join our sisters and brothers to offer communal worship. The Word, the sacraments, and the congregation nourish us in liturgy and form us into the kingdom of God on earth.

In private prayer, we maintain, clarify, and nourish our fundamental relationships. We acknowledge and keep God in the forefront of our lives; we deal with self in relation to God; and we clarify our relationships with others and the world. There is no holiness without prayer.

Love of God expressed in love of neighbor: This is an eternal challenge of Christian holiness—how to treat others with the acceptance and respect that God has for each person. The gospels say that every person is our neighbor, especially persons in need. Jesus particularly identified himself with the needy when he said, "Truly I tell you, just as you did it to one of the least of these who are members of my family, you did it to me" (Mt 25:40).

Living one's vocational commitment: We also quietly and unobtrusively live our holiness when we persevere and remain faithful to our vocational commitments. Whatever our lifestyle choice, living up to its demands is the stuff of holiness. Being faithful to a spouse in marriage, working for family harmony, staying true to dedicated singleness in the world or in the religious community setting—all are avenues of holiness.

Practicing penance and self-discipline: There is no holiness without the self-denial, control, and sacrifice that establish personal discipline. Free expression of every unbridled appetite, desire, ambition, or whim is incompatible with Christian life. Christians must, "deny themselves and take up their cross daily and follow me" (Lk 9:23).

Reaching out in discipleship: Holiness also comes from and finds its noblest expression in a life of service and ministry. Baptism initiates us into the fullness of Christian reality, which ultimately means discipleship. Being willing to share our faith and our experiences of God in community, giving witness to the presence of God in our lives, stepping forward to serve and minister to our sisters and brothers, and working for peace and justice in our world are essential elements of holiness.

For laypeople, the main arena of holiness is where they live, work, play, and struggle every day. It is there that they must proclaim "the kingdom of God is in our midst," and answer their call to holiness.

Deepening Faith

How can I deepen my faith? Sometimes I believe and sometimes I don't. Is there a secret on how to bring my faith to a deeper level?

Wanting to Believe

Dear Wanting to Believe,

Faith is one of the three theological virtues (along with hope and charity). These theological virtues pertain to our relationship to God. The Church teaches that if we truly live a virtuous life (practicing the virtues of faith, hope, and charity), we will cultivate our truest and deepest self and be happy beyond our dreams. Thomas Merton wrote: "Faith is the only key to the universe. The final meaning of human existence, and the answers to the questions on which all our happiness depends cannot be found in any other way" (*Book of New Christian Quotations*, p. 82).

But how do we "get" more virtue? It is too bad that there isn't a "virtue store" in the neighborhood, so that if we needed more virtue we could just go down to the local store and purchase some. We only deepen or "gain" virtue by practicing various behaviors that are linked to that virtue.

For example, to become more faith-filled, we have to practice believing more. Every circumstance of life gives us a chance to believe more or to believe less. Each day we can choose to live according to others' expectations, societies' values, and what is popular; or we can choose to ask God to lead us through the day, and then attempt to listen to where God is taking us. The Letter to the Hebrews states it quite clearly: "Faith is the assurance of things hoped for, the conviction of things not seen" (Heb 11:1). We build our faith by daily trusting that God will be our strength and will lead us through decisions and difficulties. Faith, at its most basic level, is a friendship between God and us. Faith is continuing to acknowledge that God made us, knows us, loves us, and will never abandon us.

How to Pray

Recently, a parishioner told me that when I have a problem, I should sit in church, be quiet, and let Jesus speak to me. I tried this. Jesus was silent. He didn't say a word. I'm tired of pious platitudes. Are there other ways to reach the Lord?

Searching for Something

Dear Searching,

Sometimes prayer can be very frustrating. We ask for things and don't get them, or we ask the Lord to speak to us or direct us, and nothing seems to come from the Lord's end of things. This is perhaps why Jesus took the time to teach his disciples how to pray. Jesus, in Luke 11:1–13, outlines very clearly for his disciples, and for us, how we should pray, what we should pray for, and what attitude to have in prayer. The task of the follower of Jesus is to learn this system of prayer that Jesus outlined for us, copy it, and then trust in God to do the rest. The system of prayer that Jesus gives us is a very active endeavor. We are to ask God for what we need (our daily bread), and if we don't get an answer, we pound on God's door again and again. We trust that God will hear us and will act in our favor. In fact, Saint Luke tells that we must trust in God to take care of us like God takes care of the flowers of the earth and the birds of the sky (Lk 12:22–32).

We do know that there are times in the Gospel when Jesus goes off by himself to pray (Lk 4:42, 6:12, 22:39). We know that in those times, Jesus talked to God as a son talks to a father, but we don't know exactly what Jesus said or what God said in return. We must trust that, in the Scriptures, Jesus taught his disciples to pray in the manner in which Jesus himself prayed. I would encourage you to study these and other passages in the New Testament that speak of prayer, and then to copy them in your own life.

12

Jesus

INTRODUCTION
Jesus, God, and Man

The second Person of the Blessed Trinity became a man, Jesus Christ. His mother was Mary of Nazareth, daughter of Joachim and Anne. Joseph, Mary's husband, was like a father to Jesus. Jesus' true and only Father is God: he had no human father (CCC 525–526).

Conceived in Mary's womb by the power of the Holy Spirit, Jesus was born in Bethlehem of Judea, probably between 6 and 4 B.C. A relatively young man, most likely in his early thirties, he died on Calvary outside of the old city of Jerusalem (CCC 595–623).

Jesus is only one Person, but he has both a divine nature and a human nature. He is truly God, and he is also truly a human being. As God, he has all the qualities and attributes of God. As a human, he has a human body, human soul, human mind and will, human imagination, and human feelings. His divinity does not overwhelm or interfere with his humanity—and vice versa (CCC 464–478).

On Calvary, Jesus really died; he experienced the same kind of death that all human beings experience. But during his dying, at his death, and after his death, he remained God.

After his death, Jesus "descended to the dead." The older English translation of the Creed said, "descended into hell"—which means the same thing. *Hades* refers to the nether world, the region of the dead, the condition of those who had passed on from this life. (This is clear from New Testament references such as 1 Pet 3:19; Eph 4:9; Rom 10:7; Mt 12:40; Acts 2:27, 31.) Basically, therefore, "descended to the dead" means Jesus really died and entered among the dead as their Savior. Liturgically, Holy Saturday expresses this aspect of the mystery of salvation—the "death" or absence of God (CCC 631–637).

The prayer of the dying Jesus—"My God, my God, why have you forsaken me?" (Mk 15:34)—finds its echo in the lives of many Christians. "Descended to the dead" expressed Jesus' outcry of agony—his experience of clinging to his Father in his moment of absolute anguish. It also expresses what many Catholics experience as God deepens their love of him by making them realize the hell life is without a sense of his presence (CCC 618).

Jesus rose from the dead on Easter morning. He is living today with his Father and the Spirit—and in our midst. He remains both God and man—and always will.

He lives. And his passage from death to life is the mystery of salvation we are meant to share (CCC 655, 658).

Why Was Jesus Baptized?

I am stumped. I have never been able to figure out why Jesus allowed himself to be baptized by John the Baptist. When we are baptized, we are told that we are baptized into Jesus' death and resurrection, and that baptism is necessary for our salvation. Jesus, being the Son of God, couldn't have possibly been baptized for these reasons, could he?

George

Dear George,

You are right. Jesus was not baptized by John in the Jordan River for the same reasons we receive baptism today. Exactly why Jesus received John's baptism is known to Jesus alone. Your question will be one of those that goes into the "everything you always wanted to ask Jesus when you meet him in heaven" box. In the meantime, scholars have studied the question diligently and have some reasonable assumptions about why Jesus requested baptism from John.

John's baptism was not a baptism of salvation. Rather, it was a baptism of repentance for sinners. The Jews held a unique belief about repentance. This belief held that if Israel could repent perfectly for even one day, the Messiah would come. It was only the hardness of their hearts that was delaying the coming of God's redeemer into the world. John, too, was aware of this conviction, and his actions cemented his reputation as the forerunner of the Messiah.

A further interesting feature of John's baptism was the fact that Jews did not need baptism; only converts to the Jewish religion were baptized. No Jew ever conceived that he or she, a member of the chosen people, a son or daughter of Abraham assured of God's salvation, could ever need baptism. Yet, Jews, after hearing John preach his message of repentance, were submitting to his baptism as a way of demonstrating their change of heart, and of experiencing God's forgiveness of sins.

When Jesus requested baptism from John, he wanted to demonstrate that he identified himself with his people's search for God. Scholars speculate that after years of faithfully performing the simple duties of the home and of the carpenter's trade, Jesus had become increasingly conscious of his mission in life, and it was time to seize the moment and begin his ministry. At first, John balked. He thought that he should be accepting baptism from Jesus—the long-awaited one. But Jesus prevailed, and the voice that came from heaven ratified his action. "This is my Son, the Beloved, with whom I am well pleased" (Mt 3:17). "This is my Son, the Beloved" is from Psalm 2:7, an accepted description of the Messiah. "...with whom I am well pleased" is from Isaiah 42:1 and describes the Messiah and the Suffering Servant. In the moments of Jesus' baptism, there was set before Jesus both his task and the only way to fulfill it.

After Jesus' baptism, John's mission was accomplished. Jesus took center stage. Identifying with his people's sinfulness, Jesus allowed himself to be baptized at the hands of John to demonstrate his solidarity with the people and to signal the beginning of the Messianic Age that John had promised.

We know the rest of the story. Later, Jesus would commission his apostles to go baptize all nations. This baptism would not be a baptism of repentance, however, but a baptism of water and the Spirit, which would signify that the baptized had found Jesus and were living in forgiveness and freedom.

Was Jesus an Only Child?

Why does the Catholic Church teach that Jesus was an only child? Some of my Protestant friends believe that he had brothers and sisters, and the New Testament mentions the "brothers and sisters" of Jesus.

Carol

Dear Carol,

The New Testament does speak of "brothers and sisters" of Jesus. For example, the Gospel of Matthew relates that when Jesus preached in his hometown of Nazareth, the people took offense at him, saying, "Where did this man get this wisdom and these deeds of powers? Is not this the carpenter's son? Is not his mother called Mary? And are not his brothers James and Joseph and Simon and Judas? And are not all his sisters with us? Where then did this man get all this?" (Mt 13:54–56).

Brothers and sisters, however, may be used in many ways. When we hear a speaker address his audience as "brothers and sisters," we assume that the words refer not to blood relatives but to friends or members of a particular nation, group, or race. In the Old Testament, the term *brothers* could refer to members of the same tribe or race. *Brother* is also used as a means of polite address. Depending on which translation of the Bible you have, Scripture frequently uses *brothers and sisters* to refer to relatives such as nephews and cousins and relatives in general. Other translations simply use the term *kinsmen* instead of *brothers and sisters*.

In the New Testament, two of those who are called brothers of Jesus (namely James and Joseph in Mt 13:54–58) are later identified as the sons of another woman in Matthew 27:56. The word *brothers* is often used for the followers of Jesus, as we see in John 20:17–18, where the risen Jesus asked Mary Magdalene, "Go to my brothers." Then Mary "went and announced to the disciples, 'I have seen the Lord!'" In the New Testament, believers are called *brothers* more than a hundred times, and Jesus said that they who hear the word of God and act on it are his brothers (Lk 8:21). The New Testament never speaks of other children of Mary or Joseph, so it is impossible to prove from the Bible that Jesus actually had blood brothers or sisters. If there were such siblings, it is difficult to explain why Jesus, as he hung on the cross, gave Mary into the care of the beloved disciple. "When Jesus saw his mother and the disciple whom he loved standing beside her, he said to his mother, 'Woman, here is your son.' Then he said to the disciple, 'Here is your mother.' And from that hour the disciple took her into his own home" (Jn 19:26–27). If Mary had other children, wouldn't they have cared for her?

Mary was a virgin when she conceived Christ by the power of the Holy Spirit. When the angel told Mary that she would have a son, Mary asked, "'How can this be, since I am a virgin?' The angel said to her, 'The Holy Spirit will come upon you, and the power of the Most High will overshadow you; therefore the child to be born will be holy; he will be called Son of God'" (Lk 1:34–35).

The Church teaches that after the birth of Jesus, Mary remained a virgin all her life. Why? Because she and Joseph would have witnessed the incredible miracle of Jesus' conception and birth. They would have realized that God had entrusted them with the greatest treasure in the history of the world: his only Son. They would have understood that their task in life was to nurture and protect the Savior of the human race. Many years later, Jesus would speak of those who renounced marriage "for the sake of the kingdom of heaven" (Mt 19:12). It is not surprising, then, that Mary and Joseph would have wanted to dedicate their lives to the care of God's only Son and, for this purpose, would have renounced the right to have other children.

"Did Jesus Know That He Was God?"

Did Jesus know that he was God? Some Bible texts seem to say that he did, and others that he didn't.

Tom

Dear Tom,

One difficulty in understanding the gospels is that we must enter the minds of people who lived in an ancient culture much different from ours. For example, our creeds state that Jesus was (and is) "true God and true man." But is that the way the people of those early days would have expressed the same truth? Hardly. For Jews in the first third of the first century, *God* meant a divine being in heaven—Lord and Creator of all. But then Jesus came. His life, death, and resurrection so impacted his followers that it forced them to expand the term *God* so it would refer to not only the God in heaven but also the Son on earth.

This faith of the early Christians is what the evangelists tried to convey in their gospels. Although writing under the inspiration of the Holy Spirit, they had nothing but imperfect human language to carry the earth-shaking message that Jesus was both truly human and truly divine. Especially susceptible to misinterpretation are certain individual texts that, when taken out of the context of the whole Gospel, seem to focus on one of Jesus' natures more than the other.

We have seen what the term *God* means now, and what it meant then. We should also look at the word *know*, especially when applied to Jesus. Saint Thomas Aquinas stated: "If there was not in Christ a form of knowledge [that he possessed as second Person of the Trinity], he would not have known anything at all." Thomas understood that purely divine knowledge (which includes omniscience) must not have been available to the human mind of Jesus. That's why it is not surprising to find texts indicating that Jesus had to learn certain things, much as we do.

All human beings have self-knowledge, at least in principle. But even though we know very well that we are individual human beings, we still find it almost impossible to formulate what that really means. Saint Thomas explains that our knowledge of all things is conceptual—we make abstractions, express them in concepts, and think by combining these concepts. But self-knowledge is the one exception—it is intuitive knowledge, not conceptual, and extremely difficult to formulate in concepts.

Did Jesus know that he was God? Yes, intuitively. But it's hard for us to express what we somehow sense as our basic humanity; imagine how difficult it would have been for Jesus to express what he profoundly grasped as his divine/human self-identity. His knowledge of his radical selfhood would have been a genuine self-awareness of who he truly was—both God and human—but he wouldn't have been able to express it in a conceptual way.

Jesus was able to build upon this profound, intuitive self-knowledge. Human beings perceive they are human early in life, but they know even more when they're forty than when they are twenty. A similar deepening perception took place in Jesus. Through life experiences, Jesus constantly discovered what being divine in human circumstances implied. That's why Hebrews 5:8 says he "learned obedience through what he suffered."

How wonderful it is to have Jesus, true God and true human, as our Savior.

The Good Shepherd

Someone told me that the image of the Good Shepherd is a pagan image. I tend to think that this person is wrong, but I wonder. What do you think?

A Defender of Jesus

Dear Defender,

In Christian art, the Good Shepherd illustrates the gospel parable of the lost sheep being carried back to the fold by the shepherd (Lk 15:3–7). In John's Gospel, Jesus himself declares that he is this "Good Shepherd" (Jn 10:11–18). The image of the Good Shepherd became one of the oldest and most favored subjects of early Christian art. This image of Jesus, the Good Shepherd, appears in the burial places of the early Christians (called *catacombs*), especially in the areas of Rome, Naples, Sardinia, and Sicily. In later centuries, this image was also found carved into the chalices used by Christians for the Eucharist, painted on the walls of chapels, developed in stone in baptistery mosaics, imprinted on medals, and even engraved on glassware. The most frequent image is of Jesus as a young, beardless man, carrying a lamb on his shoulders.

The image of the Good Shepherd does predate Christianity. There were reliefs discovered in Syria and Assyria that date back to the eighth and ninth centuries before Christ's birth, which show a man carrying a gazelle on his shoulders. In later centuries (still before Jesus), this figure of a man carrying a lamb or gazelle came to be understood as the great civic virtue of charity toward others (known today as *philanthropy*). As a practicing Jew, Jesus would certainly have been aware of these and other traditions. Jesus takes this image and fills it with a new Christian meaning. Jesus is the Savior, the one who is all-loving, who carries us and all people to salvation.

Seeing Jesus Now!

The disciples of Jesus were lucky to get a glimpse of Jesus as he was transfigured in glory. Do we have to wait until death to see Jesus in this way, or am I just looking in the wrong places?

Waiting for Glory

Dear Waiting,

I think that what the disciples saw at Jesus' Transfiguration was a radiant flash of Jesus' promise of eternal glory. In that marvelous moment on the mountain, the disciples glimpsed, however momentarily, their friend Jesus as the fulfillment of all God's Old Testament promises found in the Law and the prophets. Jesus' prayerful radiance, in a flash and for a moment, broke through their confusions, fears, doubts, and self-consciousness, illuminating him as the promise for which they had been longing. However, in an earlier section of Luke's Gospel, they wondered if that radiance, that promise, was to be trusted.

> *So John [the Baptist] summoned two of his disciples and sent them to the Lord to ask, "Are you the who is to come, or are we to wait for another?" When the men had come to him, they said, "John the Baptist has sent us to ask, 'Are you the who is to come, or are we to wait for another?'....[Jesus] answered them, "Go and tell John what you have seen and heard: the blind receive their sight, the lame walk, lepers are cleansed, and the deaf hear, the dead are raised, the poor have good news brought to them" (Lk 7:18–22).*

Indeed, we can sometimes find ourselves so haphazardly swayed by the desire for spiritual clarity that we fail to see Jesus and his promise in the places he really is, that is, in all those settings of suffering that call forth his compassion from us. Where, then, are you to look if you are to see Jesus transfigured? Perhaps in that single moment when you visit someone who is sick and receive a smile of radiant gratitude. Or when you help out at a food pantry and a child's enjoyment of your bounty brings a smile (or tear) to your face. Perhaps, too, in that moment when, despite personal discomfort, you attend a wake or funeral and your very presence radiates the promise of consolation even more than your words. In fact, probably the best place to look is wherever and whenever you encounter someone vulnerable and your awkward self-consciousness is transfigured into generous, self-giving love, because that is both Jesus' promise and his glory.

The Heavenly Kingdom

Why does the Church continue to use the image of a king to describe Jesus? Jesus certainly didn't act like a king, or expect his followers to treat him like a king.

A Humble Servant

Dear Servant,

Hereditary kings ruled over most of the nations in the ancient Near East. In some countries, like Egypt, the king was actually recognized as a god. In Israel, God was considered to be the one true king, and God's covenant was the treaty that united God and the people.

But there came a time in their history when the Israelites thought they needed to strengthen themselves militarily and politically. At that point, the elders came to Samuel and asked him to appoint a king to govern them like the other nations (1 Sam 8:5). The king of Israel was considered the instrument of God, but was also subject to the existing codes of civil and religious law. The three great kings of Israel were Saul, David, and Solomon.

Throughout the New Testament runs the theme that Jesus, a descendant of the royal Davidic line, is a ruler or king. Jesus was first proclaimed a king by the Magi, who said they were looking for the one who has been born "king of the Jews" (Mt 2:2).

At the heart of Jesus' message was the good news that all people could enter the kingdom of God if they turned away from sin. Jesus used the parable of the mustard seed (Mk 4:30–32) to show that his kingdom is one that continues to grow until all life can be contained within its branches. Jesus also hands the kingdom to his disciples. In Luke's Gospel, Jesus tells us that God has handed over the kingdom to us (Lk 12:32).

The kingdom, which was first manifested in simplicity and love in the countryside of Galilee, is to reach its fulfillment in a great love among all people. Jesus as king is an image that hopefully compels us to recognize our commitment to love and serve others in his kingdom.

The Kingship of Jesus

Why was the notion of kingship so important to Jesus and the disciples? Didn't the kings and rulers of Jesus' day oppress Israel? You would think they would have been distrustful of the idea of Jesus as king.

An Equality Advocate

Dear Equality Advocate,

Even though the notion of kingship is not that important to our modern-day thought, it was very important to Israel. In the early years of the Hebrew nation, the population felt a need to strengthen itself both politically and militarily. The people went to Samuel, who was their leader, and begged him to appoint a king so that Israel could be the same as the other nations (1 Sam 8:4–5). Samuel, in response, appointed Saul as Israel's first king. In Israel, the king became the prime instrument of God. David, the shepherd, was considered the greatest of the kings of Israel.

The kingdom was relatively short lived, however. It was split into two kingdoms after the death of Solomon. The southern kingdom, Judah, finally fell to the Babylonians about 587 or 586 B.C. Later, the area came under the domination of a series of foreign powers—the Persians, the Macedonians, and ultimately Rome (63 B.C.). Many of these empires exercised their power by appointing a king, often a foreigner, to rule locally. Such was the case with Herod the Great, appointed as king of Judea by the Romans. You remember Herod from the story of the Three Kings who came looking for the Baby Jesus.

Because both the people of Israel and the early Christians understood the notion of kingship and remembered the glory days of David and Solomon, they developed a basic theology of the king as the saving instrument of God. The theme of Jesus as king and prime instrument of God runs through the New Testament, and reaches its fullness in Jesus' victory over death and his ascent to power at the right hand of the Father.

In the gospels, Jesus preached that the kingdom of God is now in our midst. The good news is that all of us can enter this kingdom (Mk 1:15).

Why Did Jesus Visit Hell?

I have always been confused by the phrase in our creed that says Jesus "descended into hell" before he rose on Easter. What does that mean?

Pam

Dear Pam,

In the Old Testament, everyone who died, good or bad, ended up in Sheol. Sheol was portrayed as a shadowy place where the dead dwelt in a miserable sort of existence. In the New Testament, this place was referred to as *Hades* or *Gehenna*. *Hades* is the Greek word for "the land of the dead." *Gehenna* is a Hebrew word that referred to the valley of Hinnom. This valley was a narrow gorge, south of Jerusalem, that was used for a garbage dump. This image was used by Jesus for the place of punishment for the wicked after death (Mt 5:22; 18:8).

When the creed states that Jesus "descended into hell," it means that Jesus *really* suffered the effects of death—and did, indeed, die—and that every human being has to suffer. Jesus died, and went to Hades, where all the dead had to go. The Church has traditionally taught that Jesus also had a mission to perform when he went to Hades. Because everyone, whether evil or righteous, ended up in Hades, Jesus came to free the just ones who had gone before him. This is the so-called "harrowing of hell," which was a very popular devotion in medieval times. Jesus went to hell and released those holy souls who were stranded there. Some of the icon art of the Eastern Church portrays Jesus rising from the tomb and bringing all those people out of the underworld and up to heaven with him.

What Happened to the Body of Jesus?

It says in the gospel account of the Ascension that Jesus was taken up body and soul into heaven. Why would Jesus need a body in heaven? It would seem to be useless there.

Evelyn

Dear Evelyn,

In the Old Testament, there was a great chasm between our bodies and heaven. We are told that no one could see the face of God and live, let alone live *with* God in heaven. Jesus came to bridge that gap through his body and blood.

Jesus keeps his glorified body in heaven to show us that we, too, will be glorified like him, and to show that, as part of God's creation, our bodies are inherently good and worthy of heavenly life. Jesus' Ascension into heaven will be followed by our ascension into heaven. Our bodies will become like Jesus' glorified body. Our life with God will become like Jesus' life with God. We see in Jesus our own future. Our lives and our loves will not be snuffed out like a spent candle. Rather, we will carry them in our spiritual and glorified self, leaving behind pain, death, and the inadequacies of being human.

Christianity is a material, flesh-and-blood religion. We cannot bypass the physical to reach the spiritual. Jesus ascended into heaven body and soul. We do not reach higher, spiritual truths by rejecting the material world. Heaven will not contain disembodied spiritual beings, but will be full of glorified human bodies without the inadequacies we suffer now. Saint Paul, in 1 Corinthians 15:35–40, tries to explain this truth to the people of Corinth. He tells them that the splendor of the heavenly bodies is of one kind and the splendor of the earthly bodies is of another kind.

13
The Last Days

INTRODUCTION
A New Earth and a New Heaven

Belief in the Final Judgment on the last day is clearly expressed in the creeds of the Church. On that day, all the dead will be raised. Through divine power, we will all be present before God as bodily human beings. Then God—the absolute Lord of history—will conduct a panoramic judgment of all that humankind did and endured through the long centuries in which the Spirit struggled to bring us forth as one people (CCC 1038–1041).

When will that day come? In a remarkable passage filled with hope for all human beings, Vatican II addresses this question and expressed the Church's vision: "We know neither the moment of the consummation of the earth and of man nor the way the universe will be transformed. The form of this world, distorted by sin, is passing away and we are taught that God is preparing a new dwelling and a new earth in which righteousness dwells, whose happiness will fill and surpass all the desires of peace arising in the hearts of men" (*Pastoral Constitution on the Church in the Modern World*, §39).

Meanwhile, during the time that is left to us, "the body of a new human family grows, foreshadowing in some way the age which is to come" (*Pastoral Constitution on the Church in the Modern World*, §39).

After we have "spread on earth the fruits of our nature and our enter-prise—human dignity, brotherly communion, and freedom—according to the command of the Lord and in his Spirit, we will find them once again, cleansed this time from the stain of sin, illuminated and transfigured....Here on earth the kingdom is a mysteriously presence; when the Lord comes it will enter into its perfection (*Pastoral Constitution on the Church in the Modern World*, §39).

That kingdom is already present in mystery. The day has already begun when God will "wipe away every tear from their eyes, and there shall be no more death or mourning." The day has already begun when he says to all living things, "Behold, I make all things new....They are accomplished. I am the Alpha and the Omega, the beginning and the end" (see Rev 21:4–6).

Meanwhile, we all work and pray for the full flowering of that kingdom to come. Along with the early Christians, we call out: *Marana tha!* Come, Lord Jesus! We seek you.

What Is Christ's "Second Coming"?

What is this "Second Coming of Christ" all about? My neighbor belongs to a Pentecostal church, and she has told me that the end of the world can happen any day now. She believes that we will soon see some terrible things, and after that will be the Second Coming of Christ, with all bad people left shriveled up. This sounds scary. What am I supposed to believe?

Nat

Dear Nat,

Your neighbor has some good support in the Bible for her belief that the world is going to come to an end. All you need to do is read the twenty-fourth chapter of Matthew's Gospel. Here Jesus describes the fearful disturbances in the sky and on earth that will be signs of the approaching end of the world. Then he goes on to say that people will see "the Son of Man coming on the clouds of heaven with power and great glory" (Mt 24:30).

In chapter 25 of Matthew's Gospel, Jesus describes the Last Judgment, in which the "sheep" will be separated from the "goats." The faithful will then go to their reward and the unfaithful to their punishment.

It should be noted that Jesus used symbolic and figurative language to make his point. Not everything he said should be taken literally. For example, virtually no Christian believes the "sheep and goats" passage literally means that Christ will come to earth and divide up animals. Christians know he is referring to human beings. The message behind the figurative language is clear: Christ will call us to a final accounting. Our Savior will, in the end, be the judge of the world. Catholics witness to this belief at Mass when they proclaim: "Christ has died, Christ is risen, Christ will come again." Also, in our profession of faith at Mass, we say that we believe Christ will "come again to judge the living and the dead."

Where Catholics differ with your Pentecostal friend is in setting an actual timetable for all this to happen. The gospels show that the apostles were curious about this, just as we are. They asked Jesus point-blank: "Tell us, when will all this occur?"

Jesus essentially told them that it was better for them not to know. "But about that day and hour no one knows, neither the angels of heaven, nor the Son, but only the Father" (Mt 24:36). Several times in the last century, groups of people, fired up by their religious enthusiasm, thought that the signs of the end were so clearly being fulfilled that they could pinpoint the exact day when Christ would return. So they sold all their possessions and waited expectantly for a final curtain to come down. Of course they were disappointed—the world went about its business as usual. They had to pick up the pieces of their shattered faith and pinpoint another time for the end.

History has demonstrated that certain people will always be pointing to the present turmoil in the world as signs that the final blaze is near at hand. And it is always possible that they could be right. But what God expects of us is to keep working for a better world, and not get too preoccupied with exactly when the end will arrive. Jesus said, "We must work the works of him who sent me while it is day; night is coming when no one can work" (Jn 9:4). To do anything less than that would be to fail in our present Christian duty to respond to the world's needs. Therefore, we should live our lives as fully as we possible can.

What Is "Eternal Life"?

Jesus, the Good Shepherd, says that he offers us "eternal life."
What does eternal life mean in practical terms? What is it, exactly,
that we get?

Heaven Help Me

Dear Heaven Help Me,

What exactly do we receive? No one knows exactly. We do have some general clues. Saint Paul tells us that eye has not seen, ear has not heard, nor has it so much as entered our minds what God has prepared for those who love him. In the Book of Revelation, we are told there will be no more tears, no more sadness, no more mourning or pain in that place. All sad and bad stuff will be done away with. Eternal life will be good, better than we can imagine.

That said, let me share with you some of my imaginings about eternal life. I look forward to at least three things. First, I look forward to meeting Jesus face to face, eyeball to eyeball. I imagine hearing his voice and seeing what he looks like. I have seen lots of artists' representation of Jesus, and none has ever satisfied me. In this vein, I also look forward to meeting Mary, his mother. Statues and paintings of her just don't do it for me. I also imagine the conversations I would like to have with both of them. Some days, I am full of "whats" and "whys" that I would like to have answered: What is the meaning of evil? Why is there suffering? Other days, there is in me a depth of gratitude, and I imagine what it will be like to personally thank Jesus and Mary for the many, many gifts I have been blessed with.

Second, I look forward to and imagine being reunited with my family and friends who have died. A couple of my friends have been killed in car accidents, so I never got the chance to say good-bye to them. The promise of eternal life means to me that we will see one another again. We will be reunited with one another forever.

Third, eternal life means, for me, a sorting out and fixing up of all we struggle with here on earth, both individually and with others. This gift will bring ultimate healing to our entire load of human inadequacies and sinfulness. We will, at last and forever, be able to give and receive love as we were meant to.

When I think about what eternal life will be like, those imaginings have a direct and positive effect on my present moment. When I ponder what meeting Jesus will be like, I am reminded to keep my eyes open for Jesus' presence in my neighbor. This is especially the case for those people who do not appeal to me for one reason or another.

When I imagine being reunited with my family and friends on the "other side," I am reminded to do the best I can to love my family and friends here on earth. Even ordinary things, such as writing a short note, calling, or sending birthday cards, let them know of my love and care for them.

When I think about the "great fixing" that will be eternal life, it gives me courage to keep up the struggle in the present moment, to not be ultimately defeated by my own or anybody else's weaknesses. That "great healing" is, for me, the hope and promise that no present darkness or evil will defeat us.

So we come full circle. What exactly will we get? It will be good. It will be forever. It will be better than the best we can imagine. With your feet firmly rooted in the present, let your own imaginings keep your heart, soul, and life fixed on this gift. May its promise be a source of strength in the difficulties of the present moment. Some day we will meet one another in heaven. Then we can compare notes on how our imaginations were outdone by God's great generosity.

Is the End Near?

When I hear stories about the end of the world, I always think about the story of Noah, when God actually did destroy most of the world. How are we to think about these stories? Are they fact or fiction?

An End-Timer

Dear End-Timer,

Most biblical scholars generally consider the story of Noah and the Ark to be a figurative or legendary account of God's new covenant with the people. Life here is temporary, but life with God is eternal. The story of the Flood itself was probably based on some factual, historical event that was recounted in oral traditions for hundreds of years before the actual story of Noah was written. In fact, there is a theory that the Black Sea was created by a catastrophe that may be the basis for the Noah story.

The National Geographic Society, in their research of that region of the world, discovered that the Mediterranean Sea broke through a natural dam over seventy-five hundred years ago, filling a fresh-water lake with seawater and creating the Black Sea. This natural catastrophe could have been the basis for the biblical story of Noah and the Ark. The catastrophic events of the world, whether war, floods, typhoons, earthquakes, or tornadoes, remind us again and again how fragile and temporary our lives are.

The biblical truth of the Noah story, and of Jesus' accounts of the end of the world, tells us that God is our beginning and our end. Everything else is temporary. The world will end, but God will not end. Also, God's love for us will never end. There is a spiritual transformation that will happen, both at the end of our lives and at the end of all time. What we can be certain of is that, in the end, sin and death will be no more, and God's love will reign forever.

My Fundamentalist Friends Insist That
This Is the "End Time"

A few of my fundamentalist friends are certain that the end of the world is near. They cite Scripture passages that point to definite signs of when that is going to happen, and they insist these signs are now appearing. Could it be true?

Monica

Dear Monica,

Scripture scholars agree that Jesus warned his contemporaries that both Jerusalem and the Temple would be destroyed. For any Jew, a cataclysm such as that would amount to the end of the world. But scholars are not so sure that these other warnings ascribed to Jesus were actually spoken by him. Some of the words may have been put into his mouth by the gospel writers of the late first century, as they struggled to interpret the upheavals that were taking place around them.

The early Christians expected Jesus to return soon, and sought to confirm their expectation in the events of their time. When it became evident that Jesus' return was not imminent, the Christian community tempered their "end-of-the-world" rhetoric as can be seen in some of Paul's later writings and those attributed to Paul.

Throughout the centuries, fervent literalists have always used certain biblical texts to frighten people. These texts were used as indicators of how bad things were. But it is also true that, through the centuries, there have always been earthquakes, plagues, wars, and famines—and the world has not come to an end. If today it seems there are more of these occurrences, it is probably because modern communication brings news of these events instantly. In former times, it took months, even years, before news of these happenings made it around the world.

So what are we to think? Well, it is a fact that the world has at its disposal the means to end itself. That is a constant threat we live with and must work to overcome. It is also true that natural disasters and diseases of one sort or another can claim the lives of huge numbers of people. However, that being the case, we are probably not witnessing the end of the world, as it is theologically understood—as the Second Coming of Christ.

But in understanding the fragility of life, the Church asks us to consider what is more likely to occur first—that is, our own personal death and consequent encounter with the Lord. Will we come to that event confident of the Lord's welcome or fearing his judgment?

We are also asked to consider our corporate time and place in the history of salvation. Our bishops, for example, often challenge us to work wholeheartedly in building up the kingdom of God here on earth, even as we await its final establishment in the Second Coming of Jesus. There is a lot we can do for the benefit of our society and our world.

This is not the time to sit around wringing our hands in speculation about the world's demise. Now is a time to dig in, providing compassion, relief, and justice for the millions of suffering brothers and sisters in Christ with whom we share this planet. In this way, we will live up to our calling as members of the kingdom of God, world without end.

End of the World

How will it happen that Jesus will come again and lead us "through the gates"? Do you think that this will happen any time soon?

Pondering Eternity

Dear Pondering,

We have it from the best of authorities that the date of the world's end is hidden. Jesus said: "But about that day and hour no one knows…but only the Father" (Mt 24:36).

In spite of Christ's admonition that the day of his Second Coming is known but to God, there have been countless false prophets who have confidently but incorrectly predicted a date for the end of the world. Most of these foolish forecasters based their claims on misinterpretations of the Book of Revelation.

The main purpose of the Book of Revelation is to assure us that God's power will prevail. In the ongoing struggle between good and evil, there are times when evil seems to have the upper hand. No matter. Evil will be conquered and God's rule will extend over all creation.

Throughout history, many have attempted to use the Book of Revelation as a timetable. They misinterpreted symbols and numbers as a forecast of what would happen in their own century. Over and over again, such people have used Revelation to predict the end of the world.

The world might end tomorrow, or in five billion years. Jesus tells us we can't know for sure. We are sure, however, that this world will pass away. And for each one of us the world will end at the moment of death. What matters is that we should always be ready to meet Christ, our Judge. And we shall be ready if we follow Christ, our Shepherd. Jesus leads us safely through this life by his teaching, his example, and his grace.

The Last Judgment

I recently saw a picture of Michelangelo's fresco of The Last Judgment, *which covers one wall in the Sistine Chapel. The picture looked really scary, with many more people being dragged into hell than into heaven. Is this a true picture of what the Last Judgment will be like?*

Looking for Mercy

Dear Mercy-Looker,

When Michelangelo's picture of the Last Judgment scene was finally finished (it opened to the public on All Saints' Day in 1541), many of the people, like you, were shocked and scared by what they saw. In this painting, Jesus is the great judge. His right arm is raised in a gesture of condemnation, and he actually looks toward the damned, who are being bludgeoned, dragged, and pulled into hell. In the picture, even Mary is looking away, as if she has no power to help those who are going to hell. This picture fit many of the medieval notions of the judgment scene, which placed more emphasis on the gruesome punishments of hell than on the love, compassion, and beauty of heaven. Many say that this is because of the bubonic plague, during which the cruel suffering of so many people was evident and so many were dying. Many artists used this outside reality to portray what hell might be like. It seemed important to the Church to scare these people into repenting and seeking complete union with God before the black death could take them.

But this is not the scene of judgment that is given to us by Jesus in the gospels. The great judgment scene in the gospels can be found in Matthew 25:31–46. In this scene, Jesus is not a vindictive condemner; rather, he is a shepherd. Jesus separates the goats from the sheep. The only criterion of judgment is how you treated or mistreated your fellow human beings. If you gave your fellow human the simplest consideration of food, drink, lodging, clothes, and visitation, then God will call you righteous and gather you into the kingdom. This is the true picture of the judgment scene. Jesus is gentle, loving, and compassionate. May we follow Christ's example and become more gentle, loving, and compassionate.

What Does the Church Teach About Heaven?

I have been a Catholic all my life. Heaven is supposed to be our final goal, yet we rarely hear sermons on this topic. What does the Church teach about heaven?

Melba

Dear Melba,

It may seem odd, but many preachers find it hard to talk about heaven. After all, they have no direct knowledge or experience of it. Life in heaven is a radically new form of existence, beyond human grasp, knowable only through the Spirit: " 'What no eye has seen, nor ear heard, / nor the human heart conceived, / what God has prepared for those who love him'—these things God has revealed to us through the Spirit…" (1 Cor 2:9–10).

Because of these limitations, heaven tends to be pictured in mostly materialistic images—pearly gates, streets of gold, life of ease and comfort, and so on. Biblical and Christian tradition present heaven in more spiritual metaphors. These images depict personal relationships with God, the absence of pain and sorrow, the fullness of life.

The New Testament describes the glory of heaven as the face-to-face vision of God. "Beloved, we are God's children now; what we will be has not yet been revealed. What we do know is this: when he is revealed we shall be like him, for we will see him as he is" (1 Jn 3:2). Or "For now we see in a mirror, dimly, but then we will see face to face. Now I know only in part; then I will know fully, even as I have been fully known" (1 Cor 13:12).

This face-to-face vision of God is called, in the formal teaching of the Church, the *Beatific Vision*. Those in heaven will see the very essence of God in all God's beauty and goodness; and in this vision, they will know and love God forever.

The Scriptures also describe heaven as the dwelling place of God and the angels and the saints, the place of eternal happiness for all who are saved. "Then I saw a new heaven and a new earth;…I heard a loud voice from the throne saying, / 'See, the home of God is among mortals. / He will dwell with them as their God; / they will be his peoples, / and God himself will be with them; / he will wipe every tear from their eyes. / Death will be no more; / mourning and crying and pain will be no more, / for the first things have passed away'" (Rev 21:1, 3–4).

Saint Thomas Aquinas, probably the greatest theologian the Church has ever known, put a human touch on the happiness of heaven. "Eternal life consists of the joyous community of all the blessed, a community of supreme delight, since everyone will share all that is good with all blessed. Everyone will love everyone else as oneself, and therefore will rejoice in another's good as one's own. So it follows that the happiness and joy of each grows in proportion to the joy of all."

According to Catholic teaching, heaven is perfect love, love without limitation, without imperfection, without end. Heaven is fullness of life—without illness, without strife, without death.

Saint Augustine reminded all God's children that whatever is found beautiful or desirable in this world is but a faint reflection of God. In the course of our lives, we experience powerful hints that enable us to imagine what it will be like when we are in the presence of God.

Do Non-Christians Go to Heaven?

Can you help me understand what happens to non-Christians after they die? I can't accept that those who follow another faith, who love God and try to do God's will, cannot enter into heaven. That seems so heartless and unfair.

A Heavenly Interest

Dear Heavenly Interest,

You can entrust your loved ones to the caring Jesus, the Good Shepherd who laid down his life for his sheep (Jn 10:11) and the Savior who died in order to gather all the scattered children of God into one family (Jn 11:52). Our Catholic Church teaches that God's compassionate hand is extended to all people in Jesus Christ, even those who do not know him by name.

It is true that Jesus said, "No one can enter the kingdom of God without being born of water and Spirit" (Jn 3:5). Some Christians think this passage means that anyone not actually baptized in water is condemned to hell. But Catholics believe that John 3:5 must be interpreted in light of Jesus' words at his Ascension: "The one who believes and is baptized will be saved; but the one who does not believe will be condemned" (Mk 16:16). This passage implies that the condemned are those who hear the gospel and refuse to accept it. So the Catholic Church teaches that those who learn of Christ's gospel and culpably reject it are rejecting eternal life. But there are many who are not baptized through no fault of their own, and the Church believes that they can be saved.

This understanding came very early because some catechumens preparing to enter the Church were martyred before they could be baptized. The Church maintains that those who shed their blood for Christ are joined to him by "baptism of blood." Others desire baptism but die before they can receive it; these people have an explicit "baptism of desire." Still others sincerely try to do what is right but have no opportunity to learn about Christ. These are said to have an implicit "baptism of desire," and the Church teaches that they, too, can be saved.

This teaching has its basis in Scripture. The parable of the Last Judgment, in Matthew 25, implies that some will be saved because they ministered to Christ in the poor and the hungry, even though they were unaware of his presence. Anyone knowing the gospel would be aware of this. It is also common sense. We cannot expect people to follow rules they could not have known. Similarly, God would not expect people to obey the command to be baptized if they had no opportunity to learn about it. People who love and do what is right can be saved. They may not know Christ by name, but they know God, who is love: "Everyone who loves is born of God and knows God" (1 Jn 4:7).

Obviously, we should do our best to bring knowledge of Jesus Christ and of his true Church to all the world. But many people have no real opportunity to know about Christ. Perhaps they live in an area where Christ has not been proclaimed. Perhaps they were raised in another creed and have been conditioned not to question that creed. If they are in good conscience and do their best to follow God's will as they see it, they can find salvation. This is the official teaching of the Church as explained in the *Catechism of the Catholic Church* (1257–1261).

If those who have never been baptized can find salvation, then certainly those who have been baptized in other Christian communities can be saved. In the past, as the *Catechism* notes, divisions did not occur without sin (on both sides), but those who are born into separated Christian communities today cannot be charged with the sin of separation. They can find salvation, and they are our brothers and sisters in Christ (817–818).

Do Suicide Victims Go to Hell?

I recently learned that a friend of mine killed himself. He was only twenty-five, talented, loved, and respected by many. I wonder if suicide victims go to hell. Is there any hope for my friend?

Depressed

Dear Depressed,

We know for sure that God is merciful beyond our imagining, and we commend those who die by suicide to the mercy and compassion of God. But we do not know for certain the fate of those who commit suicide.

The Bible and the Church teach that it is wrong to commit suicide, to take one's own life. God's commandment is: "You shall not murder" (Ex 20:13). We are not to kill others or ourselves. That is because God gives life, and only God has the right to determine when our lives here on earth will end. It is also true that some people utterly reject God's dominion over human life. These are the "professional advocates" of suicide, those who promote groups like the Hemlock Society. They deliberately encourage suicide.

But most people who commit suicide apparently do so because they are mentally ill or under great emotional distress. They may be so overwhelmed by depression that they lack the ability to see clearly what they are doing. Their ability to make a free choice may be short-circuited by images and feelings that simply overwhelm their desire to live. Such people may not be capable of a fully human choice, and their suicide may not necessarily separate them from God forever.

We Catholics express our hope for the salvation of those who commit suicide in our willingness to have a funeral Mass for them, and in our readiness to pray for and commend the deceased into the hands of our loving God.

One of the most consoling facts of Catholic belief is that those who die are not beyond our reach. We can pray for them and help them on their journey from this world to eternal life. This doctrine is all the more comforting when those who die leave this world in a state of turmoil and distress. In the "time" after their suicide, they may need strength, guidance, and light. Our prayers can help them find their way to the light of God's love.

I've read about people who attempted suicide but were revived; they said that their experience was frightful. They had the same problems on the "other side" as they had here. For them, death was not an escape but a continuation of their anguish and distress. Death left them wandering in a state of darkness and confusion. These people experienced "near death," not actual death, but their experience brings to mind the state of those in purgatory. Such individuals, we believe, can be helped and guided by our prayers. Our prayers can touch them and assure them that they are not alone. Our prayers can lead them into the arms of Jesus, who died for them, and whose love can purify them of all their failings.

So I encourage you to imitate the Church in praying for your friend. Ask Jesus to let your love for your friend ease his pain and guide him to eternal life. I am praying for you and for him. God bless you!

14
Lent and Easter

INTRODUCTION
Lent, the Popular Understanding

Lent. Forty Days before Easter. Ashes. Penance. Fasting. Giving up something that is enjoyable. Completing your Easter duty. Penance services. Parish missions. Stations of the Cross. Purple vestments. Palm Sunday. The passion of the Lord. Good Friday.

Each of these symbols, experiences, and expectations somehow comprise the popular understanding of that time of the liturgical year identified as *Lent*. For some people, each concept is necessary for a full experience of Lent. For others, a selection of the "liturgical menu" provided by the season is enough.

Even to the most casual observer of the Catholic experience, there seems to be an awareness of this forty-day period before the feast of Easter. Lent, which comes from the Anglo-Saxon *Lencten,* which means "spring," is a time that seems marked with peculiar rituals. The most obvious ritual is the reception of ashes on Ash Wednesday, but certainly Lenten rituals are not limited to this. Discussion around the water cooler might reveal that a person has "given up chocolate" or "given up dessert" as a Lenten practice. Still others may reveal that they not only have up given something but also have added something to their normal Catholic practice. "I go to the Stations of the Cross on Wednesday night." Every other Wednesday during the year is available for socializing but, for some reason, the Wednesdays of Lent have been reserved for other things.

What is Lent? What is the purpose of each of these peculiar rituals? Do they have something to say to each of us who live in the modern age, or are they rituals and practices left over from a time that can almost be remembered as "once upon a time"?

What Is "Metanoia"?

One of our deacons was preaching about Lent and he kept mentioning that the Church calls us to "metanoia." This sounds like some kind of mental illness. What was he talking about?
Down to Earth

Dear Down to Earth,

Most of us think of Lent only as a time of penance. We receive our ashes and then take up some traditional practice of giving up something or doing something for Lent. But there is more to the season of Lent than just practices of piety or acts of penance and mortification. Your deacon is correct. In Lent, the Church calls us to metanoia.

Metanoia is a Greek word, and it means "a change of mind and heart." We begin a whole new way of thinking and acting. We take a long hard look at the way we are living our lives, and we compare this to the values that Jesus offers us. Then we change our lives to match the values of the Lord. This, of course, is very difficult to do by ourselves. The Church asks us to pray during Lent that the Lord's power will come into our lives and give us the wisdom to see a new direction, and the courage to move in that direction. The Church suggests that we can strengthen our resolve through acts of personal mortification and sacrifice for others. This will tighten the belt of our discipline, and get us in training for the more sweeping changes that we need to make.

The Scripture readings for the first three weeks of Lent center on metanoia. The readings direct us to understand what exactly is involved with "changing our hearts" and seeking a new direction for our life. Listen to them well and they will lead you to metanoia.

The History of Lent

Was Lent always associated with sacrifice, sin, and penance?
Did Lent have some other purpose in Church history?

Manfred

Dear Manfred,

A set period of Lent was not observed during the first centuries of Christianity. Rather, Christians prepared for the Easter celebration with an all-night vigil and a fast. This vigil concluded with a morning Eucharist. Gradually, Christians extended this celebration to include Jesus' own Passover (the supper on Holy Thursday and the death of Jesus on Friday). By the end of the second century, baptism became linked to the Easter Vigil, and the time leading up to Easter became a period of intense preparation for baptism. At first, this preparation period lasted only three weeks, to correspond to the three gospel readings used for preparation: the woman at the well, the man born blind, and the raising of Lazarus. We still use these gospels today on the third, fourth, and fifth Sundays of Lent in the catechumenate program. This baptismal preparation program eventually extended to forty days. The idea of forty days came out of Mark's Gospel (1:13), where we read about Jesus going into the desert for forty days to prepare for his ministry.

Today the season of Lent serves a double purpose. The Lenten period is still a time of intense preparation for the catechumens, as they anticipate celebrating the sacrament of baptism at the Easter Vigil. But Lent also has become a time for baptized Christians to reflect on their own baptism. During Lent, the baptized are challenged to turn away from sin and choose again the deepest meaning of their baptism: the fact that they have died and risen with Christ and are now alive anew in Jesus. This renewal is done through the traditional penitential practices of fasting, prayer, and works of charity.

Why Do We Fast, Especially in Lent?

I know that there must be some spiritual reason for fasting, but the practice tends to make me just that much hungrier. Already, I can hear the Lenten growls in my stomach!

A Lenten Grouch

Dear Grouch,

The popular understanding of Lent is that it is a penitential period of time during which people attempt to become more sensitive to the role of sin in their lives. Lenten sermons will speak of personal sin, communal sin, and the effects that these sins have on others and on ourselves. Originally, the sacrament of penance was celebrated before Lent began. The penance was imposed on Ash Wednesday and practiced during the forty days of Lent. One of the traditional penances was fasting. The chosen foods Christians fasted from were milk and eggs. The money not spent on the purchase of dairy products was collected and donated to the church. In fact, there is a church tower in Germany that is known as the "butter tower" because it is built from the proceeds of Lenten fasting from dairy products. The common practice of Easter eggs is directly related to this practice as well. Easter Sunday involved decorating and eating the eggs to mark the end of the fast and the end of Lent.

Fasting is one of the three Christian practices called for in Lent. The other two practices are *prayer* and *acts of charity*. Fasting allows us to "empty ourselves" so that we can fill ourselves with God. When we feel hungry, it will be a reminder to pray to God from whom all life, health, food, and goodness come. We might consider fasting from not only food but also television, the Internet, movies, shopping, and other distractions that keep us from thinking about God. Fasting is also a discipline, it is used to strengthen our will power so that we can abstain from the larger evils of anger, slander, maliciousness, jealousy, and the desire to obtain and possess more material things.

What Makes Ash Wednesday So Special?

My wife, a convert of one year, wonders about the fascination of Ash Wednesday. We go to Mass on holy days of obligation, and there's a fair crowd. But on Ash Wednesday, not a holy day, the place is packed. How would you explain this?

John

Dear John,

Indeed, pastoral experience corroborates your observation. Holy days of obligation draw fairly well—but it's "standing room only" on Ash Wednesday. I can only surmise that, although it is not a day of obligation, it is considered a "holy" day by most Catholics.

There's something undeniably elemental about the ugly smudge of ashes on the forehead. People wear it without embarrassment or shame. No matter our walk of life or social status, we want that sooty cross. It's like a badge of identification, reminding Catholics in a graphic and startling way that it's "spiritual gut-check" time. It jogs us from our numbing routines and spurs us on to more important realities, to go back to being who we are supposed to be—fully and totally Christian. It is as if Catholics are saying, "I'm Catholic and proud of it. I may not be the best or greatest. I may slack off a little on my church attendance and commitments. I have my faults and sins. But I'm not a bad person. I know deep down that being Christian is the way to live, and I'm going to try again."

We all know in our hearts that the cross of Jesus Christ is the only way to salvation. We also know how difficult it is to internalize this truth, to pick up the cross daily and live it in all of life's circumstances. We know we need more prayer and discipline in our life, more genuine concern for others and less self-centeredness, more involvement in church and community. So we suck it up, get our ashes, and turn back to the Lord.

Ash Wednesday is unique because it signals the beginning of Lent, the Church's special time of confession and renewal in preparation for Easter. It is what Christians are all about—a people who have died with Christ in the waters of baptism in order to rise with him to a new life. We renew our baptismal commitment to be his people in the world. As we recall and celebrate Christ's passage through death to life, we renew our own death to old sinful ways to rise and live with recaptured vigor.

The symbols of Ash Wednesday touch us in a powerful way. When we hear the words, "Remember, you are dust and to dust you shall return," we are reminded of our vulnerability and utter dependence on God. Despite our mechanisms of power, ultimately, like dust in the wind, we can be whisked away in an instant and brought to our knees. At the same time, we are called to scale the spiritual heights, to "turn away from sin and be faithful to the gospel," affirming that we are a people with an enduring destiny and a sacred mission in the world.

Ash Wednesday's insistent call to renewal strikes a responsive cord deep within us. It is difficult to resist the charm and pull of this fascinating day. Together we get our ashes and turn back to the Lord.

Why Bless Palms on Palm/Passion Sunday?

I recently converted to Catholicism. Last year was the first time I attended Holy Week services as a Catholic. I am wondering about the significance of the blessed palm branches that we receive on Palm Sunday. Can you tell me more about their meaning and symbolism?

Sarah

Dear Sarah,

There are two levels on which we can consider the meaning of the palm branches.

On the first level, we commemorate a historical event—Jesus' triumphal entry into Jerusalem: "The great crowd that had come to the festival heard that Jesus was coming to Jerusalem. So they took branches of palm trees and went out to meet him" (Jn 12:12–13).

In biblical times, people saw the palm tree as a "kingly" tree because of its lofty height and majestic appearance. Palm trees have slender, graceful trunks that rise high in the air, their tops crowned with green branches. It is easy to understand why the palm tree became a sign and symbol of royalty and victory. The Jews carried palm branches in their processions on festive holy days. Roman soldiers carried palm branches in their victory parades in Rome. In public games, the winners of the various contests and sports received palm branches as a sign of their victories. Thus, when people greeted Jesus with branches of palm upon his entrance into Jerusalem, they were greeting him in the spirit of joy and triumph that they usually showered on victorious kings, armies, and athletes. It was the biblical equivalent of a ticker-tape parade!

That brings us to the second level of meaning for the palm branches. They do signify a joyful victory, but not a victory in the worldly and military sense of the word. It is a victory that we can understand and celebrate only in the light of the other events of Holy Week and Easter Sunday.

The ultimate victory of Jesus was his Easter triumph over death and sin. But it was a victory won only through suffering and dying. This is the victory we begin to recall on Palm Sunday. Even though we must relive the sad events of Holy Thursday and Good Friday, we know the triumphant outcome of the story. And knowing the outcome enables us to make Palm Sunday the beginning of a victory celebration, and the palms are a sign of the Easter victory.

As Catholics, our custom is to take the palm branches home and display them throughout the year. Many of us entwine palm fronds in the crucifixes we have displayed in our homes. When we do this, we remind ourselves that we share in the victory of Jesus over death and sin. It is a victory, however, that will be ours only in the way that Jesus has shown us—through suffering and dying. We, too, will endure the many sufferings that are a part of life—sickness, hardship, disappointment, failure, worry, and, eventually, death itself. But personal suffering and death no longer lack meaning or purpose. Jesus has taught us that passing through suffering and death is the way to a victorious resurrection and everlasting life. The palm branches, then, also become a symbol and reminder of the victory that awaits each one of us as followers of Jesus.

Through his own suffering, dying, and rising, Jesus has called us to live in great hope. We need not become discouraged with the burdens of this life; we need not despair over our sinfulness; we need not fear the darkness of death itself. These are the "Good Fridays" we must endure on the way to our Easter mornings. On Palm Sunday let the palm branches symbolize that great hope—a sign of the great triumph that Jesus made possible for each and every one of us.

Holy Week's Special Place

I'm a new member of our parish's liturgy committee, and I understand that Holy Week is the most important time of the year as far as Church liturgy is concerned. How would you summarize Holy Week and its special place in our lives as Catholics?

Just Wondering

Dear Just Wondering,

The Triduum of Easter is the three-day celebration of Jesus' Paschal Mystery. It presents us with the central mystery of the Christian life, perhaps of life itself—dying to rise, death to life. Even though the Church spreads the Triduum liturgies over three days (Holy Thursday, Good Friday, and the Easter Vigil), what we commemorate is one single movement: Jesus' passage through the pain, humiliation, and suffering of death, to the glory and triumph of resurrection and new life. Because Holy Week has so many implications for the Christian life, the Church savors its richness and complexity. The Church knows we need time, perhaps a lifetime, to make this dying and rising with Christ the central moving force in our lives.

The distinction of the Triduum cannot be emphasized enough. It is the year's principal liturgy, summarizing in marvelously rich celebrations what being Christian is all about. During these days, the Church's basic symbols are especially highlighted. These symbols appear again and again as we use them extensively to mark the passages of life and the ongoing flow of life. But their singular importance is underscored in the sacred Triduum.

On Holy Thursday morning, there's the Chrism Mass that's held in the cathedral of each diocese. During this Mass the bishop consecrates the oils used for baptism, confirmation, holy orders, and the anointing of the sick. Later that day we commemorate the Last Supper—the first Mass—with a special Mass that also re-creates the scene of Christ washing the disciples' feet.

Good Friday is perhaps the most difficult liturgy of the Triduum, because it commemorates the gruesome death of Jesus Christ. The tendency might be to overemphasize death to the point of having a wake service or funeral for him with the pounding of nails and taunts of "Crucify him, crucify him." But we must remember that this death is not once and for all. Rather, Jesus is *alive*. So Good Friday must be celebrated with an eye to Sunday's Resurrection. It is the premier day to highlight dying to selfishness and sin in order to live a new life.

Holy Saturday's liturgy is the queen of all liturgies. The Church outdoes itself on this night. This is what it is all about. This is what we celebrate in one way or another all year long. We light the new fire, proclaiming Jesus to be our light and our life. We hear the readings that tell the primal stories of who God is and of who we are— and before that, the exultant song proclaiming the night of nights when Jesus rose. We bless the waters of baptism through which new members are initiated into the Church. Along with these new members, we celebrate the renewal of old members, ensuring a Church alive and ever new. Finally, the Eucharist celebrates our coming together to nourish ourselves at the font of all life: the Lord's table.

There are those who say all parish planning should start and end with the sacred Triduum. The key to an authentic and fruitful celebration of the Triduum is not to restage historical events but rather to renew what these events mean in our lives. The historical occurrences took place centuries ago. Now our goal is to recommit ourselves to dying to the old way in order to rise with Christ to a new life.

What Is the Triduum?

A friend of mine told me that he was looking forward to celebrating the Triduum. I didn't know what that word meant. Can you explain it to me?

Peter

Dear Peter,

The word *triduum* is a Latin word meaning "three days." In the early part of the 1900s, most major feasts of the Church were preceded by three days of prayer and pious exercises in preparation for the feast at hand. Today we use the word to refer to the paschal Triduum. These three days of Holy Thursday, Good Friday, and Holy Saturday celebrate Christianity's most sacred events—the passion, death, and resurrection of Jesus.

The official beginning of the paschal Triduum takes place the evening of Holy Thursday, when we celebrate the Mass of the Lord's Supper. This day is also referred to as *Maundy Thursday*, because Jesus gives a command (*mandatum*) to his followers to be an example of love and service to others. The Mass of the Lord's Supper ends in somber stillness, as the tabernacle is emptied and the altar is stripped bare. The priests, ministers, and congregation then exit in silence. Good Friday is a day of somber quiet, as we relive the passion and death of Jesus. The service centers on the solemn veneration of the cross. Holy Saturday is characterized by the spirit of waiting and quiet anticipation, until the festive Easter Vigil, celebrated in the evening, when the Church comes alive with the new Light of Christ and catechumens are joyfully received into the eucharistic community. These are the Christian high holy days.

Is Faith Based on an Empty Tomb?

I've just returned from a visit to the Holy Land. It was a once-in-a-lifetime experience, but one thing disappointed me greatly. When we visited the tomb of Jesus, I was expecting a powerful witness to Jesus' Resurrection. Instead, in the Church of the Holy Sepulcher, we saw a simple marble slab in a small chapel. Even then, the guide said that the original tomb was probably five feet below the chapel. Is this marble slab the foundation of our belief in Jesus' Resurrection?

Jerry

Dear Jerry,

I am happy that I can answer your question on this highest truth of our faith—the Resurrection of Jesus. Our faith in Jesus' Resurrection is not based on an empty tomb or the little marble slab that you saw. There are many plausible explanations for "an empty tomb," most of which would not contribute to the belief in Jesus' Resurrection.

Our faith in the Resurrection rests not only on the physical reality of the empty tomb but, more importantly, on the eyewitness accounts of those who saw Jesus, talked to him, and walked with him after his Resurrection.

There are many reports in the gospels and the Acts of the Apostles that chronicle the appearances of Jesus after the Resurrection. The details and circumstances vary, but one constant fact is found in all the accounts: those who saw the risen Lord had such a powerful experience that they could not keep it to themselves. They had to run and tell somebody.

Just think of this experience as the Christian version of the "big bang theory." The followers of Jesus had such a tremendous initial experience of the risen Lord's presence that they could not hold it in. They were compelled to tell their friends, their neighbors—anyone who would listen. The excitement spread to neighboring villages and hamlets. Then the news traveled to surrounding countries and cultures. Eventually, Christianity expanded, sometimes under great oppression and persecution, throughout the world. Could such endurance and dynamism result from just an empty tomb? Certainly just an empty tomb cannot be responsible for the faith of generations. Rather, only an experience of the risen Jesus could bring this about.

We who live in the twenty-first century are heirs to the truth and power of Jesus' Resurrection. The powerful experience of the resurrected Jesus can be our experience today. But in our modern day, some say that we have reached the end of the expanding "Christian big bang," and Christianity has begun its last days. Is this true?

History seems to favor the continued life of the Church, and the risen Lord has assured us that he will never abandon us, no matter what the difficulties and no matter how large or how small the community of loyal followers becomes (Mt 28:20). But if we are to be credible witnesses to Jesus' Resurrection and presence in our world today, we must live in a way that is meaningful. We must commit ourselves to lives of true conversion. Our faith and external observances must not be superficial, but a true response to the risen Lord— a commitment that touches our hearts, our homes, and our relationships. Only then can the world see and believe.

15
Marriage and Family Life

INTRODUCTION
Jesus and Marriage

In the time of Jesus, marriage was not so much a religious matter as it was a family matter. This is not to say that marriage did not have religious meaning or consequence. My attempts here are to position marriage within its proper sociological context, or at least within the context of how Jesus may have experienced marriage and how he may have understood what he experienced. For example, marriage in the first century was a state in life, expected in the normal course of events for all men and women. Marriage was understood as an agreement, contract, or covenant that was arranged between two families; our modern notion of romance rarely influenced the choice of a spouse. Rather, the fathers of the bride and the groom mutually agreed upon the union, determined the gifts that would be exchanged, and even presided over the ceremony.

In the culture of first-century Palestine, as it was in most of the ancient Near East, marriage was understood as a kind of partnership, and each partner had specific duties and responsibilities that he or she was were expected to fulfill. The husband was expected to provide some kind of living for the family, either through a learned trade or perhaps as a day laborer, and to provide the necessary leadership and make required judgments and decisions. The wife was expected to bear children and manage the normal tasks of the household. No one assumed that the partnership was one of equality, but it was routinely understood and accepted by all that if the man and the woman in the marriage performed their tasks and completed their responsibilities, the marriage would be a successful partnership, effectively contributing to their eventual happiness and the stability of the society in which they lived. There were no doubt religious concerns—fidelity to the requirements of the covenant, for example, and a regular practice of the traditions—but the overriding consideration was the specific roles and functions to be fulfilled.

A core value within this kind of partnership was the assumption that both spouses would be faithful to their appointed tasks and to each other; if this was not the case, the partnership would be weakened and the stability of the family, and by extension the stability of the society, would be threatened. For this reason, a very severe penalty for adultery was imposed: death by stoning. A secondary concern was if, despite the best efforts of the man and the woman, the partnership became intolerable, some remedy would need to be applied. For this reason, divorce was accepted and could be initiated by the man; in such an instance, the woman would be sent back to her family and certain gifts (dowry) would be returned to the woman's family. However, there was no remedy available to a woman who found herself in an intolerable situation; the best she could possibly hope for would be to convince her husband to divorce her.

Marriage: New and Old

I recently attended a wedding ceremony. Much of the ceremony centered on personal choice and the love of one partner for the other. I was thinking that marriages should be based on firmer foundations than just personal choice. Does the Church agree?

Pro Strong Marriages

Dear Pro Strong Marriages,

For many centuries, marriage was understood as a financial and political alliance arranged by families. Marriage had nothing to do with personal choice or with love. This practice of "arranging marriages" continues in some cultures, even to our present day. Actually, it was the Canon Law of the Catholic Church that first gave women and men a "legal right" to marry because of love. In the twelfth century, the Church proclaimed that two people were married when they exchanged their mutual consent, in the present moment, to marry. No one could be married "against his or her will."

Today things are going in different directions. Married couples are encouraged to look beyond their little garden of love and personal choice, to see marriage as a commitment to family, neighborhood, faith community, and society. Marriage is a commitment to build the spiritual family and the temporal society. The Coalition for Marriage, Family, and Couple Education is spearheading a movement to promote marriage as an asset to society. This means promoting marriage education in high school, mandatory pre-marriage counseling, and changes in the divorce policy. Most dioceses demand that couples attend a premarriage program of some kind. This program stresses that the task of every Christian couple is to build their marriage on the foundation of Christ. The love the couple has for each other must eventually turn outward, toward creating a family, being a contributing member of a church community, and actively caring for their relatives and friends. As it says in the nuptial blessing: "Give this couple the strength which comes from the Gospel so that they may be witnesses of Christ to others."

Divorce and Remarriage

I am a divorced Catholic and I would like to get remarried in the Church. How do I do that? I am a bit frightened to reexamine the pain of my first marriage and divorce.

Tracy

Dear Tracy,

Congratulations on your courage to seek a new beginning. Before you can be remarried in the Catholic Church, you need to obtain a Declaration of Nullity. This is also called an *annulment*. Many dioceses offer annulment workshops for people, like yourself, who seek to be remarried in the Catholic Church. Call your local parish and find out the dates of such a workshop. This will also provide you a support group to help you through the pain and struggle of reexamining your first marriage.

The annulment process can take up to a year and a half, and involves several steps. The first step is to visit your parish priest. He will help you fill out an application form, which is then sent to the Office of the Marriage Tribunal. Each diocese of the Catholic Church has a marriage tribunal. This is a court system where thousands of marriages are brought for examination.

Once your application form is accepted, you will receive a questionnaire and instructions on how to answer it. This questionnaire centers on retelling the story of your marriage. After you complete the questionnaire, you will be asked to have an interview with a person from the tribunal office, who will go over your testimony with you. These people are sworn to confidentiality and are usually psychologists.

The tribunal will also ask others, whom you name, to witness the history of your marriage. It is only when all the testimony and evidence is complete that the presiding judge studies your case and then makes a decision. Another panel of three judges reviews this decision. If all goes well, you will then receive your Declaration of Nullity, signed by the judge and stamped with the official seal of the diocese.

There is a fee for this process, set by each diocese, but when people are unable to pay, no fee is requested.

Good News About Marriage

For years we have heard that 50 percent of the people who get married end up getting divorced. Has religion made any difference in stemming this tide?

Planning to Marry

Dear Planning,

Some of the recent good news about marriage stems from the Catholic Church's premarriage programs. A national study completed by the Center for Marriage and Family at Creighton University showed that 66 percent of the couples married in the Catholic Church responded that marriage preparation had helped them build a stronger and better marriage. More than 90 percent of the couples surveyed were still married to their original partner.

For the past twenty-five years, the Catholic Church has been a leader in programs for both engaged couples and married couples. These programs offer a unique mix of the practical and the spiritual, including communication and conflict resolution skills, and they rely on the peer witness of happily married couples who share their own successes and failures. Two of the most popular programs are Marriage Encounter and Engaged Encounter. For those experiencing serious difficulties in their marriage, the Church offers the Retrouvaille program, an intensive weekend that teaches the couple to reestablish communication, rediscover love, and work together toward reconciliation.

The commonly held belief that 50 percent of all marriages fail is an exaggeration. Statistics prove, however, that the more intense the common bond of faith is between husband and wife, the less likely the couple will become a divorce statistic. One study pointed out that the divorce rate among couples who share the same religion, worship together, and pray together was one in fifteen hundred.

It would seem that premarriage preparation and a deeply shared faith are two keys to a loving and lasting Catholic marriage.

Annulments: Information Please?

I recently received an annulment of my first marriage from the marriage tribunal of our diocese. I am grateful for the way everything was handled. Through my experience, however, I learned that many Catholics need correct information about Church annulments. These are a few examples of what I heard from other Catholics: "You won't get an annulment because you were married more than three years." "...because you have two children." "...because you're not wealthy enough." Why don't we educate Catholics on these matters?

Lynn

Dear Lynn,

The basic teaching of the Catholic Church on marriage is this: when a baptized man and a baptized woman, who are free to marry, exchange their marriage vows before an authorized priest or deacon and two witnesses, and then consummate their union, their marriage is a true sacramental marriage. This sacramental bond of marriage is unbreakable; it cannot be dissolved by any power on earth.

To enter such a marriage, however, the man and the woman must be able and willing to give their free and informed consent. The Code of Canon Law emphasizes the importance of this consent: A marriage is brought into being by the lawfully manifested consent of persons who are legally capable. This consent cannot be supplied by any human power. "Matrimonial consent is an act of the will by which a man and a woman by an irrevocable covenant mutually give and accept one another for the purpose of establishing a marriage" (Canon 1057, §2).

Let us now suppose that a couple who was married in the Catholic Church runs into serious difficulties in their marriage, and finally the marriage "breaks down." The couple obtains a civil divorce. In the course of time, one of the spouses may wish to enter into a new marriage. Desiring to retain full, active participation in the Church, he or she may approach the parish priest about the possibility of an annulment of the first marriage.

An annulment is a declaration by the Church that, although there was a legal marriage in accord with state law, there was never a valid sacramental marriage in this particular case. The Church arrives at this decision only after careful and objective investigation of the marriage by the marriage tribunal of the diocese.

This investigation seeks to discover whether an essential ingredient for a valid sacramental marriage was lacking in this case and, if so, whether there is solid evidence to prove this. For example, true freedom is an essential ingredient for matrimonial consent. If a person was to marry because of grave fear or force, the marriage would not be valid. If a person entered marriage with the explicit intention to exclude permanence or fidelity or the right to have children, this person would be excluding an essential ingredient of Christian marriage. Or perhaps one party entered the marriage suffering from a serious mental illness or a grave lack of discretionary judgment concerning the essentials of marriage or from a true psychic incapacity to fulfill the responsibilities of marriage (see Canon 1095). In all these examples, an essential ingredient of marriage is lacking and an annulment is a possibility.

It's clear that being married for more than three years or having two children does not automatically mean that the marriage was a valid sacramental marriage. And I'm sure you can testify that you don't have to be rich to receive an annulment.

Finally, in an effort to be as clear and concise as possible, I think the following statement from a document on the annulment procedure from the Archdiocese of Chicago might also be helpful in understanding the question that you asked: "The effect of Formal Annulment is to declare that parties are not bound to a specific marital relationship, stating that the marriage in question was not a binding sacramental union. It is important to understand the meaning of an annulment. The annulment does not deny that a real relationship existed, nor does it imply that the relationship was entered into with ill will or moral fault. Rather, an annulment is a statement by the Church that the relationship fell short of at least one of the elements seen as essential for a binding union. Therefore, the union in question cannot be seen by the Church as a source of continuing marital rights and obligations."

I'm Tempted to Be Unfaithful

After only nine months of marriage, I am attracted to another man. I never thought that this could happen. I love my husband, but the feelings between this man and myself are very strong and difficult to resist. Can you help me?

Lena

Dear Lena,

If you are tempted to have an affair, it's important to remember three things. First, you aren't evil for feeling tempted. Feelings are neither good nor bad; they are *just feelings*. What can become harmful is how you might choose to behave in response to your feelings.

Second, the temptation to have an affair happens to many people. You aren't abnormal. What you are going through has probably happened to a number of other married people around the world.

Third, the temptation to have an affair does not necessarily mean you have a bad marriage.

Here are a few ideas that have helped others successfully overcome this temptation.

1. Take responsibility for your behavior and your decisions. You are not a helpless victim at the mercy of some evil tempter. God has given you a free will to choose what you will do and how you will respond. Also, remember that you are not totally to blame for this predicament. Both parties have a moral responsibility in this situation.

2. Focus on your relationship with your spouse. If you can safely do so, openly discuss your feelings with your spouse. It would help to visit a marriage counselor together. Emphasize that you have not been unfaithful. Bringing the topic out in the open can help to strengthen your relationship. If

you fear that such a discussion might incite abusive behavior or abandonment, seek out a friend or a counselor to help you. This is especially important if your spouse has a history of reacting abusively in the face of other marital problems.

3. Remove yourself completely and permanently from this temptation. This may be as easy as changing where you take your morning coffee break or as difficult as changing jobs. Whatever it takes, it is *necessary*. If, and only if, it is completely impossible for you to remove yourself from the person to whom you are attracted, establish strict boundaries. That means making sure you are never completely alone with this person and that there are never any opportunities for intimacy.

4. Take things one day at a time. If your attraction to the other person did not develop overnight, it will probably not go away overnight. Give yourself time to get over the feelings of attraction, and don't waste time feeling guilty about the past or worrying about the future.

5. Invite God to help you. Turn the problem over to God in prayer, and admit that you need help. Be honest and tell God about all your conflicting feelings and desires. Ask God to lead you out of your feelings of helplessness. Do this every day—and remember Christ's promise: "Ask and you will receive. Seek, and you will find. Knock and it will be opened to you" (see Mt 7:7).

I'm Divorced, Can I Go to Communion?

I am the divorced mother of three young children. My daughter, Mary, is making her first Communion and I want to go to Communion with her. But I haven't been to Mass in three years because of my divorce. I am nervous and embarrassed about returning to the Church. What can I do?

Carol

Dear Carol,

Your daughter's first Communion certainly will be an important day in her young life. It will be a nice chance for the family to get together, and they will always remember it.

Your daughter's first Communion, however, should be more than just a happy day to remember. It is a major step in her growth as a Catholic, strengthening the faith that was promised for her at baptism. Sit down with your daughter before her first Communion and ask her questions about what this day will mean to her. Tell her why she was baptized when she was a baby. Even if you haven't been getting to Mass as often as you should, tell her about the place that the Church has had in your life.

Your sharing in your daughter's preparation for holy Communion is a good chance to look closely at your own faith. It can be a time for you to ask yourself this important question: *Am I allowing my child to receive first Communion in a faith that I rarely practice?* If you are, then let her first Communion be a chance for you to get back to full communion with the Church.

You mentioned that you haven't been to church in three years because of your divorce. It seems that you may be confused about the teachings of the Church concerning divorce. Divorced Catholics are still full members of the Church. If you have remarried outside the Church, it is a more complicated issue, yet not hopeless. Your parish priest would be happy to discuss your situation with you.

Your daughter's first Communion can be the little push you need to get back to Mass on a regular basis. She needs to see in you someone who is strong in faith and filled with deep love and commitment to her Church. You should take her and your other children to Mass on Sunday. They should see you with them at church to make your faith credible.

Remember, you sacrificed a lot to give your daughter and your other children what you think they need: nice clothes, a good school, and a comfortable home. But they need more. Give them something to believe in. Your example as a good Catholic can set a tone for your children that will last for years and years.

It is not easy for a single parent to round up the troops on Sunday morning, get into the car, and drive to church. But when you come to Mass week after week, you also teach your children about the importance of faith and Church. In time, they will appreciate that lesson.

Since you haven't been to Mass in three years, the first step you need to take is to call your parish and ask to speak with a priest. Be honest. Tell him you are nervous. Explain why you have stayed away from the Church. Then set up a time to go to confession. And please, please, don't be ashamed or embarrassed about coming back to Church. There are at least fifteen million Catholics in America who no longer practice their faith. No matter how long it has been and no matter what you have done in the meantime, the Church wants you to come home.

I'm Worried About My Teenagers

I am a Catholic parent with teenage children. I am constantly wondering and worrying about them. Does the Church have anything to say to parents like me?

Pam

Dear Pam,

Most parents tend to be on the alert for trouble with regard to their children's well-being. Parents of teenagers seem to increase their vigilance during these years. Parents want to know where their teenagers are going, with whom, where they can be reached, and when they will be home. Many times, the parents present an avalanche of advice on jobs, school, friends, what to do, and how to do it. This pattern can cause adolescents to feel resentful, and parents can become overprotective. This is a lethal combination that results in shouting matches, insults, demands, and various disciplinary threats and measures.

Jesus was never a parent, nor did he give specific instructions about raising children. But by examining Jesus' style of being with others, we can find some guiding principles for parenting.

We see in the gospels that Jesus never forced instruction or cures on others. Those who had faith in Jesus freely came to him for help. When they did, Jesus usually helped them. Jesus left alone those who either had no faith in him or did not want to hear his instruction.

A good approach for guiding teenagers is using statements like: "If you need help in any area, I am here to talk with you. I believe you are capable of handling most situations, so I will trust you to let me know when you need my advice." It is good for parents of teens to remember that their sons and daughters are attempting to shed the skins of childhood in order to let the new adult skins shine through. The only way they can do this is by trial and error. Like Jesus, parents can trust that the best time to give advice is when teens ask for it.

We also notice in the gospels that when Jesus came into his hometown and was not accepted, he still offered good example and right teaching; then he left. Jesus didn't scream at the folks or condemn them. Nor did he call down fire from heaven to punish them. He simply let them be. The art of backing off is essential for parents of teens. Parents should continue to set a good example and promote the values of the family, but it's not wise to condemn teens when these teachings are not fully accepted.

Another belief that Jesus embodied in the gospels is that of openness and acceptance of people, no matter what gossip, events, or deeds they were involved with. Some were caught in adultery or filled with demons. Others were beggars from birth or they were hated tax collectors. Jesus loved them as individuals, and this brought about healing, faith, and growth.

As a parent of teens, you are attending a performance of growth. Support that growth, allow enough space for growing, and above all, love the ones who grow.

Marrying a Non-Catholic

*David, my nephew and godson, is getting serious about marriage.
He's Catholic, his fiancée is Protestant. He often asks me for
information and has already raised a few questions about
"mixed" marriages. For example, could he be allowed to get
married in her church? I would appreciate knowing what the
Catholic Church says about "mixed" marriages.*

Aunt Margaret

Dear Aunt Margaret,

The Catholic Church, like most other religions, does not favor mixed
marriages. This position strikes some people as narrow and preju-
diced, I know, but in truth, it is based on long experience with the
special difficulties of such marriages. Religion, which should be a bond
of unity in marriage, can easily become a bone of contention. This is
especially true when the couple have children. Common worship by
parents and children is almost impossible. The religious education of
the children raises tough questions. This is not to say that mixed marriages can never be successful. Some are remarkably so. Yet their success demands extraordinary generosity on the part of the couple—
and many couples are not capable of such generosity.

While remaining opposed to mixed marriages, the Church wants
to offer pastoral support to those couples who enter a mixed marriage. This support emphasizes how important it is for the couple to
prepare themselves as well as possible for such a marriage. Both the
Catholic party and the non-Catholic party should be aware of mutual
expectations and potential hazards. In addition to the preparation
that applies to all marriages, there are certain points that apply precisely to mixed marriages.

First, because the Catholic faith has many implications for marriage and family life, the non-Catholic party is asked to spend time
learning about basic Catholic beliefs and practices. The purpose of
this is not to try to convert the non-Catholic but to inform him or her
of the religious values and obligations of the Catholic party. It is equally

important that the Catholic party become familiar with the religious beliefs and practices of his or her future spouse.

Second, the Catholic who wishes to marry a non-Catholic must have the express permission of the bishop of the diocese (Canon 1124). This permission is usually requested through one's parish priest. The bishop will grant this permission if there is a good reason and provided the norms of the Church are fulfilled.

Third, the Catholic party in a mixed marriage must declare "that he or she is prepared to remove dangers of falling away from the faith" and must make "a sincere promise to do all in his or her power to have all the children baptized and brought up in the Catholic Church" (Canon 1125, §1). It is essential that the non-Catholic party have a clear understanding of this declaration and promise. Very early in the preparation of a mixed marriage, therefore, the couple should discuss this matter most carefully.

Fourth, Catholics are obliged to be married in the presence of an authorized priest or deacon and two witnesses. In mixed marriages, the pastor of the non-Catholic party is usually encouraged to take part in the ceremony. For the Catholic party to be married before a non-Catholic minister in a non-Catholic church, the express permission of the bishop is required (Canon 1127, §2). If this permission is granted, a Catholic priest may be present and take part in the ceremony.

I hope this reply is helpful to you and to others who may be looking for the same information.

Do We Have to Be Married in a Church?

My fiancée and I were hoping to be married outdoors in a park. When we talked to our priest about the ceremony, he informed us that in this diocese, all Catholic weddings are to take place in a Catholic church. Why is that?

A Nature Lover

Dear Nature Lover,

It is true that Catholic weddings always take place in a church, unless specific permission is granted by the bishop for the ceremony to be performed in another sacred place. First of all, there is a purely practical reason for Catholics to get married in their parish church. It is a way of recording when and where Catholics marry. Parish records serve a useful purpose in both civil and Church matters.

But a more important reason is that marriage, in the eyes of Catholics, is a sacrament—one of the seven sacred signs through which God communicates God's love to us. When Catholics marry, they believe that God ratifies their union. The love of the couple for each other is a sign of God's love for each of them. This is expressed during the wedding ceremony with the words: "What God has joined together, let no one put asunder." The union of the couple themselves is also a continuous sign of Christ's love for the Church. Saint Paul tells us that husbands should love their wives just as Christ loved the Church (Eph 5:25). So when Catholics marry, they do not look upon it simply as a contract that a man and woman make between themselves. Rather, they see it as something in which God is deeply involved, and which also involves the whole Christian community.

The church building, which contains the presence of Christ himself, is thought of as the most sacred place to make this most sacred of commitments.

I Want My Spouse to Be Catholic!

I am getting married soon and my spouse is a baptized non-Catholic, but has never practiced his faith. I, on the other hand, am Catholic and very religious. How can I get him to believe more deeply, or even to become Catholic?

Marsha

Dear Marsha,

I commend you for your farsightedness in preparing for your marriage. I am glad that you are working on spiritual compatibility with your future spouse. Your community and your family need your visible witness of commitment to Christ and his Church through your public worship and your unselfish service to others.

I asked a parishioner of mine, who was in your exact situation, what she would advise you to do. She and I offer the following ten strategies for developing spiritual compatibility in marriage:

1. Pray and don't preach. Every day ask the Lord to open the heart and mind of your future spouse so that he might receive God's love and life.

2. Accept and love your future spouse as he is. Only the Holy Spirit can prompt him to inquire about Christ and the fullness of Catholic faith. Any kind of pressure from you or other Catholics can have a negative effect.

3. Discover the elements of spirituality the two of you share in common. As a baptized Christian, hopefully he embraces the fundamental beliefs revealed by Christ: the Holy Trinity, Jesus' divinity and humanity and virgin birth, his atoning death and bodily resurrection, the Bible as the inspired Word of God, and many other teachings regarding social ethics and personal morality.

4. Let your future spouse know that you are eager to discuss any of his questions about the Catholic faith. This will also be an opportunity for you to grow in faith as you seek for answers you do not readily know.

5. Strive to live the moral teachings of Jesus as proposed by the Catholic Church throughout your marriage, thus providing a powerful witness of faith. Show your concern for the poor and the disadvantaged; root your attitudes about sexuality, love, natural family planning, and child rearing in the truth taught by the people and the bishops.

6. Invite your future spouse to pray with you. Use the psalms and other scriptural prayers such as the Lord's Prayer or conversational prayer with Jesus.

7. Invite your future spouse to celebrate Mass with you each

week, leaving the choice entirely up to him. God bestows special grace during Mass, even upon those who are not yet able to receive the holy Eucharist.

8. Be patient. I find that many non-Catholics begin showing interest in the Church only when their children became involved in catechesis and sacramental preparation.

9. Put your participation in parish activities in the right perspective, so that it does not overshadow your commitment to your future spouse and your family. Use the sacrament of penance often to experience ongoing conversation to Jesus.

10. Offer special sacrifices, novenas, and prayers for the sake of your future spouse's conversion.

I hope these suggestions will get you thinking about the many possible ways God can help you grow in faith.

My Son Attends a Protestant Church!

My son and his wife attend the Christian Unity Church. They like the minister there and the "upbeat" service. My son was raised Catholic and still claims that he is Catholic, even though he doesn't go to a Catholic church. I feel frustrated by the whole affair!

Frustrated

Dear Frustrated,

Your frustration is certainly shared by many parents and grandparents today. They raised their children Catholic, even sent them to Catholic schools, but the children have grown up and chosen to be more eclectic about the practice of their faith. A recent survey on religion showed that nine out of ten people say they believe in God, and seven out of ten consider spirituality important in their lives. But this doesn't mean that they are committed to a single religion or house of worship. About half of the people questioned attend religious services less than once a month, or never. Many of them are interested in exploring different teachings and attending different churches. The loyalty to one religious sect that was evident in our own lives, or in our parents' and grandparents' lives, is lacking in today's under-55 crowd.

What can one do about this situation? The traditional method is to pray for your children and to continue to give a good example through your own loyalty to the Catholic Church and attendance at Sunday Mass. It would even be good to invite your son and his wife to attend with you when they are visiting. As we age, we often become more religious and traditional. We may become more interested in our family's history, photo albums, and traditions. The religion of our childhood begins to appear very attractive again. Try to be patient and continue to pray that your children will return to the Church of their roots.

I Lost My Son

Several months ago my son died in a tragic car accident. Life, work, family, and even religion seem so meaningless now. How can I find my way back?

Lost in Grief

Dear Lost,

You have suffered a great loss. But you must now choose to live in a way that will respect both your son's memory and your own ongoing life. Here are ten gentle steps to recovery:

- Find a friend to help you deal with your loss. It is most important that you find someone to talk to, take a walk with, or share coffee with. The old saying is true: "Sorrows shared are sorrows lessened."
- Expect to feel numb at first. This numbness and meaninglessness that you feel is nature's protective mechanism to help you build up your strength. Keep following the normal patterns of your life and, eventually, meaning will return.

- If you are sad, let the tears come! Tears are essential to the natural healing process. Even Jesus cried at the death of his friend Lazarus (Jn 11:32–35).

- If you are angry, look for a healthy release. Focus the energy of your anger into exercise, cleaning sprees, helping others who have lost children, or joining a church ministry. Turn your inner storm outward!

- If your symptoms become severe, seek professional help. You might not have the inner resources for complete healing. A therapist has the expertise to help you talk about your loss and guide you through the steps of grief.

- Join a support group that shares your kind of loss. A support group will help you sort through your feelings with people who are on a similar journey. Call your parish office for the nearest support group.

- Take time alone to sort out your loss and encourage healing. A loss can turn your world upside down. There is nothing more healing than a day in the woods, a walk on a beach, or a quiet evening of listening to music.

- Pray to and with the Lord about your loss. Jesus is the great healer (Mk 6:53–56). Speak to the Lord and he will heal you.

- Let go and let God. After you have done everything you can, leave your loss in God's hands. The Lord will do for you what you cannot do for yourself.

- Use your experience to help others. Helping others in their time of need will also heal you. It often happens that, while helping others, the Lord reveals to us the meaning of our own losses.

You don't feel like it right now, but God is with you during this time of sadness. May you come to know God's presence.

In Need of a Miracle

Is it wrong to hope for a miracle? One of my children has been diagnosed with cancer, and I am praying for a miracle!

Trusting

Dear Trusting,

When my mother was a teenager, she suffered from internal problems. Her mother took her across Detroit to a famous healer, Father Solanus Casey. He talked to her, prayed over her, and sent her back home. After that visit, my mother's internal problems disappeared.

As Christians we believe in miracles. It is the legacy handed on to us by the Lord Jesus. Remember that once Jesus had trained his disciples, he sent them out in pairs to cure the sick and drive out demons (Lk 9:1–6). They, like the Lord, became miracle workers. Jesus worked his miracles "out of compassion" (Lk 7:13). Jesus wanted to show us that our God was a personal God, genuinely kind and loving.

The first step to asking for a miracle is to believe deeply in the power of Jesus. Jesus always demanded that an initial faith be present before he performed a miracle (Mt 21:22). The miracle would then deepen, strengthen, and stabilize this faith. The second step is to be tireless in your asking. Saint Luke's section on prayer in chapter 11 (1–13) promises success for those who keep knocking on God's door. The final step is to accept whatever the Lord gives. Perhaps the Lord has greater plans for your children than even you might know or fathom.

The Lord's greatest miracle for us is the Eucharist. Here would be the proper place to lay your request before the Lord.

16
The Saints

INTRODUCTION
Catholics and Saints

D evotion to the saints is rooted in a belief in the communion of saints, which Catholics affirm each time we pray the creed. Catholics believe that we are linked in a close-knit spiritual relationship, bonded in the grace and the love of God. The saints, the souls in purgatory, and we pilgrims on earth "form one body, the good of each is communicated to the others" (CCC 947). Those in heaven assist us here on earth, and we on earth pray for those in purgatory.

The saints provide a sense of contact and fellowship with us by maintaining an interest in worldly affairs. When we pray to the saints we ask them to pray to God for us. In life, too, we often use intermediaries to plead on our behalf. When we were children, for example, we may have asked our mother to ask our father for something we wanted. "You ask for me" is a common ploy we use when we want others to solicit favors for us. So also we ask the saints to help us.

Contrary to popular opinion, however, Catholics do not worship the saints—although exaggerated piety gives that impression at times. The tributes we render to the saints differ from our adoration of God. Nonetheless, as models of virtue, the saints are worthy of honor and imitation.

In English there are no specific words to make the distinction between divine worship and veneration of the saints. Thus, we use Latin terms. *Latria* is the adoration we pay to God and Jesus alone. Honor paid to the saints and angels is a different kind and degree, called *dulia*, which can be translated as "fitting and appropriate respect."

When a person is canonized a saint, the Church proclaims that the person can be publicly honored. Over the years the Church has venerated saints in liturgy and official commemorations.

How Are Saints Made?

I am curious as to how a person is declared a saint these days. I've heard that there have been some changes in the process initiated by Pope John Paul II. What are these changes and why were they made?

Helen

Dear Helen,

On January 25, 1983, Pope John Paul II issued an apostolic constitution, "Divine Teacher and Model of Perfection." This document brought about the most sweeping changes in the canonization ("saint-making") process since the time of Pope Urban VIII (1623–1644).

This reform was designed to make the process simpler, faster, cheaper, and more collegial. To accomplish this, the document called for a basic change of procedure. The process used to be a battle between Church lawyers, one of whom was actually called the "devil's advocate." These lawyers would examine and argue about the good and bad sides of the potential saint.

Canonization now takes place in an academic situation. A competent researcher (*realtor*) writes a complete critical and historical biography (*positio*) about the candidate. This is presented to the *prefect* (usually a cardinal) of Congregation for the Causes of Saints and other theological advisers. If these officials approve the candidate, the cause is passed on to the Holy Father for beatification and canonization.

The new process now begins at home, or in the place (or places) where the candidate lived and was recognized as a holy person. In the case of martyrs, the procedure is somewhat different. Their cases are shortened (no miracles are required for beatification, for example) and are almost automatically accepted, except when their deaths resulted from political activism.

The case of the saint (even for a world traveler like Mother Teresa of Calcutta) begins under the authority of the local bishop. Before beginning his investigation, however, he consults other bishops of the region and of other places where the candidate has become known. This is to make sure that the candidate's reputation for holiness has gone beyond the neighborhood. The local bishop and/or his delegate thoroughly examines the candidate's life, virtues, and martyrdom (where applicable). He also records the testimony of any witnesses who knew the candidate. Theologians collect the candidate's published and unpublished writings and evaluate them for orthodoxy. If all is well, the case goes to Rome. There, if the case is considered acceptable, the *positio* is presented to the authorities of the Congregation.

Even after all this, the case must be confirmed by miracles attributed exclusively to the intercession of the saint-to-be. These miracles are considered to be signs that God confirms the individual's holiness. One miracle is needed for beatification, and a second is required before the candidate is officially canonized a saint. Although this is still a lengthy process, the results offer us fine examples to imitate and follow.

All Saints and All Souls

I've often wondered about the feast of All Saints and the feast of All Souls. Are not all the souls we pray for also saints? Why not just celebrate a feast day for all who are in heaven?

Carmen

Dear Carmen,

In the New Testament, the word *saint* meant "Christian." In some way, then, all followers of Jesus were originally considered to be saints of God. But over the centuries, the word *saint* has gradually come to connote the holy men and women who have been declared saints by the Catholic Church. The formal process of becoming a saint is called *canonization* and sometimes can take centuries. (For example, it took nearly five hundred years for Saint Joan of Arc to be canonized.) In the two thousand years of Roman Catholic history, more than twenty-five hundred saints have been recognized as such. On the feast of All Saints, we honor these holy men and women, especially our patron saint and those saints for whom we have some special admiration.

The feast of All Souls is a day to honor our loved ones who have died. It is safe to say that the Church has not officially canonized most of those among our family and friends who have died. As the Church gives official status to a deceased holy person by canonizing them as a saint, so too Christ's Paschal Mystery gives meaning to the death of a faithful Christian. As it says in the First Letter of Paul to the Thessalonians: "For since we believe that Jesus died and rose again, even so, through Jesus, God will bring with him those who have died" (1 Thess 4:14). When we pray for our dead on the feast of All Souls, we acknowledge the mystical body of Christ, which includes us, our family and friends who have died, and the officially canonized saints of the Church.

Do Saints Ever Smile?

Do saints ever smile? That question comes to me every year on the feast of All Saints (November 1). As a child I used to stare at the huge pictures and statues suspended high above the altar in church. The faces were so somber and serious. What are the saints really like?

Carlos

Dear Carlos,

Artists through the centuries may have portrayed sanctity in very subdued tones. The saints, however, and their biographers tell a different story. The holy men and women who make up the communion of saints are an incredibly fascinating array of diverse personalities.

Jesus characterized his personal choices in colorful ways. Peter was called *Rock*. The impulsive Peter gloried on the mountaintop with the transfigured Lord (Lk 9:28–36) but crumbled in the courtyard as the same Jesus stood trial before Pilate (Lk 22:54–62). John and his brother James were called sons of thunder (Mk 3:17) because of their fiery nature (Lk 9:54). Bartholomew is probably the witty Nathaniel who teased Jesus about the rivalry between Cana and Nazareth, saying, "Can anything good come out of Nazareth?" (Jn 1:46).

The feast of All Saints celebrates our universal call to holiness. Our challenge is to imitate the characteristics these unique individuals share in common.

Genuine holiness requires total commitment to God and his ways. Saint Augustine (354–430 A.D.) is one of the great conversion stories of all times. He once prayed, "Lord, give me chastity, but not yet." Later in life he would pray, "I now hunger and thirst after you; you touched me, and I burn again to enjoy your peace."

Saint Irenaeus (125–202 A.D.) said that the glory of God is the human fully alive. Jesus' own words, "I came that they may have life, and have it abundantly" (Jn 10:10). Saints enjoy life! The nearsighted Saint Alphonsus Liguori (1696–1787), founder of the Redemptorists, sat in the back row of the Naples theater with his glasses off so he could enjoy the music he loved without the distraction of the half-naked chorus line. Saint Teresa of Ávila (1515–1582), caught devouring partridge in the convent kitchen, said, "When I pray, I pray; when I eat partridge, I eat partridge!" Saint Joan of Arc (1412–1431) loved horses, and Saint Charles Borromeo (1538–1584) loved chess. Indeed, saints do smile—even laugh.

Whatever image may be conveyed in the plaster and oils of the artists, the saints were all human. The saints are like us. And we can be just like them. Prayer is the key. Take the advice of Saint Ignatius of Loyola (1491–1556), "Pray as if everything depends on God and act as if everything depends on you."

Patron Saints

The pope recently proclaimed Saint Thomas More as the patron of statesmen and politicians. How does one become a patron saint?

Saint Watcher

Dear Saint Watcher,

Saint Thomas More has to do double duty now as a patron saint. He was previously designated as the patron of lawyers, and now he has taken on added responsibilities as patron of statesmen and politicians. Thomas More, who was the Lord Chancellor of England under King Henry VIII and beheaded in 1535, became famous in modern history through the movie, *A Man for All Seasons*.

Patron saints are nominated by various groups (like politicians) and reconfirmed by the Holy See. The patron saint then becomes the heavenly protector of the individuals, institutions, or specialized activities that are placed under the saint's care. Those under the saint's patronage are encouraged to call for the saint's intercession and to follow the example of the saint's life (1 Cor 14:12).

The choosing of patrons dates back to the early centuries of the Church, when Christians were named after the apostles and martyrs, and churches were named after angels. The popularity of patron saints grew in the Middle Ages, when every circumstance of life had a heavenly protector. Examples of this are Saint Michael, as the patron invoked to protect bell towers against lightening strikes, and Saint Maurice, the patron of sword smiths. In the age of exploration, whole cities and even newly discovered countries were put under the protection of the saints (San Francisco is protected by Saint Francis; the islands of Saint Lucia and Saint Vincent, in the Caribbean, are named after saints).

If you wish to see a listing of all the patron saints, a good place to go is the Internet site: www.catholic-forum.com/saints/ indexsnt.htm. May your patron saint always watch over you and protect you!

Why Pray to the Saints?

I am a person who always prays to the saints. I light candles to them and I also pray and light candles for members of my family who are deceased. Sometimes I wonder if that really does any good. What do you think?

A Devout Wonderer

Dear Devout Wonderer,

What a wonderful question. The part about lighting candles poses the issue in a most thought-provoking way, so I raised your question at a recent gathering of priests. One pastor had recently removed the votive candles from his church, proclaiming them a superstitious moneymaker whose wax ruined his carpets. Others, however, spoke gratefully of candles; they represent a person's desire to pray always. The candle's flame continues to burn, steady and faithful, even as we go about the business of daily living. Another priest suggested that the flame's consuming itself suggests people's desire to consume themselves in love for God and service to others in daily life.

For myself, I recall my own diagnosis of cancer in 1986, and my doctor's statement that my own prayer, my family's prayers, and the prayers of others would be as important in my recovery as his treatment plans. He would not allow me to attempt a faith healing, but his medicines would be much less effective if faithful prayer did not accompany them. In fact, despite very difficult side effects, my chemotherapy proceeded so successfully that it was impossible to doubt the power of prayer. Prayer was clearly central to the whole healing event.

Interestingly, science itself has begun to address the effects of prayer in healthcare. Dr. Randolph Byrd reported on a study he did (*Southern Medical Journal*, July 1988, p. 826) to determine the effects of intercessory prayer on 393 patients admitted to a coronary-care unit. He found that the patients who were prayed for had fewer complications. His conclusion was that intercessory prayer to God has a beneficial therapeutic effect on patients admitted to a CCU.

If such experiences and data can be trusted, it only makes sense that prayer also links us, however mysteriously, to those who have gone before us in faith. If prayer can change people, opening them to God's healing, then surely the saints and our deceased loved ones can facilitate that healing openness from their communion at God's right hand. Such prayer also calls us, however subtly, to the central mystery that we too shall one day die and be a part of that communion. Thus, even as we seek the intercession of the saints for our earthly cares, such prayer reminds us that the fire of our own lives is daily being consumed, and that each of us will inevitable receive a call to death when it becomes God's will.

When the late Sister Thea Bowman—brilliant, creative, beautiful, and passionately alive—was diagnosed with cancer, she wondered how to pray. "I didn't know if I should pray for healing or death. Then, I found peace in praying for what my folks call 'God's perfect will.' As it evolved, my prayer became 'Lord, let me live until I die.' By that I mean I want to live, love, and serve fully until death comes. If that prayer is answered, I am able to truly live until I die. How long really doesn't matter."

Are Catholic Statues the Same As "Graven Images"?

Some friends have asked me why Catholics worship statutes. They say the Bible forbids the making of images. Aren't our statues the same as images?

Chris

Dear Chris,

The Book of Exodus portrays God as giving Moses the commandment: "You shall not make for yourself an idol, whether in the form of anything that is in heaven above, or that is on the earth beneath, or that is in the water under the earth. You shall not bow down to them or worship them" (Ex 20:4–5). God forbade the making of *idols*, images of false gods. But God obviously did not forbid the making of all images, for images of cherubim were placed on the Ark of the Covenant (Ex 37:7–9), and the Book of Numbers tells how God commanded

Moses to make a bronze serpent and put it on a pole as a sign of healing (Num 21:7–9).

Not only is the making of images or representations of people not forbidden by God, it is so common and so human that we take it for granted. No doubt you've seen the bumper sticker, "Ask us about our grandchildren." Go ahead, ask them! They'll tell you all about how wonderful their grandchildren are, and they'll have a pocketful of pictures to show you. It is human to praise the ones we love and keep photographs or images to remind us of them.

We Catholics love the saints as family members who have gone before us, and we keep statues and paintings of them in our homes and churches. The statues and paintings, like the pictures of our grandchildren, are "sacramental," that is, they serve as signs that bring our loved ones to mind. We value the signs and the saints they represent.

As you mentioned, Catholics are often criticized for "worshiping" the saints because we keep images of them and pray before those images. We do not, of course, "worship" the saints. We worship and adore God alone. But we do honor the saints. We remember their holy lives and we try to imitate them.

The Bible teaches us to do this: "Remember your leaders, those who spoke the word of God to you; consider the outcome of their way of life, and imitate their faith" (Heb 13:7). The Bible honors heroes of old, in some cases with entire books, such as Ruth, Judith, and Esther. Surely we follow God's word when we memorialize and honor the saints in word and song, in marble, stained glass, and canvas.

Actually, most non-Catholic Christians do erect statues of saints at Christmastime when they put up nativity scenes with images of Mary and Joseph. Catholics, however, do not reserve this practice to Christmas; we have our statues all year. And there is really nothing unusual about keeping statues and paintings in prominent places. Almost any city in the world has statues of great leaders and prominent citizens. Images of saints are signs of a special kind of greatness: dedication to Jesus Christ.

At times, Catholics may seem overly enthusiastic in their veneration of saints. But if we consider the adulation commonly paid to movie stars, sports figures, and singers, we will probably have to admit that saints come in second best. The real problem is not that we honor saints too much, but that we honor them too little.

People will have their heroes one way or another. If we all, adults and children, are given only secular models to imitate, we will be denied models who can guide us to Jesus and to eternal life.

I grew up in a small town and attended weekly Mass in a church built in the 1830s. Its walls are covered with paintings of martyrs, and its altars are populated with statues of saints. These were not great works of art, but they taught valuable lessons. They taught that many great people made Jesus Christ the Lord of their lives. They proclaimed Christ as a leader people would gladly die for. For example, statues of Saint Vincent de Paul and Saint Louise de Marillac spoke volumes about the importance of caring for the poor and the needy. A painting of Mary's Assumption pointed toward heaven as a final goal.

Statues and paintings are not false idols. Rather, they are signs to God's grace and goodness fleshed out in the lives of people very much like us. They are reminders that we are called to the only kind of greatness that matters: lives of dedication to Jesus Christ.

Do the Saints Remember Us?

I know the Catholic Church teaches that saints in heaven pray for us. But Isaiah 65:17–21 tells me that the new heaven and the new earth are so wonderful that no one will think about the old ones anymore. I take this to mean that I will be so in awe at seeing my heavenly Father that nothing else will come to mind or matter. I would appreciate hearing from you on this.

In Awe

Dear In Awe,

It is certainly true that our vision of God in heaven will be an awesome experience! But our adoration of God in the Beatific Vision of heaven will not cut us off from our loved ones on earth. The New Testament points out that love of God and love of neighbor are closely linked. Being one with God, the Creator of all, will not make us oblivious to the people God has created. If this were so, angels in heaven could not take care of us. But Jesus said: "Take care that you do not despise one of these little ones; for, I tell you, in heaven their angels continually see the face of my Father in heaven" (Mt 18:10). Obviously, angels see God and yet watch over the people committed to their care.

There are many clear indications in the Bible that the saints in heaven are aware of us, and that there is interaction between those in heaven and those of us on earth. The most obvious passage is found in Hebrews 12:1: "Therefore, since we are surrounded by so great a cloud of witnesses [those in heaven], let us also lay aside every weight and the sin that clings so closely, and let us run with perseverance the race that is set before us." The Book of Revelation pictures the saints in heaven as offering to God the prayers of God's people on earth: "Each of the elders held a harp and gold bowls filled with incense, which are the prayers of the holy ones" (see Rev 5:8). The Second Book of Maccabees 15:12–15 reports a vision in which the martyred high priest Onia, and the prophet Jeremiah pray for the Jewish nation. The gospels portray Moses and Elijah appearing with Jesus at the Transfiguration and talking with him about his coming passion and death (Mt 17:1–9; Mk 9:2–9). Jesus speaks of "joy in heaven over one sinner who repents" (Lk 15:7). All these passages imply interaction between heaven and earth, and show that union with God does not blot out everything else.

In Isaiah 65:17–21, the prophet seems to be referring to the fact that God would bring back the Jewish people from exile in Babylon and create a new life for them in Jerusalem. Isaiah is saying that the joy of those returning to Jerusalem will be such that it will make their past misfortunes fade from memory. The actual experience of the returning exiles was less blissful than they expected, but they did find much joy in returning home. A deeper meaning can be read into the passage in the light of the New Testament. Christ's death and resurrection opened heaven for us, "new heavens and a new earth," where we will find the immense joy foretold by Isaiah. This joy will make any misfortunes we experienced on earth fade from memory. Saint Paul says, "I consider that the sufferings of this present time are not worth comparing with the glory about to be revealed to us" (Rom 8:18). We will "forget" the troubles we endured on earth, but we will be aware of the sufferings of those who are still on earth, and we will want to help them. Why? Because the greatest happiness, as Jesus himself said, is in giving (Acts 20:35).

So the Church has always taught that through the communion of saints we are untied to those who have gone before, and they are with us. The *Catechism of the Catholic Church* explains that the communion of saints includes those here on earth, those being purified after death (in purgatory), and those in heaven. Through the communion of saints, all can share spiritual goods. The saints in heaven pray for us on earth; union with them brings us closer to Christ. We pray for those who are being purified after death, and they pray for us. We are one family under God, one holy Catholic Church (CCC 954–962). The closer our union with God, the closer our union with one another. We have a wonderful goal in life: the promise of union with God and with all those joined to God.

"You have come to Mount Zion and to the city of the living God, the heavenly Jerusalem, and to innumerable angels in festal gathering, and to the assembly of the firstborn who are enrolled in heaven, and to God the judge of all, and to the spirits of the righteous made perfect, and to Jesus, the mediator of a new covenant, and to the sprinkled blood that speaks a better word than the blood of Abel" (Heb 12:22–24).

Who Was Saint Valentine?

Do our Valentine Day traditions of love and romance have anything to do with the actual Saint Valentine?

Hoping for More

Dear Hoping,

There were actually three Saint Valentines. One was a priest who was beheaded in Rome on February 14 in the year 269; the other was a bishop, who was also martyred in the third century. Both are buried on the Appian Way in Rome. The third Saint Valentine is a lesser-known saint who died in Africa with a number of companions during the early centuries of the Church.

The tomb of the priest Saint Valentine became a center of considerable popular devotion in the early Middle Ages. In 496, Pope Gelasius set aside February 14 to honor this Saint Valentine.

The popular romantic customs that surround our present Valentine's Day trace their origins back to the Middle Ages. The English writer, Chaucer, noted that halfway through the second month of the year, February 14, the birds began to choose their mates. For this reason, the day was looked upon as especially consecrated to lovers, and as a proper occasion for writing love letters and sending lovers' tokens. People who gave or received these tokens or letters were referred to as "valentines."

In the Middle Ages, a legend began to be attributed to Saint Valentine, the priest. The legend says that Saint Valentine left a farewell note for his jailer's daughter, who had become his friend, and he signed that note: "From your Valentine."

Saint Joseph, Our Guardian

Why does the Church honor Saint Joseph, and is there a prayer to Saint Joseph that I can use?

Honoring the Saints

Dear Honoring,

Saint Joseph was chosen by the Lord to be spouse of Mary and guardian of the Word Incarnate, Jesus Christ. The little we know about Joseph is taken from the gospels. In Matthew's Gospel, for example, we learn that Mary is betrothed to Joseph, a "righteous man." When Joseph learns that Mary is already with child, he decides to dismiss her quietly so as not to disgrace her publicly. But an angel of the Lord appears to him in a dream and tells him not to be afraid to take Mary as his wife, and informs him that she will bear the child of the Holy Spirit, the one who will come to save people from their sins. Joseph obeys the angel without question (Mt 1:18–25).

Joseph heeds God's call once again, when he is instructed by an angel of the Lord to flee Bethlehem to escape the murderous Herod. Matthew tells us: "Joseph got up, took the child and his mother by night, and went to Egypt" (Mt 2:14).

It is this faithfulness, this steadfast and complete trust in God, that makes Joseph such a wonderful example for us, and for this, the Church honors him.

Why Is Saint Joseph Called "the Worker"?

Why is Saint Joseph called "the Worker"? I would think that he should be honored primarily as the father of Jesus. Is he honored by other titles as well?

Scott

Dear Scott,

Historically, traditionally, and theologically, the development of devotion to Saint Joseph has had an interesting path. It was not until the eighth century that Joseph, underneath the title "Spouse of Mary," was even publicly acknowledged—except perhaps as an afterthought or as silent participant in the Christmas story—primarily because of the theological difficulties that were present in acknowledging the father of a son who, "was born of a virgin."

The Church has always acknowledged that Joseph was in a unique fatherhood relationship with Jesus, but there was, and continues to be, reluctance to call him the *father* of Jesus. We understand the father of Jesus is not Joseph, but rather God the Father. As a result of this reluctance, Joseph's role was able to develop only in our continued understanding of what his unique contributions may have been in the development of the Church and our own spiritual story. Early attempts to understand the role of Joseph were not entirely satisfactory.

Since Joseph was not the biological father of Jesus, some tried to explain him as an older, widowed, protector for Mary; but that role did not seem to make sense within the context of the times in which he lived. Still others tried to explain his role as the adoptive father of Jesus; but again, that did not seem to be accurate or even satisfying. The development was slow, but historically, it seems there was a consistent effort.

A consensus about the role of Joseph in the plan of salvation seems to be in place by the early fourteenth century. In 1324, we are able to discover clear references to the celebration of his traditional date of birth on March 19 of each year. By 1870, Pope Pius IX was able to declare Joseph the Patron of the Universal Church. Still later, in the nineteenth century, worldwide devotion to Saint Joseph was able to find a home at St. Joseph's Oratory in Montreal, Canada. Today the Oratory dominates the Montreal religious skyline and is a popular place for devotion and pilgrimage.

Reflection upon the known and assumed life of Saint Joseph in the life of the Church lent itself to the development of still other insights into his unique contribution. He is known as the Patron of Families, the Patron of Virgins, and Patron of the sick and Dying. Still others, especially Saint Teresa of Ávila, identified Joseph as Patron of Prayer and Interior Life.

Of all the titles associated with Saint Joseph, it seems that "Worker" is used most often by Pope Pius XI, in his references to Saint Joseph as the patron of the Church's battle against atheistic communism. Pope Pius XII further developed this approach in 1955, when he established the feast on May 1 that was to counteract the communist celebration of May Day and to emphasize the Catholic teaching concerning the dignity of labor.

My own devotion to Saint Joseph is best summarized by my understanding of him as a man who tried to do the best he could when the will of God became clear to him. For me, that is the best example of all, and the most helpful for each of us.

17
General Questions

INTRODUCTION
A Human Being Who Seeks God

From the time you learned to talk, you asked questions—which reveals something absolutely basic about you: the fact that you have a questioning intellect.

Throughout your life, you have always wanted things, and you find yourself making constant decisions—saying yes to this, no to that. These experiences reveal something else very basic about you: the fact that you have a free will, the power to want and to choose.

As time passes, you are changing in bodily appearance, and your way of viewing life is shifting and deepening. But the basic you—the "I" behind your eyes—remains the same person. At your core you are constantly reaching out, seeking that for which you are created. This questing, spiritual core or your being has been called by many names. Common names for it are *soul*, *spirit*, and *heart* (CCC 356–368).

The Ultimate Reality you seek—which is present in everything you reach out to—has also been called by many names. The most common name for this Ultimate Reality is God. You are so bound to God that without God you would not live or move or have your being. You are so bound to God that if you did not sense his presence in some way, you would view life as pointless and cease to seek.

What Do the Stars Tell Us?

I'm into horoscopes, and I faithfully read the astrology column in the daily paper. A friend told me that astrology is a lot of nonsense and against the Catholic faith. What do you say?

Gemini Gerry

Dear Gemini Gerry,

What I say is: "Don't give credit or blame to the stars for what you do and what you are."

Stargazing is, of course, as old as the human race. We know with certainty that ancient Chaldea was celebrated for its stargazers. Many of the constellations' names originated in that time. One opinion has it that the three wise men that came from the East to pay homage to the newborn Savior were themselves Chaldean stargazers. These men supposedly found an omen in the new star that was not recognized by ordinary folk.

The science of *astronomy* developed from such early stargazing. Astronomy is a perfectly respectable branch of learning that seeks to understand the nature and limits of the astral bodies of the mighty universe around us. Astronomy is what allows us to know things like how the powerful gravitational relationship between earth and moon influences ocean tides. This science studies things like how sunspots, huge disturbances on the sun's surface, have a definite influence on our atmospheric conditions. The science of astronomy studies these and many other observable phenomena.

Perhaps it was natural enough that from the early stargazing there should also develop the pseudoscience of *astrology*. Astrologers believe that people and the world are heavily influenced for good or evil by the position of the stars. The development of astrology is intimately connected to the innate human desire to know and control the future. The pagan religions all had their various forms of divination— whether by listening to oracles or by observing the direction of birds in flight or by examining the entrails of animals. These people tried to probe beyond the curtain that divides the future from the present. But of all these pseudoscientific means of foretelling the future, astrology was one of the earliest and certainly seems to have held the field the longest.

Astrologers believe that the zodiac signs under which we were born largely control our human destiny. The main objection that Christians have to astrology is that, taken seriously, it insults almighty God, who alone knows the future. God alone, in cooperation with the free will of humans, controls the future. To suppose that stars, planets, animals, or inanimate objects can, independent of God, direct or influence our lives opposes the first commandment: "I am the Lord your God; you shall not have strange gods before me."

The Old Testament clearly spells out that it is vain to imagine "either fire or wind or swift air, or the circle of the stars, or turbulent water, or the luminaries of heaven were the gods that rule the world" (Wis 13:2).

Remember also that astrologers are often careful to make their predictions vague so that they can apply to just about anyone. Here is a horoscope sample, picked at random: "Mercury, Venus, Jupiter and Uranus all move together in the eleventh house of your Virgo chart. It rules your social life, income, and friendships. You could have remarkable developments in these matters, despite strife or strain in your life." Does this tell a person anything not already known?

My advice on astrology is this: Don't stop at stars. See past them to the God who made them, and who made us, and who watchfully cares for all creation.

Can Catholics Believe in Reincarnation?

A recent poll indicated that 21 percent of the population believes in reincarnation. Shirley MacLaine has become a kind of high priestess of reincarnation with her books and seminars. Even some Catholics, according to the poll, see no problem in accepting the idea. Does reincarnation contradict any basic Catholic teachings?

Confused Charlie

Dear Confused Charlie,

Reincarnationists believe in a perpetual cycle of rebirth into this world. According to this belief, you live for x number of years, you die, and then you come back to earth in a new form. The idea of reincarnation began as an ancient Hindu belief that the world is fundamentally unreal. According to this belief, the purpose of life is to pierce this unreality and thus reach spiritual perfection, or so-called "Absolute Reality." This may require millions of successive reincarnations.

The teaching of Christ is opposed to this cyclic, unfinalized view of existence. While reincarnationists believe in a succession of lives, our Christian belief is well expressed in Hebrews 9:27: "It is appointed for mortals to die once, and after that the judgment...."

In Christian belief, each human being is unique and unrepeatable. With very few exceptions, all of us are responsible for our actions. We live our lives, add our own unique contributions to history, and then cross the boundary into eternity to face God's compassionate but fair judgment. In Matthew's Gospel, Jesus says that some will "go away into eternal punishment, but the righteous into eternal life" (25:46).

The Gnostics, who were heretics of the second and third centuries, taught *transmigration* of souls, another name for reincarnation. Early Church Fathers, like Tertullian, Origen, and Saint Irenaeus, soundly refuted Gnostic teachings. This ancient heresy, however, is experiencing new life as a popular fad. Robert Baldwin of *Our Sunday Visitor* recently reported that at a New Age Fair in San Francisco most of the 650 exhibitors were reincarnationists.

How do we account for this? Perhaps it is connected with the tendency today to escape the burden of personal responsibility—to deny the reality of sin. Dr. Karl Menninger a world-famous psychiatrist, wrote a book on this phenomenon entitled *Whatever Became of Sin?* He saw people's lack of awareness of sin as a prime cause of prevalent deep neurosis.

Belief in reincarnation can be a convenient way of avoiding responsibility. The danger exists that if I am destined to repeat my life indefinitely, I can stop worrying about any final accounting for my actions.

But bear in mind that popular New Age fads don't guarantee truth. I don't see how anyone who truly believes in Christ and what he stood for can reconcile this with belief in reincarnation.

My advice is to put your faith in Christ who said, "I am the way, the truth, and the life" (Jn 14:6), and who said he was going to prepare a place for us in a better world to come (Jn 14:2).

Organ Donors, Givers of Life

Should I sign a statement donating my organs in case I die suddenly? What are the pros and cons of this? Do you have any solid figures on the real need?

Tobias

Dear Tobias,

Jesus said, "No one has greater love than this: to lay down one's life for one's friends" (Jn 15:13). Therefore, it would be a great act of charity to donate a kidney, a liver, your corneas, or some other organ to someone in great need, as long as your own life is not at high risk in doing so.

Although all organs are needed, there are only two that we can't live without—the heart and the liver. Doctors can only transplant these two organs from persons who have died. Doctors must transfer organs within hours of the donor's death. In such cases, the law requires that a deceased person's next of kin must consent to any organ transplants.

A woman whose husband received a transplant wrote to me saying, "We know very little about Peter's donor. A husband and thirteen-year-old daughter both died. The wife and mother, certainly in a moment of unimaginable pain, consented to donate their organs. We know for sure that two livers, a kidney, and a pancreas were transplanted. Three lives were saved... I pray each day for this wife and mother, who lost so much and still gave so that others could live."

Almost 80,000 persons in the United States alone await organ transplants. The United Network for Organ Sharing lists 3,883 heart patients in critical need of a heart. People needing a kidney number around 57,000; only a small percentage will find a compatible organ. In the last four years, the average wait for a kidney has doubled to two years. Thousands of blind or partially blind people wait for corneas. Transplant surgery techniques are always improving, but ironically the supply of organs has declined by 10 percent in the past year.

Some people hesitate to donate organs because they fear that medical personnel who know that a dying person is an organ donor might not work as hard to save the life of the seriously injured. If you have these sorts of fears about medical personnel, remember that liver and heart donations can take place only after all efforts to save a life have been exhausted and death has actually occurred. Doctors take the Hippocratic oath, which requires them to do all that is possible to save a life before giving up.

Anyone of any age can be a donor, and there is no charge or payment for organs or tissue used in transplants. Social and financial status is never a factor in selecting recipients; vital organs are transplanted into those whose need is most urgent. Blood and tissue type and body size must be compatible.

If you feel drawn to this great act of charity, now is the time to tell your family, close friends, and attorney. Many regions of the country allow people to state their intentions on the back of their auto licenses.

Patients and families waiting for transplants have a saying: "Don't take your organs to heaven. Heaven knows we need them here."

Organ Donations

Hospitals often request donation of organs and/or bodies to medical science. What are the views and the requirements of the Church regarding this practice?

B.L.

Dear B.L.,

The ability to transplant living organs from one human being to another is a dramatic advance in modern medicine. Thousands of people are alive today or are living healthier because they have received a new cornea, kidney, liver, or heart. It is certainly not a duty or an obligation to give your organs for transplant, or your body for medical research. It is a free gift made out of your charity and concern for others. An ethical decision like this is built on four cornerstones.

The first cornerstone is good education. You need to understand clearly the benefits and the burdens of both transplant surgery and donating your body to science. To choose well, you should acquaint yourself with all the details of such procedures and decisions.

The second cornerstone is communication. You should include all your family members in your decision. Most hospitals will not remove organs if the family objects, even if the potential donor has signed a donor card.

The third cornerstone is facing your own mortality. Some individuals feel forced into donating an organ because of pressure from family or friends. This should be discussed with your minister and family members.

The fourth cornerstone is to be conscious of the justice issues involved in making such a decision. You must be sure that donating an organ, receiving an organ, or giving your body to medical science will not in any way be cooperating with an evil or unlawful effort.

Certainly, the final gift of life to another is a profoundly Christian act. Donating your organs at the end of your life can be such a gift.

Can Catholics Be Cremated?

My friend's mother died recently after a long and painful illness. She was Catholic and let it be known clearly that she wanted her body to be cremated. So that is what my friend arranged for. I didn't say anything to him, but isn't cremation against Church teaching?

Stuart

Dear Stuart,

For more than a century Catholics have seen cremation as not being in line with Catholic tradition and practice, even though, in itself, cremation is not opposed to any specific article of faith. In the pre-Vatican II Canon Law, there was a definite proscription against cremation. The principal reason behind this disapproval was that historically the practice had, for some, represented ridicule of the Christian belief in the resurrection of the body. Bodily resurrection is an ancient teaching of the Church, going back to the very first letter written by Saint Paul to the Christian community in Thessalonica: "If we believe that Jesus died and rose, God will bring forth from the dead those also who have fallen asleep believing in him" (see 1 Thess 4:14). Saint Paul later wrote: "If the dead are not raised, then Christ has not been raised. If Christ has not been raised, your faith is futile" (1 Cor 15:16–17).

In the nineteenth century, at the time of great scientific discoveries, it became fashionable to regard religion as unscientific. Certain freethinkers boasted about their rejection of the resurrection, and thus advocated cremation, to demonstrate that Christians were foolish in saying that a body reduced to ashes could be raised up to new life. The obvious response to this claim is that if God could create the universe out of nothing, divine power is surely great enough to bring about a resurrection, even from a few ashes!

On May 8, 1963, the Roman Congregation for the Doctrine of the Faith circulated an instruction to bishops throughout the world. This document upheld the traditional practice of Christian burial as the one to be followed under ordinary circumstances. But it also modified anti-cremation provisions that Canon Law had previously contained.

Cremation is now permitted for serious reasons of a private as well as a public nature, provided it does not involve any contempt of the Church, religion, or any attempt to deny or belittle the doctrine of the resurrection of the body. A public reason could involve a time of epidemic, with the danger of widespread infection. As for "private reasons," as in the case of your friend's mother, we can probably safely presume that she acted without any intention of casting ridicule toward the doctrine of the resurrection of the body. Beyond that, she obviously felt that she had good and serious reason for her decision. It may have had something to do with expense (cremation is less expensive than burial) or with a personal desire to save land (cremation does not involve taking up space with a burial plot).

Whatever the reason, whether we are buried deep in the ground or cremated with our ashes spread across the ocean, our Catholic belief in the resurrection of the body remains. "The trumpet will sound, and the dead will be raised imperishable, and we will be changed" (1 Cor 15:52).

May Catholics Be Masons?

For many years any Catholic joining the Masons was excommunicated. Now I hear that the Church changed its stand and that Catholics can be Masons. Where does the Church stand now?

I.M.C.

Dear I.M.C.,

Yes, for many years Catholics were forbidden to join the Masons under penalty of excommunication. The Code of Canon Law before 1983 stated: "Those who join a Masonic sect or other societies of the same sort, which plot against the Church, or against legitimate civil authority, incur an excommunication simply reserved to the Holy See" (Canon 2335).

Why did the Church impose such a severe penalty for joining the Masons? While the origins of Freemasonry are shrouded in mystery, its modern manifestation began in England in 1717, with the organization of the first Grand Lodge. Just twenty-one years afterward, Pope Clement XII said Roman Catholics were forbidden to seek membership in any Masonic group. His basic reasons were that this fraternal order fosters a view of religion that is incompatible with Christian faith, demands secret oaths of its members, fosters religious indifferentism, and is openly hostile to the Church and its teaching. These are still the basic objections of the Catholic Church to Masonic membership.

You are also correct in thinking that there has been confusion about the Church's stand on this matter. The confusion apparently stemmed from a letter written in 1974 by Cardinal Franjo Seper, head of the Congregation for the Doctrine of the Faith (a key Vatican office). That letter was widely interpreted to say that Catholics could join those Masonic lodges that were not opposed to religion or to the Catholic Church. I remember news items at that time discussing this apparent change in the Church's stand, and also some heated debates about it.

Later, however, that interpretation of Cardinal Seper's letter was called erroneous. In 1981 and again in 1983, the same Congregation for the Doctrine of the Faith restated the Church's prohibition against Masonic membership. "The Church's negative position on Masonic association...remains unaltered, since their principles have always been regarded as irreconcilable with the Church's doctrine. Hence, joining them remains prohibited by the Church. Catholics enrolled in Masonic associations are involved in serious sin and may not approach Holy Communion."

This declaration does not include a penalty of excommunication for Catholics who join the Masons. Neither does the 1983 revised Code of Canon Law, but this technical change does not entail any fundamental change in the Church's stand toward Masonic membership. Such membership is still prohibited.

I've heard it argued that some people who belong to Masons don't subscribe to Masonic beliefs and that Catholics should be allowed to join the Masons for business or philanthropic reasons. It remains true, however, that even passive membership does promote the organization. Whatever benefits may flow from membership in the Masons can also be obtained through other religious or civic organizations.

Do I Need to Monitor Movies?

During the winter months my family turns into a pack of media hounds. We are constantly renting movies, going to them in theaters, or watching them on TV. Does the Church give any guidelines for what we should and shouldn't watch?

Movie Lover

Dear Movie Lover,

The bishops of North America have an Office of Film and Broadcasting that is specifically devoted to the media and communications. This office suggests that it is the task of parents to educate their children in the influence of the media, to take responsibility for monitoring what media the family uses, and to become role models in the appropriate use of media.

The duty of the Catholic family is to affirm Christian values in its media choices. The first area to look at is how the film or program portrays human life. Is human life shown to be a precious gift from God? Is sexuality linked to life? How is the act of dying presented? Are there moral consequences connected with the actors' actions?

The second "yardstick" is how the family is presented in the movie. Does the plot promote lasting commitments within the context of marriage and the family? Is exploitation, oppression, or neglect of any group of people condoned or even promoted? Is respect shown for a variety of cultures?

The final area to consider concerns Scripture and Christian belief. Do your media choices foster a sense of the divine, of human destiny beyond this life, of our obligation to forgive and our need for forgiveness? Are compassion, reconciliation, thanksgiving, and moral responsibility affirmed?

All parents must take full responsibility to affirm strong Catholic morals when choosing their family's movies and television programs.

Is Gambling a Sin?

I enjoy going to the casino and gambling, but I have seen people gambling and losing all of their money. Is gambling considered a sin?

Mark

Dear Mark,

To play games of chance, to bet on horse or dog races, or to buy lotto tickets are, in and of themselves, innocent undertakings that can be sources of fun, and even of financial returns. But circumstances can change an "innocent" game into something morally suspect, even downright wrong. When a person gets so involved with gambling that it becomes addictive, when the welfare of the gambler and the gambler's family is jeopardized, gambling ceases to be a "harmless" amusement. Instead, it becomes an irresponsible practice—indeed, objectively, a sin. The sin lies in the neglect of one's responsibilities to self, family, and God.

The *Catechism of the Catholic Church* says this about gambling: "Games of chance or wagers are not in themselves contrary to justice. They become morally unacceptable when they deprive someone of what is necessary to provide for their needs or those of others. The passion for gambling risks becoming an enslavement" (CCC 2413).

A survey of a local group of Gamblers Anonymous highlights the potential destructive nature of this activity. Within this group, the gambling addiction has led 22 percent to divorce, 40 percent to lose their jobs, 49 percent to steal money with which to pay their gambling debts, and 63 percent to contemplate suicide. Hopefully, we and others will seek healthier ways to relax or seek out our fortunes.

18
Appendices

GLOSSARY OF TERMS

absolution: the form (words) prayed by an authorized priest for the forgiveness of sin in the celebration of the sacrament of penance. The actual words of absolution are, "God, the Father of mercies, through the death and resurrection of His Son, has reconciled the world to himself and sent the Holy Spirit among us for the forgiveness of sin. Through the ministry of the Church may God give you pardon and peace, and I absolve you from your sins in the name of the Father, and of the Son, and of the Holy Spirit."

abstinence: a penitential practice of doing without (abstaining from) meat or another food or drink. According to the Code of Canon Law, "Abstinence from eating meat or another food according to the prescription of the conference of bishops is to be observed on Fridays throughout the year unless they are solemnities," and also on Ash Wednesday and Good Friday (Canon 1251).

adoration: a conscious act of an intelligent creature by which God alone—infinitely perfect and having supreme domination over nature—is recognized as worthy of supreme worship. Adoration is essentially an act of the mind and will, but is commonly expressed in external acts of sacrifice, prayer, and reverence. Adoration in the strictest sense is due to God alone (CCC 2096–2097).

Advent: a liturgical season and a time of waiting and expectation, approximately four weeks in length, in preparation for the feast of Christmas. In the Latin Church (commonly known as the Roman Catholic Tradition) the season of Advent begins on the Sunday closest to the feast of the Apostle Andrew (November 30) and is considered the beginning of the liturgical year.

age of reason: the time of life at which a person is believed to be morally responsible and able to distinguish between right and wrong, normally at about the age of seven (CCC 1244). In sacramental practice, the age of reason in the Latin Church is the age when a person first celebrates the sacrament of penance and receives his or her First Holy Communion. It is also the required age for the celebration of the sacrament of the anointing of the sick (CCC 1511–1513).

annulment: a term for what is known in the Code of Canon Law as a decree of nullity—namely, a declaration by a competent authority of the Church that a marriage was invalid from the beginning because of the presence of a diriment (invalidating) impediment, a basic defect in consent to marriage, or an inability to fulfill the responsibilities of marriage, or a condition place by one or both of the partners on the very nature of marriage as understood by the Church. The annulment procedure may be started at the parish level; the investigation of the facts is usually carried out by a marriage tribunal (ecclesiastical court) under the leadership of a bishop (CCC 1628–1629).

anointing of the sick: one of the seven sacraments of the Church; celebrated by the Church to offer the healing power of Christ to the sick and to the infirm. The scriptural roots of this sacrament can be found in Mark 6:13, "They cast out many demons, and anointed with oil many who were sick and cured them," and also in James 5:14–15, "Are any among you sick? They should call for the elders of the church and have them pray over them, anointing them with oil in the name of the Lord." Only a bishop or a priest can administer the sacrament. It is properly administered to "a member of the faithful who, after having reached the use of reason, begins to be in danger (of death) due to sickness or old age" (Canon 1004.1; CCC 1511–1513).

ashes: symbols of penance and reconciliation made by burning the palms blessed on the previous Passion Sunday. These ashes are blessed and then used to mark the forehead of the people on Ash Wednesday.

baptism: the first of the seven sacraments of the Church, considered the gate to the sacraments, and necessary for salvation, in fact or at least in intention. It is the way by which men and women are reborn as the children of God and welcomed into the Church. The sacrament is conferred by immersion or the pouring of water on the person to be baptized and the required words (form) is: "I baptize you in the name of the Father, and of the Son, and of the Holy Spirit. Amen."

Benediction of the Blessed Sacrament: a liturgical service for the purpose of acknowledging the presence of Christ in the reserved sacrament. The service consists of songs, prayers, and biblical readings, which focus the attention of the gathered congregation on the meaning and importance of the Eucharist.

The practice of Benediction dates back to the Middle Ages when people felt a desire to see the Holy Eucharist, especially since personal reception of the Blessed Sacrament occurred infrequently. The popularity of Benediction was furthered by the celebration surrounding the solemnity of Corpus Christi (the Body and Blood of Christ), including the exposition of the host in a *monstrance* or *ciborium,* and processions.

Body of Christ: the ways in which Christ is present to humankind and to the world. The term has many meanings that stem from the human body of the historical Jesus. This biblical image and its extension to other images are well developed by the Second Vatican Council's document entitled *Dogmatic Constitution on the Church* (§7).

Catechism of the Catholic Church: a universal text summarizing the doctrines of the Catholic Church, first published in French in October 1992. It was prepared by a Vatican commission and is intended to help bishops in formulating local catechism programs adapted to the cultural and other concerns of the local church. It is seen as an organic presentation of the Catholic faith in its entirety (CCC 18).

Catholic: from the *Greek,* meaning "universal," part of the official title or designation given to the body of Christian communities in union with the Bishop of Rome (the pope). Saint Ignatius of Antioch first used the term in the year 107, as a description of the Church. The word is now used in a variety of different ways. For example, it describes the universality of the Church as intended for all human beings; it identifies a particular institution in the Church (that is, Catholic schools); it refers to individual members of the Church (that is, Mary and Robert are Catholic parents).

Christian: name used by Pliny the Younger in 112 B.C. in a report to the Emperor Trajan. The word is used only three times in the New Testament (1 Pet 4:16; Acts 11:26, and 26:28). More often than not, the early communities described themselves as "believers," "disciples," or "Followers of the Way."

Church: that "visible religious society" founded by Jesus Christ, under one head (Saint Peter and his successors), whose purpose is to preserve and proclaim the teachings of Jesus and to make present his sacrifice and sacraments for the salvation of all people until the end of time.

The Church may also be defined, or perhaps more accurately, "recognized," by the "marks" that characterize it: one, holy, catholic, and apostolic. Vatican II, in the *Dogmatic Constitution on the Church*, offered many images and descriptions to try to communicate the total meaning of the Church. It is the new people of God; the Mystical Body of Jesus Christ; "the whole Christ, head and members"; a sacrament or sign of God's presence; a community of believers united with Christ, especially in and through the Eucharist; an assembly of the faithful, committed to carrying forth the mission of Christ under the guidance of the Holy Spirit (CCC 763–766).

clergy: title referring to those men who receive the sacrament of holy orders for the service of God and the Church, including deacons, priests, and bishops. A distinction may be made between diocesan clergy, those ordained for a particular diocese and committed in obedience to a particular bishop, and religious clergy, those who belong to a religious institute in the Church (that is, Jesuit, Franciscan, Redemptorist) and owe primary obedience to their religious superiors as well as pastoral obedience to the bishop in whose diocese they exercise this ministry (CCC 1562–1571).

Code of Canon Law: the official body of laws for Catholics of the Roman, or Latin, Rite. The first code was promulgated in 1917. The present code contains 1,752 codes (laws) and was promulgated in 1983. It contains laws that apply to all members of the Catholic Church, others that define and govern the hierarchy of the Church and members of religious communities, and norms for all of the sacraments of the Church. Pope John Paul II, on the occasion of the publication of the Code in 1983, reminded all Christians that the code is not to be seen as a substitute for faith or grace, but is rather to be viewed as a help and as a necessary discipline.

crèche: from the Old French meaning "manger," used specifically to designate the manger in which Jesus was placed when he was born in Bethlehem. It is also used to designate any representation of the Nativity in which the principle characters of the event are portrayed. The essential representations would include Jesus, Mary, Joseph, the ox and the donkey, the shepherds with their sheep, and often an angel. On the solemnity of the Epiphany, the three kings (Magi) and their camels might also be added to the scene.

divorce: The teaching of the Church, based on the teaching of Christ himself (Mk 10:2–12 and Lk 16:18), is that a "ratified and consummated marriage cannot be dissolved by any human power or for any reason other than death" (Canon 1141). Thus, although civil law may claim to dissolve the bond of marriage and render a person free to marry again, the Church maintains that the civil law has no power to do this. For serious reasons, such as adultery or serious danger to spirit or body of the other spouse or the children, a person may have a legitimate cause for separation (CCC 1650–1651, 2384–2386).

Easter: a movable feast, celebrated on a Sunday between March 22 and April 25, commemorating the Resurrection of Jesus Christ from the dead (Mk 16:1–7). It is considered the greatest of all Christian feasts and holds a central place in the liturgical year. The celebration of the Resurrection continues for a period of fifty days, from Easter Sunday to the feast of Pentecost.

Easter duty: a popular term for the obligation that is described in the Code of Canon Law: "All the faithful, after they have been initiated into the Most Holy Eucharist, are bound by the obligation of receiving Communion at least once a year." It is understood that this precept must be fulfilled during the Easter season, unless it is fulfilled at some other time during the year.

Emmanuel: Hebrew for "God is with us," or "May God be with us." The name is given to Jesus in the Gospel of Matthew (Mt 1:23). May also be spelled Immanuel.

Epiphany: from the Greek *epiphaneia,* which means "manifestation." The term refers primarily to the solemnity of the Epiphany, celebrated every year on January 6 (or the Sunday closest to this date in some countries), and celebrates the manifestation of the Lord to the entire world, as represented by the Magi, or the three kings (Mt 2:1–12).

Eucharist: from the Greek *eucharistia,* which means "thanksgiving"; one of the seven sacraments of the Church; is the sacrament of the body and blood of Christ. In the Eucharist, Jesus is present, body, soul, and divinity, under the forms of bread and wine. The Eucharist was instituted by Christ at the Last Supper (Mt 26:26–28, Mk 14:22–24, Lk 22:17–20, and 1 Cor 11:23–25).

eucharistic adoration: devotional practices focused on Christ's presence as Lord and Savior in the consecrated bread and wine. These devotions include exposition of the Blessed Sacrament, usually followed by Benediction, eucharistic processions, visits to the Blessed Sacrament, and holy hours of adoration.

Public or private devotions to the Eucharist were inspired by the desire of the thirteenth-century faithful to look at the consecrated host in order to achieve interior communion with Christ. These outside-the-Mass devotions became popular almost to the point of becoming as important as the celebration of the Mass—sometimes replacing it in the minds of ordinary Catholics.

After Vatican II (1962–1965), these eucharistic experiences were seen as an extension of the eucharistic liturgy itself, which is the summit of Christian life. Thus, they provide people with additional time to contemplate and revere the mysteries celebrated in the Eucharist, and to seek from Christ strength for the journey of discipleship.

ex cathedra: from the Latin meaning "from the chair." When the pope speaks *ex cathedra* in matters of faith and mortals, he is speaking infallibly (CCC 891).

extreme unction: the sacrament of the anointing of the sick, celebrated when a person is very near death. Until the liturgical reforms of the Vatican Council II, the ordinary celebration of the sacrament of the anointing of the sick was almost exclusively celebrated with those who were at the point of death. However, even in this practice, there remained the hope that sick persons would recover their health (CCC 1512).

faith: one of the three (faith, hope, and charity) theological, or God-given and God-directed, virtues or powers or graces, by which, in the words of the First Vatican Council, "a person is enabled to believe that what God has revealed is true—not because of its intrinsic worth is seen with the rational light of reason—but because of the authority of God who reveals it, that God who can neither deceive nor be deceived." Also Romans 1:5; 16:26; and 2 Corinthians 10:5–6 (CCC 1814–1816).

Gabriel: archangel whose name means "man of God." Archangel Gabriel was sent by God to the town of Nazareth to announce the conception of Jesus to the Blessed Virgin.

Guadalupe, Our Lady of: On December 12, 1531, the Blessed Mother appeared at Tepeyac, Mexico, to Juan Diego, a native Indian. She requested that a church be built on the spot, and in 1555, a church was erected. By 1746 Our Lady of Guadalupe was the Patroness of Spain, and in 1910 she was declared the Patroness of Latin America. In 1946 she was declared Patroness of the Americas and in 1988 Pope John Paul II directed that her feast day be celebrated in all dioceses in the United States.

guilt: a state or condition of mind and soul that follows upon a personal, free, deliberate transgression of God's law. Awareness that one has done wrong gives rise to what are often referred to as "guilt feelings," feelings of spiritual unrest or discomfort. Guilt feelings, in their turn, urge the sinful person to repent and seek reconciliation, and thus once again to experience inner peace. In contrast to "true" guilt, which follows upon actual sin, "false" or "neurotic" guilt seems to arise from a general lack of self-worth or a scrupulous conviction that one is almost always in sin.

heaven: the dwelling place of God and the angels, and the place of eternal happiness for all those who have been saved; it consists primarily in the face-to-face vision of God and the possession of eternal peace.

hell: the dwelling place of Satan (the devil) and the evil spirits of all those who die deliberately alienated from God. The primary punishment is the pain of loss and the deprivation of the face-to-face vision of God and eternal happiness and peace. There is also the pain of the senses caused by an outside agent, described as fire in the New Testament (Mt 25:41 and Mk 9:43). Hell is the dire destination for one who freely chooses his or her own will against the will of God.

holy water: water that is blessed by a priest for use by the people of God, ordinarily while one is blessing oneself with the sign of the cross. It is a symbol of spiritual cleansing and, by custom, is used in time of physical or spiritual dangers. It is used in all of the Church's blessings (CCC 1668).

incense: a grainy substance made from the resins of various plants that gives off an aromatic odor when burned; used in divine worship as a symbol of the ascent of prayer to God (CCC 2581).

Jansenism: a particularly destructive heresy, rooted in French pietism of the seventeenth century. Jansenism emphasized human sinfulness before God and the need to go to confession before the reception of holy Communion. As a result of this heresy, people developed the habit of going to Communion, usually only once a year, during the Easter season, because it was perceived to be so difficult to attain the proper disposition to worthily receive the sacrament. Saint Alphonsus Liguori, the founder of the Redemptorists, was one who struggled with this notion and heroically preached against it.

judgment: according to Catholic teaching, there is a distinction between "general" judgment and the "particular" judgment. The general or Last Judgment is the final judgment of the human race by Jesus Christ (Mt 25:31; 2 Thess 2:3–10) who "will come in glory to judge the living and the dead" (Nicene Creed). The particular judgment is the judgment that takes place immediately after an individual's death and determines whether the person will spend eternity in either heaven or hell (CCC 678–679).

justification: the process by which a sinner is made right with God. In the teachings of Saint Paul, God makes a person "just," free from sin and pleasing to God, through grace, attested by faith (Rom 3:2–30). According to the Council of Trent, "justification is the change from the condition in which a person is born as a child of the first Adam into a state of grace and adoption among the children of God through the second Adam, Jesus Christ our Savior." Thus, justification includes a true removal of sin by the power of God and a true supernatural sanctification through the gift of sanctifying grace or participation in the life of God (CCC 1266).

laity: all members of the Church, the people of God, the Christian faithful. According to Canon Law, "the Christian faithful are those who, inasmuch as they have been incorporated in Christ through baptism, have been constituted as the people of God; for this reason, since they have become sharers in Christ's priestly, prophetic and royal office in their own manner, they are called to exercise the mission which God has entrusted to the Church to fulfill in the world, in accord with the condition proper to each one" (Canon 204, §1). Among the Christian faithful, the laity are all the faithful except for those in holy orders (clergy) and those who belong to a Christian state approved by the Church (religious men and women). According to Vatican Council II, the *Decree of the Apostolate of the Laity,* §8, the special mission of the laity is to renew the temporal order and to witness to Christ in a special way in order to aid secular affairs (CCC 897–900).

magisterium: a Latin word meaning "teaching authority." According to Catholic doctrine, this teaching authority is vested in the pope, the successor of Saint Peter and the head of the Church, and in the bishops together in union with the pope. This teaching authority is at times infallible, and then demands from the Christian faithful the assent of faith. At other times, this teaching authority, though not explicitly infallible, does express authentic Christian Catholic teaching, and demands from the Christian faithful the loyal submission of the will and the intellect (CCC 83–88).

Mass: in Latin, *missa,* which means to be sent or dismissed. The Mass is the center and heart of Catholic worship. The Mass is in two parts, the Liturgy of the Word and the Liturgy of the Eucharist. In the earliest expressions, the Mass was a simple meal, but it evolved over time and with the influence of many different cultural expressions. In the sixteenth century the Council of Trent reformed and standardized the celebration of the Mass and the directives of this council became normative for four hundred years. The document entitled *Constitution on the Liturgy,* from the Second Vatican Council, implemented the renewal of the Mass as it is celebrated today.

ministry: from the word *minister,* which means "to render service." In the viewpoint of Catholic theology, there is one essential ministry—the ministry of Jesus Christ. His ministry is extended, however, through the members of his Body, the Church. In the Church, the term is used in a variety of ways, among which are the following:

> *ordained ministry,* the service of the people of God by those who have received the sacrament of holy orders (that is bishops, priests, and deacons) and who have specific functions determined by the teaching of the Church itself.
>
> *non-ordained ministry,* the service of the people of God undertaken by baptized Catholics either (a) with a formal commission from the Church (for example, lector, catechist, acolyte) or (b) without a formal commission from the Church (for example, performing the corporal and spiritual works of mercy).
>
> The Second Vatican Council calls attention to both the variety and the unity of ministries in the Church: "In the Church not everyone marches along the same path, yet all are called to sanctity and have obtained an equal privilege of faith through the justice of God (2 Pet 1:1). Although by Christ's will some are established teachers, dispensers of the mysteries and pastors for the others, there remains, nevertheless, a true equality between all with regard to the dignity and to the activity which is common to all the faithful in the building up of the Body of Christ" (*Dogmatic Constitution on the Church,* §32; CCC 873–879, 1590–1596).

mortal sin: from the Latin word meaning "deadly"; synonymous in Catholic teaching with "grave" or "serious." A mortal sin is a personal sin involving a fundamental choice against God in a serious way, a free and willing turning away from God's love and law in a grave matter. Traditional Catholic theology has emphasized three conditions for mortal sin: (1) the matter be grave or serious; (2) there be sufficient reflection or advertence or awareness of the seriousness of the choice being made; (3) there be full consent of the will, that is that one freely chooses to do what one knows to be seriously wrong, even though one could stop from doing it.

novena: from the Latin word meaning "nine," and referring to a public or private devotion that extends for nine consecutive days or, in less common usage, for nine consecutive weeks, with the devotion beginning on a particular day for those nine weeks. The Church approves of such devotional practices, provided there is no superstition connected with the number nine and such externals are used as a help to prayer.

Ordinary Time: the period of time (consisting of thirty-four weeks) within the liturgical calendar of the Church that is not the Advent/Christmas season or the Lent/Easter season. During this period, four solemnities of the Lord are celebrated: Trinity Sunday, the Body and Blood of Christ, the feast of the Sacred Heart, and Christ the King.

ordination: the ritual by which candidates receive one of the three orders that are part of the sacrament of holy orders: bishop, priest, and deacon. Ordination is conferred by the imposition of the hands of the ordaining bishop(s) with the accompanying prayer of the Holy Spirit, proper to the order the received.

parish: a defined community, usually within a specific geographical territory, of the people of God, entrusted to the care of a pastor and under the jurisdiction of the local diocesan bishop. The parish is the ordinary place where the sacraments are administered and celebrated (CCC 2179).

Parousia: the Second Coming of Christ to earth (1 Cor 15:23), when his triumph over all evil will be complete and his kingdom definitively established (1 Thess 4:15–178; Lk 23:3–14; CCC 671–674).

penance, sacrament of: also known as reconciliation; one of the seven sacraments of the Church. It is the sacrament by which sins committed after baptism are confessed and forgiven by the absolution of a priest. Jesus Christ conferred the power to forgive sins to the ministry of the Church in John 20:21–23: "As the Father has sent me, so I send you... .Receive the Holy Spirit. If you forgive the sins of any, they are forgiven them; if you retain the sins of any, they are retained."

precepts of the Church: obligations imposed on Catholics by the law of the Church. Traditionally six are listed: (1) to participate in Mass on Sundays and holy days of obligation; (2) to fast and abstain on days designated by the Church; (3) to confess one's sins once a year; (4) to receive holy Communion during the Easter season; (5) to contribute to the support of the Church; (6) to observe the laws of Church governing marriage.

priest: the ordained minister who presides at the Eucharist. The priest is considered one of the ordinary ministers of the sacraments, with the exception of holy orders and confirmation. The word derives from the Greek *hiereus* and from the Latin *sacerdos.*

purgatory: according to Catholic teaching, the state or condition of the elect (those who have died in sanctifying grace or the friendship of God) still in need of purification before they see God; this purification is altogether different from the punishment of the damned. The faithful are encouraged to pray for the souls in purgatory, especially on the feast of All Souls, celebrated each year on November 2 (CCC 1030–1032).

Real Presence: the substantial presence of Christ in the consecrated bread and wine. The *Constitution on the Liturgy,* teaches that there are five prominent means by which Christ is present. The first is in the person of the minister; the second is through the power of the sacraments; the third is in the Word of the Scripture; the fourth is in the gathered and the praying community; and the fifth is under the appearance of bread and wine in the Eucharist. It is the teaching of the Church that Christ is substantially present in the Eucharist, and as such, the Eucharist is to be understood as the Real Presence.

reconciliation: the act of reestablishing a damaged or destroyed relationship between two parties. Reconciling humankind to God was the primary work of Jesus Christ and is an essential part of the Good News (2 Cor 4:17–19). According to Catholic teaching, reconciliation with God after one has gravely sinned against him and reconciliation with the Church that is wounded by sin are basic results of the sacrament of penance.

Sabbath: the seventh day of the week (Saturday), prescribed in the Decalogue (the Ten Commandments), as a day to be kept holy, a day of rest and religious observance (Deut 5:12–14), held in special reverence by religious Jews. The manner of observing the Sabbath became a source of conflict between Jesus and some of the Pharisees (Mk 2:27). In apostolic times Christians transferred the Sabbath to the first day of the week in honor of the Resurrection of Christ, and designated it the "Lord's Day" (CCC 2168–2173).

sacrament: from the Latin, *sacramentum,* which means "oath" or "pledge." Within the Catholic tradition there are seven sacraments. The sacraments are the principal liturgical rites of the Church and the primary way in which the people of God are enabled to receive the grace of God that flows from the passion, death, and resurrection of Jesus Christ. The seven sacraments are: baptism, confirmation, Eucharist (the sacraments of initiation, CCC 1212); penance and anointing of the sick (the sacraments of healing, CCC 1421); matrimony and holy orders (the sacraments at the service of communion, CCC 1533).

Second Vatican Council: the twenty-first ecumenical council of the Catholic Church held in Rome for four sessions. The first session was held during the pontificate of Pope John XXIII, October 11 to December 8, 1962. The other three sessions during the pontificate of Pope Paul VI, September 29 to December 4, 1963, September 14 to November 21, 1964, and September 14 to December 8, 1965. This was the largest (2,800 members) and most productive (16 significant documents) of all the ecumenical councils. The teaching of Vatican II had an enormous impact on the Church in all parts of the world. Of the sixteen documents enacted by the council, four were constitutions of major importance for the whole Church, nine were decrees on particular topics for particular communities within the Church, and three were declarations. The impact of the Second Vatican Council is continuing to be experienced in the Church today.

Sunday obligation: the prescription to go to Mass every Sunday. The obligation to participate in the Sunday Eucharist "is foundation and confirmation of all Christian practice" (CCC 2181). The 1917 Code of Canon Law made attendance at Mass a serious obligation for all Catholics unless there was a serious situation that would make it difficult to fulfill the obligation, such as the care of infants or illness.

tabernacle: a receptacle for the exclusive reservation of the Blessed Sacrament. According to the Code of Canon Law, it "should be place in a part of the church that is prominent, conspicuous, beautifully decorated, and suitable for prayer" (Canon 938, §2). Moreover, it should be "immovable, made of solid and opaque material, and locked so that the danger of profanation may be entirely avoided" (Canon 938, §3).

Ten Commandments: laws given by God to Moses on Mount Sinai as found in Exodus 20:1–21 and Deuteronomy 5:2–33 and interpreted by Jesus (Mt 5:17–48). As given in the Book of Exodus, the Ten Commandments are as follows: (1) I am the Lord your God and you shall have no other gods before me; (2) You shall not take the name of the Lord your God in vain; (3) Remember to keep holy the Sabbath; (4) Honor your father and your mother; (5) You shall not kill; (6) You shall not commit adultery; (7) You shall not steal; (8) You shall not bear false witness against your neighbor; (9) You shall not covet your neighbor's house; (10) You shall not covet your neighbor's wife.

Tradition: one of the sources (together with the sacred Scripture) of divine revelation. It is, as Vatican II points out, the Word of God that has been entrusted to the apostles by Christ the Lord and the Holy Spirit. Unlike many Christian communities that teach Scripture alone is the source of divine revelation, the Catholic Church professes that "sacred Tradition and sacred Scripture form one sacred deposit of the word of God, which is committed to the Church" (*Dogmatic Constitution on Divine Revelation,* §10).

Trent, Council of: the nineteenth ecumenical council of the Catholic Church held in twenty-five sessions between 1545 and 1563. Its primary work was a defense of Catholic teaching against the attacks of the Protestant Reformers. In presenting this defense it also offered a comprehensive treatment of Catholic teaching on the nature of justification, original sin, grace, faith, the seven sacraments (especially the Eucharist), the veneration of saints, purgatory, and indulgences. Trent set in motion a number of Catholic reforms in regard to the liturgy, the religious education of the faithful, the training of candidates for the priesthood, and the devotional life of the Church. Its influence was, for the most part, widespread and positive, and it is considered one of the more important of the Church's ecumenical councils (CCC 884).

unbaptized, fate of: if, as the Church professes, baptism is necessary for salvation (Jn 3:5), what can be said of the salvation of those who die without baptism? This theological question has been pondered for centuries. Briefly, Catholic teaching holds that, in the case of adults, there are two possibilities: (1) baptism of blood or martyrdom and (2) baptism of desire. In the case of infants, a rather common theological opinion has been that infants who die without baptism are excluded from heaven but spend eternity in a state of natural happiness called limbo. The Church has never explicitly taught this theological explanation. Another fairly common theological explanation has been that God in his mercy can supply for the lack of baptism in way that has not been revealed to us (CCC 1257–1261).

DIFFERENT TRANSLATIONS
OF THE BIBLE

Revised Standard Version: The RSV, published by Oxford University Press (1952/1962) along with the NRSV (*New Revised Standard Version*, 1989) is a popular choice. The reason the RSV is identified as the "revised" version is that it is a revision of the *King James Version* (KJV, 1611) of the Bible, which has been the standard Protestant version of the Bible since the time of the Reformation. The RSV has a familiar "feel" and "tone" to it, although at times it can be a little jarring to modern readers because of the use of certain antiquated words and expressions. The NRSV is very sensitive to gender specific language, sometimes referred to as "inclusive" language.

New International Version: The NIV, published by the International Bible Society (1978/1984) is a popular ecumenical edition of the Bible. It is somewhat more traditional than the RSV, probably reflective of the fact that it was produced by a group of biblical scholars reacting to the "less than enthusiastic" reception that the RSV edition received from conservative Protestant individuals and congregations who feared that the RSV might have strayed too far from the original KJV.

New American Bible: This edition of the Bible, published by the Confraternity of Christian Doctrine (1970) is most familiar to Catholics. The Lectionary that is used in the Liturgy of the Word at Mass often is based on the NAB translation, and so this is the translation that we hear proclaimed from the pulpit. The New Testament and the Psalms have been revised (1991) and the Old Testament is currently under revision. The NAB is sensitive to gender-inclusive language, whenever the reference is to a human person, but retains the traditional language and expressions used in reference to God.

New Jerusalem Bible: This translation is a favorite of those studying the Bible because of its extensive footnotes and references. It is also favored by those who use the Bible for prayer, because of its poetic language. The NJB is a translation of the French edition of *La Sainte Bible* (1966). The NJB is published by Doubleday (1985).

Christian Community Bible: This Bible is the first-ever Bible translation from the developing world, and is well known in Latin America, Asia, Africa, and Oceania. The text introduces the reader to the language, the expressions, and the feelings of the poor and the oppressed. The extensive margin notes and introductions to each of the books of the Bible provide a clear and insightful historical context for the Word of God. Published by Claretian Publications (Philippines) and Liguori Publications (United States), 1995.

One other translation of the Bible should be noted here, more for an historical perspective than anything else. Just as many Protestants viewed the *King James Version* of the Bible as the "authorized text" of the Bible, Catholics often viewed the Douay-Rheims-Challoner as the "authorized text." This version of the Bible was based on the Latin Vulgate as required by the Council of Trent. However, in 1943, with the encyclical by Pope Pius XII titled *Divino Afflante Spiritu,* which encouraged translations of the Bible from the original language, this particular translation was slowly replaced with translations that were more in line with the directives of the encyclical.

In addition to particular translations of the Bible, there are other resources available to the general reader that are more appropriately identified as a paraphrase of the biblical text. These resources attempt to present the Bible in a more popular style—a style that might be more appealing to the reader. Because they are not translations of the text, these "Bibles" are seldom used for worship or biblical study. They include the *Living Bible* and the *Reader's Digest Bible* to name just two.

Authors Referenced

The following is a partial listing of the Padres who contributed to the "Dear Padre" column through the years.

Father Tom Artz, C.Ss.R.
Father John Bandyk, C.Ss.R.
Father Rich Boever, C.Ss.R.
Father Peter Brickman, C.Ss.R.
Father Bill Broker, C.Ss.R.
Father Paul Coury, C.Ss.R.
Father Edward Day, C.Ss.R.
Father Jim Drucker
Father Robert Earl, C.Ss.R.
Father Gil Enderle, C.Ss.R.
Father John Farnik, C.Ss.R.
Father Chris Farrell, C.Ss.R.
Father Joe Guthrie, C.Ss.R.
Father Walt Halberstadt, C.Ss.R.
Father Pat Kaler, C.Ss.R.
Father Mathew Kessler, C.Ss.R.
Father James Krings
Father Gary Lauenstein, C.Ss.R.
Father Frank Lee, C.Ss.R.
Father Daniel Lowery, C.Ss.R.
Father Oscar Lukefahr, C.M.
Father Timothy McCanna
Father Bill McKee, C.Ss.R.

Father Thomas McManus
Father Steve Meyer, C.Ss.R.
Father Louis G. Miller, C.Ss.R.
Father Joe Morin, C.Ss.R.
Father John Murray, C.Ss.R.
Father Bob Newmes, C.Ss.R.
Father Joe Nolen, C.Ss.R.
Father Maurice J. Nutt, C.Ss.R.
Father Michael Parise
Father Bill Parker, C.Ss.R.
Father Gerard Pecht, C.Ss.R.
Father Robert Rietcheck, C.Ss.R.
Father Thomas Santa, C.Ss.R.
Father Frank Semyck, C.Ss.R.
Father Dick Thibodeau, C.Ss.R.
Father Eamon Tobin
Father Ray Walter, C.Ss.R.
Father Allan Weinert, C.Ss.R.
Father Dan Welte, C.Ss.R.
Father Bob Wirth, C.Ss.R.
Father Paul Ziegler, C.Ss.R.
Father Gary Ziuraitis, C.Ss.R.

Resources

Definitions and selected introductions are from *The Essential Catholic Handbook of the Bible, The Essential Catholic Handbook of the Sacraments, The Essential Lenten Handbook,* and *The Essential Advent and Christmas Handbook,* all by Rev. Thomas M. Santa, C.Ss.R. (Liguori, Mo.: Liguori Publications).

Unless otherwise noted, Scripture quotations are from the *New Revised Standard Version* of the Bible, © 1989 by the Division of Christian Education of the National Council of the Churches of Christ in the USA. Used with permission. All rights reserved.

References from the Documents of Vatican II, *Vatican II: The Conciliar and Post Conciliar Documents,* edited by Austin Flannery, OP (Northport, N.Y.: Costello Publishing Company, 1988). No part of these excerpts may be reproduced, stored in a retrieval system, or transmitted in any form or by any means—electronic, mechanical, photocopying, recording or otherwise, without express permission of Costello Publishing Company.

"Introduction: The Meaning of Advent," adapted from *The Essential Advent and Christmas Handbook,* Rev. Thomas M. Santa, C.Ss.R. (Liguori, Mo.: Liguori Publications, 2000).

"Introduction: Catholics and Sacred Scripture" and "Translations of the Bible," adapted from *The Essential Bible Handbook,* Rev. Thomas M. Santa, C.Ss.R. (Liguori, Mo.: Liguori Publications, 2002).

"Introduction: The Blessed Mother," adapted from *The Essential Mary Handbook,* Judith A. Bauer (Liguori, Mo.: Liguori Publications, 1999).

Some introductions are adapted from *The Essential Catholic Handbook,* A Redemptorist Pastoral Publication (Liguori, Mo.: Liguori Publications, 1997).

"Introduction: Catholics and Saints," from Charlene Altemose, MSC, *What You Should Know About the Saints* (Liguori, Mo.: Liguori Publications, 1997).

"Introduction: A Popular History of Lent," adapted from *The Essential Lenten Handbook*, Rev. Thomas M. Santa, C.Ss.R. (Liguori, Mo.: Liguori Publications, 2000).

The introductions entitled, "The Church Is a Sign of the Presence of God," "Jesus and Forgiveness," and "Jesus and Marriage," all from *The Essential Catholic Handbook of the Sacraments*, Rev. Thomas M. Santa, C.Ss.R. (Liguori, Mo.: Liguori Publications, 2001).

"Introduction: Jesus God and Man," "Introduction: A Human Being Who Seeks God," and "Introduction: A New Earth and a New Heaven," from *Handbook for Today's Catholic*, A Redemptorist Pastoral Publication (Liguori, Mo.: Liguori Publications, 1994).

Encyclopedia of Catholicism, Richard P. McBrien, General Editor (New York: HarperCollins Publishers, 1995). *Catholicism*, Richard P. McBrien (New York: HarperSanFrancisco, 1994).

Excerpts from the English translation of the *Catechism of the Catholic Church* for the United States of America, copyright © 1994, United States Catholic Conference, Inc.—Libreria Editrice Vaticana; English translation of the *Catechism of the Catholic Church: Modifications from the Editio Typica*, copyright © 1997, United States Catholic Conference, Inc.—Libreria Editrice Vaticana. Used with permission.

The Catholic Almanac's Guide to the Church, Matthew Bunson (Huntington, Ind.: Our Sunday Visitor Publishing Division, 2001).

The Bible Documents, A Parish Resource, David A Lysik (Chicago: Liturgy Training Publications, 2001).